i

book

Counties in this issue:

Bedfordshire
Buckinghamshire
Cambridgeshire
Essex
Hertfordshire
Norfolk
Suffolk

September 1995

British Bus Publishing

The Eastern Bus Handbook

The Eastern Bus & Coach Handbook is part of the Bus Handbook series that details the fleets of stage carriage and express coach operators. Where space allows other significant operators in the areas covered are also included. These handbooks are published by British Bus Publishing and cover Scotland, Wales and England north of London.

Quality photographs for inclusion in the series are welcome, for which a fee is payable. The publishers unfortunately cannot accept responsibility for any loss and request you show your name on each picture or slide. Details of changes to fleet information are also welcome.

More information on the Bus Handbook series is available from:

British Bus Publishing,
The Vyne,
16 St Margaret's Drive
Wellington
Telford,
Shropshire TF1 3PH

Series Editor: Bill Potter

Principal Editors for The Eastern Bus Handbook:
Keith Grimes, Colin Lloyd, David Donati and Bill Potter

Acknowledgements:
We are grateful to Mark Jameson, Geoff Mills, London Omnibus Traction Society, the PSV Circle and the operating companies for their assistance in the compilation of this book.

The front cover photo is by Malc McDonald
The rear cover and frontispiece photographs are by David Cole and Richard Godfrey

Contents correct to September 1995
ISBN 1 897990 11 1
Published by British Bus Publishing Ltd
The Vyne, 16 St Margarets Drive, Wellington,
Telford, Shropshire, TF1 3PH
© British Bus Publishing Ltd, September 1995

CONTENTS

CONTENTS

AIRPORT COACHES

Airport Coaches Ltd, 44 First Avenue, Stansted, Essex CM24 1RY

Part of Lynton Travel group

XEH254M	Leyland National 1051/1R/0402		B44F	1973	Ex Citibus, Middleton, 1994
UCY629	Aüwaerter Neoplan N122/3	Aüwaerter Skyliner	CH53/18CT	1982	Ex Ward, Harlow, 1993
BAZ7296	Leyland Tiger TRCTL11/3RH	Berkhof Everest 370	C49FT	1985	Ex County, 1993
BAZ7349	Leyland Tiger TRCTL11/3RH	Berkhof Everest 370	C37F	1986	Ex Speedlink, 1993
BAZ7336	LAG G355Z	LAG Panoramic	C53FT	1986	Ex Ward, Harlow, 1993
D526MJO	Renault-Dodge S56	Reeve Burgess	DP18F	1986	Ex Ward, Harlow, 1993
D527MJO	Renault-Dodge S56	Reeve Burgess	DP18F	1986	Ex Ward, Harlow, 1993
E473YWJ	Aüwaerter Neoplan N122/3	Aüwaerter Skyliner	CH57/18CT	1988	Ex Silver Choice, East Kilbride, 1994
G995VEU	Ford Transit VE6	Zodiac	M14L	1989	Ex van, 1994
H140WMR	Ford Transit VE6	Zodiac	M8	1990	Ex van, 1994
M889WAK	Volvo B10M-62	Plaxton Premiére 350	C53F	1995	

Previous Registrations:

BAZ7296	C128PPE	BAZ7349	C140SPB
BAZ7336	C393UPC	UCY629	NES482Y, 9492SC, OES629Y

Livery: Maroon, red, gold and yellow

Photographed in Trafalgar Square, London is Neoplan Skyliner E473YWJ of Airport Coaches. With some seven years of service behind it, the model style still looks modern and is still produced, and has been - with minor changes - for some 27 years.   Over 2500 Neoplan Skyliners have been built and sold in 24 countries. *BBP*

AMBASSADOR TRAVEL

Ambassador Travel (Anglia) Ltd, James Watt Close, Gapton Hall Industrial Estate, Great Yarmouth, Norfolk, NR31 0NX

100	F100BPW	Volvo B10M-61	Plaxton Expressliner	C46FT	1989	
101	F101BPW	Volvo B10M-61	Plaxton Expressliner	C46FT	1989	
106	F106CCL	Volvo B10M-61	Plaxton Expressliner	C49FT	1989	
107	G107HNG	Volvo B10M-61	Plaxton Paramount 3500 III	C51FT	1989	
108	G108HNG	Volvo B10M-61	Plaxton Paramount 3500 III	C51FT	1989	
109	G109HNG	Leyland Tiger TRCL10/3ARM	Plaxton Paramount 3500 III	C53FT	1990	
111	G111HNG	Leyland Tiger TRCL10/3ARM	Plaxton Paramount 3500 III	C51FT	1990	
112	G512MNG	Volvo B10M-60	Plaxton Paramount 3500 III	C51FT	1989	
113	G609MVG	Volvo B10M-60	Plaxton Paramount 3500 III	C51FT	1989	
118	H379TNG	Leyland Tiger TRCL10/3ARZM	Plaxton Paramount 3500 III	C53F	1991	
119	H380TNG	Leyland Tiger TRCL10/3ARZM	Plaxton Paramount 3500 III	C53F	1991	
121	H381TNG	Leyland Tiger TRCL10/3ARZM	Plaxton Paramount 3500 III	C53F	1991	
122	PIJ9274	Volvo B10M-60	Plaxton Paramount 3500 III	C53F	1991	
123	PIJ4317	Volvo B10M-60	Plaxton Paramount 3500 III	C53F	1991	
125	H167EJU	Volvo B10M-60	Plaxton Paramount 3500 III	C53F	1991	
122	H176EJU	Volvo B10M-60	Plaxton Paramount 3500 III	C53F	1991	
131	H833AHS	Volvo B10M-60	Plaxton Paramount 3500 III	C49FT	1990	Ex Park's, 1993
132	J438HDS	Volvo B10M-60	Plaxton Premiére 350	C53F	1991	Ex Park's, 1993
133	J437HDS	Volvo B10M-60	Plaxton Premiére 350	C53F	1991	Ex Park's, 1993
134	J431HDS	Volvo B10M-60	Plaxton Premiére 350	C48F	1991	Ex Park's, 1993
135	J432HDS	Volvo B10M-60	Plaxton Premiére 350	C48F	1991	Ex Park's, 1993
136	L979UAH	Volvo B10M-62	Plaxton Premiére 350	C53FT	1994	
137	L978UAH	Volvo B10M-62	Plaxton Premiére 350	C48FT	1994	
138	PIJ3379	Volvo B10M-62	Plaxton Excalibur	C28FT	1994	
139	M741KJU	Volvo B10M-62	Plaxton Premiére 350	C49FT	1995	
140	M742KJU	Volvo B10M-62	Plaxton Premiére 350	C49FT	1995	
141	M743KJU	Volvo B10M-62	Plaxton Premiére 350	C49FT	1995	
142	M330KRY	Volvo B10M-62	Plaxton Premiére 350	C49FT	1995	
143	M331KRY	Volvo B10M-62	Plaxton Premiére 350	C49FT	1995	
144	M332KRY	Volvo B10M-62	Plaxton Premiére 350	C49FT	1995	

Ambassador Travel operate several National Express contracts. Vehicles used include three Volvo B10M-61s with Plaxton's special version of the Expressliner bodywork. Seen in Stratford while heading for Great Yarmouth is F106CCL. *Colin Lloyd*

Six Volvo B6-9.9Ms are employed on a Park and Ride service in Norwich. These are fitted with Alexander's Dash style of bodywork and painted in a predominantly green livery. Seen in Castle Meadow, Norwich is 505, L73UNG. *Keith Grimes*

| 200 | M321VET | Scania K113CRB | Van Hool Alizée | C49F | 1995 | | | |
| 201 | M322VET | Scania K113CRB | Van Hool Alizée | C49F | 1995 | | | |

501-506		Volvo B6-9.9M		Alexander Dash	B41F	1994		
501	L67UNG	503	L69UNG	504	L71UNG	505	L73UNG	506	L74UNG
502	L68UNG							

| 507 | L938ORC | Mercedes-Benz 811D | Plaxton Beaver | B31F | 1994 | | | |

878-886		Leyland Leopard PSU3G/4R	Eastern Coach Works B51	C51F	1982	Ex Eastern Counties, 1984		
878	HCL927Y	882	HEX47Y	884	HEX52Y	885	CAH885Y	886	CAH886Y
881	HCL957Y	883	PIJ8513					

1001	JOX467P	Leyland Leopard PSU3E/4R	Plaxton Supreme III Express	C49F	1977	Ex Midland Red West, 1992
1002	RDA670R	Leyland Leopard PSU3E/4R	Plaxton Supreme III Express	C49F	1978	Ex Midland Red West, 1992
1003	XRR622M	Leyland Leopard PSU3B/4R	Plaxton Elite III Express	C53F	1974	Ex Barton, 1992
1004	GNN221N	Leyland Leopard PSU3B/4R	Plaxton Elite III Express	C53F	1975	Ex Barton, 1992
1006	ONN274M	Leyland Leopard PSU3B/4R	Plaxton Elite III Express	C53F	1974	Ex Barton, 1992
1007	ONN279M	Leyland Leopard PSU3B/4R	Plaxton Elite III Express	C53F	1974	Ex Barton, 1992
1008	RRB118R	Leyland Leopard PSU3D/4R	Duple Dominant I	C49F	1977	Ex Trent, 1993
1009	UVO123S	Leyland Leopard PSU3E/4R	Duple Dominant I	C49F	1977	Ex Trent, 1993
1010	RRB120R	Leyland Leopard PSU3D/4R	Duple Dominant I	C49F	1977	Ex Trent, 1993
1011	RNN982N	Leyland Leopard PSU3B/4R	Plaxton Elite III Express	C53F	1974	Ex Trent, 1993
1012	RNN984N	Leyland Leopard PSU3B/4R	Plaxton Elite III Express	C53F	1974	Ex Trent, 1994
1013	OAL631M	Leyland Leopard PSU3B/4R	Plaxton Elite III Express	C53F	1974	Ex Trent, 1994
1014	XRR629M	Leyland Leopard PSU3B/4R	Plaxton Elite III Express	C53F	1973	Ex Trent, 1994
1015	XRR613M	Leyland Leopard PSU3B/4R	Plaxton Elite III Express	C53F	1973	Ex Trent, 1994

Liveries: White with various contract liveries; green (Park & Ride) 501-7.

Previous Registrations:

HCL927Y	CAH870Y, PIJ5751	HEX52Y	CAH884Y, PIJ4317	PIJ8513	CAH883Y
HCL957Y	CAH881Y, PIJ3379	PIJ3379	L977UAH	PIJ9274	H163EJU
HEX47Y	CAH882Y, PIJ9274	PIJ4317	H173EJU		

AMOS COACHES

J Amos & Son, The Bungalow, Belchamp St Paul, Sudbury, Suffolk, CO10 7BS

HRT530N	Bedford SB5	Duple Dominant	C41F	1975	Ex Burton, Haverhill, 1990
SWO70N	Bedford YRQ	Plaxton Elite III Express	C45F	1975	Ex Davian, Enfield, 1990
JAR484Y	Ford Transit	Ford	M12	1983	Ex private owner, 1993
C764NRC	Ford Transit	Ford	M11	1987	Ex Andrew, Spalding

Livery: Red and cream

ANGLIAN

Anglian Coaches Ltd, Beccles Road, Loddon, Norfolk, NR14 6JJ

WDB551S	Ford R1114	Duple Dominant II	C53F	1979	Ex Phoenix Stowmarket, 1992
OXK395	Ford R1114	Plaxton Supreme IV	C53F	1980	Ex Jenkins, Skewen, 1989
UVG846	Ford R1114	Plaxton Supreme IV	C53F	1980	Ex Horton, Ripley, 1984
KSU412	Ford R1114	Plaxton Supreme IV	C53F	1981	Ex Norfolk , Gt. Yarmouth, 1985
MJI4487	Ford R1114	Plaxton Supreme IV	C53F	1981	Ex Moss, Handsworth, 1986
CSK282	Ford R1114	Plaxton Supreme IV	C53F	1981	Ex Wallace Arnold, 1987
NBX862	Ford R1114	Duple Dominant IV	C53F	1981	Ex Mullover, Bedford, 1992
LTG272X	Ford R1114	Plaxton Supreme IV	C53F	1981	Ex Sanders, Holt, 1993
LTG274X	Ford R1114	Plaxton Supreme IV	C53F	1981	Ex Sanders, Holt, 1993

Previous Registrations:

CSK282	PNW318W	MJI4487	PNB788W	OXK395	BCY249V
KSU412	SVF510W	NBX862	TND101X	UVG846	FTV546V

Livery: Red, white, yellow and blue

APT

PA & AG Thorn, Rawreth Industrial Estate, Rawreth Lane, Rayleigh, Essex SS6 9RL

CBV10S	Bristol VRT/SL3/6LXB	Eastern Coach Works	H43/31F	1977	Ex Ribble, 1993
LHG445T	Bristol VRT/SL3/501(6LXB)	Eastern Coach Works	H43/31F	1979	Ex Ribble, 1993
RIB8815	Bedford YMT	Duple Dominant II	C53F	1980	Ex Economy, Welton, 1995
BAZ6877	Bova EL26/581	Bova Europa	C53F	1981	Ex Stoddard, Cheadle, 1994
HSV673	Bova EL26/581	Bova Europa	C53F	1982	Ex Snow, Great Wakering, 1994
APT416B	Bova EL26/581	Bova Europa	C53F	1983	Ex Stoddard, Cheadle, 1994
APT42S	Van Hool T815H	Van Hool Alizée	C53F	1983	Ex Snow, Great Wakering, 1993
D342JUM	Volkswagen LT55	Optare City Pacer	B25F	1986	Ex Oaklands College, Hatfield, 1994
A20APT	DAF SBR3000DKSB570	Jonckheere Jubilee P99	C57/19CT	1987	Ex ?, 1994
E558CGJ	DAF SBR3000DKZ570	Plaxton Paramount 4000 II	C55/19CT	1988	Ex Clarkes of London, 1995
A12APT	DAF MB230LT615	Plaxton Paramount 3500 III	C49FT	1988	Ex Happy Days, Woodseaves, 1990
A16APT	DAF MB230LB615	Duple 340	C53FT	1989	Ex Tellings-Golden Miller, Cardiff, 1992
K2APT	Volkswagen Transporter T4	Volkswagen	M7	1993	
827APT	Volvo B10M-60	Jonckheere Deauville 45	C49FT	1993	Ex Park's, 1994

Livery: White with many vehicles in contract liveries

Previous Registrations:

827APT	K905RGE	BAZ6877	JHR672W, BGS71A
A12APT	E337EVH, APT42S	E558CGJ	E315AGA, BIL1878
A16APT	F213RJX	HSV673	SMY623X
APT42S	827APT, TRT182, BJS98Y	RIB8815	DHT667W
APT416B	OOU854Y, LIB4333, PMS371, PMS1M		

Much travelled but now regularly on stage runs from the Belchamps is Amos' HRT530N, a Bedford SB5 with forward-entrance Duple Dominant bodywork. *Geoff Mills*

APT Holidays operate several vehicles on holiday contracts from their base in Rayleigh. Two former Ribble, double-deck Bristol VRTs, one high-bridge and one low-bridge, are also owned. LHG445T, a highbridge version is seen here passing Marble Arch. *BBP*

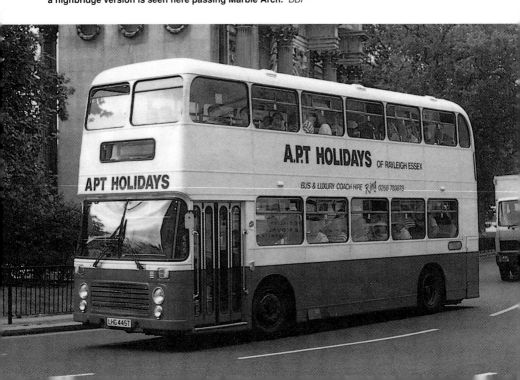

BEESTON

B Beeston's (Hadleigh) Ltd, 21 Long Bessels, Hadleigh, Suffolk IP7 5DB
C Combs Coaches Ltd, Stow Road, Ixworth, Suffolk IP31 2HZ
Constable Coaches Ltd, Station Yard, Long Melford, Sudbury, Suffolk CO10 9LQ
M Mulley's Motorways Ltd, Stow Road, Ixworth, Suffolk IP31 2HZ

Depots: Long Bessels, Hadleigh; Stow Road, Ixworth and Station Yard, Long Melford

	DFK214	AEC Regal III 6821A	Burlingham	C33F	1949	Ex preservation, 1995
M	HGA637T	Leyland Leopard PSU3/4R	Plaxton Supreme IV (1979)	C53F	1967	Ex New Viscount, Witham, 1988
B	CRO689L	Leyland Leopard PSU3B/4R	Plaxton Elite III	C51F	1973	Ex Capitol, Cwmbran, 1995
	PJI3670	Leyland National 11351/1R		DP48F	1975	Ex Wilts & Dorset, 1992
	PJI3671	Leyland National 11351/1R		DP48F	1975	Ex Wilts & Dorset, 1992
B	WUL261N	Leyland Leopard PSU4B/4R	Plaxton Elite III	C41F	1974	Ex British Airways, 1995
M	HTU164N	Bristol VRT/SL2/6LX	Eastern Coach Works	H43/31F	1975	Ex Happy Al's, Moreton, 1994
B	SJI4429	Bristol VRT/SL2/6LX	Eastern Coach Works	H43/31F	1975	Ex Wilts & Dorset, 1994
B	SJI4430	Bristol VRT/SL3/6LX	Eastern Coach Works	H43/31F	1976	Ex Wilts & Dorset, 1994
B	SJI4431	Bristol VRT/SL3/6LX	Eastern Coach Works	H43/31F	1976	Ex Wilts & Dorset, 1994
M	LDV398P	Volvo B58-56	Duple Dominant	C51F	1975	Ex Wangford, Thurston, 1992
	LDW362P	Leyland National 10351/1R		B41F	1975	Ex The Wright Company, Wrexham, 1995
B	FIL4163	Bedford YMT	Plaxton Supreme III	C53F	1977	
	OJD212R	Leyland Fleetline FE30AGR	MCW	H44/24D	1977	Ex Davian, Enfield, 1991
B	OBN502R	Leyland Fleetline FE30AGR	Northern Counties	H43/32F	1977	Ex Rossendale, 1992
M	UWA93S	Leyland Leopard PSU3F/4R	Duple Dominant I	C53F	1977	Ex ?, 1995
M	VAL55S	Leyland Leopard PSU5B/4R	Plaxton Elite III	C57F	1978	Ex Rosemary, Terrington St Clement, 1993
	WGY594S	Leyland National 11351A/3R		B49F	1978	Ex British Airways, 1993
	CFM349S	Leyland National 11351A/1R		B49F	1978	Ex Mancurian, Bradford, 1993
	CFM355S	Leyland National 11351A/1R		B49F	1978	Ex Mancurian, Bradford, 1993

Autumn tints are represented in the Beeston bus livery of sandy-brown with red, yellow black. RFS588V is one of three Leyland National 2 in the Beeston fleet acquired from Westbus in 1993, though all were new to Eastern Scottish. *Malc McDonald*

Photographed passing Cambridge fire station is TND134X, liveried in red for the Mulley's operation. New to Shearings for their tour operations, this Volvo B58 carries a Duple Dominant IV body.
Keith Grimes

	EMB363S	Leyland National 11351A/1R		B49F	1978	Ex CMT, Aintree, 1993
	WWY126S	Bristol VRT/SL3/6LXB	Eastern Coach Works	H43/31F	1978	Ex Sovereign, 1994
	GMB387T	Leyland National 11351A/1R		B49F	1978	Ex Aintree Coachlines, 1994
	SJI4423	Bedford YMT	Plaxton Supreme IV Express	C53F	1979	Ex Mitchell's Coaches, 1994
	SJI4424	AEC Reliance 6U2R	Duple Dominant II Express	C53F	1979	Ex Hants & Dorset, 1994
	SJI4425	AEC Reliance 6U2R	Duple Dominant II Express	C53F	1979	Ex Hants & Dorset, 1994
M	AFH194T	Leyland Leopard PSU5C/4R	Duple Dominant II	C50F	1979	Ex Cavalier, Ramsey, 1995
M	EWR166T	Bristol VRT/SL3/6LX	Eastern Coach Works	H43/31F	1979	Ex Millman, Buckfastleigh, 1991
M	FIL4743	Bedford YMT	Plaxton Supreme IV Express	C53F	1979	
	RFS585V	Leyland National 2 NL116L11/1R		B52F	1980	Ex Westbus, Ashford, 1993
	RFS586V	Leyland National 2 NL116L11/1R		B52F	1980	Ex Westbus, Ashford, 1993
	RFS588V	Leyland National 2 NL116L11/1R		B52F	1980	Ex Westbus, Ashford, 1993
B	LUA283V	Leyland Leopard PSU5D/4R	Plaxton Supreme IV	C57F	1980	Ex Ipswich Travel, 1989
	GHB85W	Bristol VRT/SL3/6LXB	East Lancashire	H44/32F	1981	Ex National Welsh, 1992
B	PNW296W	Leyland Leopard PSU5D/4R	Plaxton Supreme IV	C55F	1981	Ex Theobald, Long Melford, 1991
C	FIL4345	Bedford YMT	Duple Dominant II Express	C53F	1981	
C	RUT684W	Volvo B58-61	Duple Dominant II	C53F	1981	Ex Brown, Horley, 1993
M	TND134X	Volvo B58-61	Duple Dominant IV	C53F	1982	Ex Thorpe, London, 1993
B	TXI8762	Volvo B58-61	Plaxton Supreme IV	C57F	1982	Ex The Noddy Bus, Stevenage, 1995
	VKN836X	Leyland Leopard PSU3F/4R	Willowbrook 003	DP47F	1982	Ex Maidstone & District, 1995
B	219GRA	Leyland Leopard PSU5D/5R	Duple Dominant III	C57F	1982	
M	FIL4169	Leyland Leopard PSU5D/5R	Duple Dominant III	C57F	1982	
M	FIL4741	Leyland Leopard PSU5D/5R	Duple Dominant III	C57F	1982	
M	FIL4742	Leyland Leopard PSU5D/5R	Duple Dominant III	C57F	1982	
	FIL4033	Leyland Leopard PSU5D/5R	Duple Dominant III	C57F	1982	
B	FHJ565	Volvo B10M-61	Van Hool Alizée	C53F	1983	Ex Barratt, Nantwich, 1992
B	FIL4164	Leyland Tiger TRCTL11/3R	Van Hool Alizée	C53DT	1984	Ex Travellers, 1988
B	FIL4165	Leyland Tiger TRCTL11/3R	Van Hool Alizée	C51D	1984	Ex Travellers, 1988
B	FIL4166	Leyland Tiger TRCTL11/3R	Van Hool Alizée	C51FT	1984	Ex Travellers, 1988
M	WSV555	Volvo B10M-61	Van Hool Alizée	C44FT	1984	Ex Berryhurst, Vauxhall, 1986
B	FIL8613	Volvo B10M-61	Van Hool Alizée	C53FT	1983	Ex Ellard, Princes Gate, 1989
M	SXF615	Volvo B10M-61	Van Hool Alizée	C49FT	1984	Ex Crosville Wales, 1990
B	221GRA	Volvo B10M-61	Jonckheere Jubilee P599	C51F	1984	Ex Jalna, Church Gresley, 1992
C	FIL4034	Scania K112CRS	Jonckheere Jubilee P50	C57F	1985	Ex Henry Crawford, Neilston, 1988
M	B711EOF	Volvo B10M-53	Jonckheere Jubilee P95	CH54/13FT	1985	Ex Flights, Birmingham, 1990
B	RJI7972	Kässbohrer Setra S215HD	Kässbohrer	C49FT	1985	Ex Landtourers, Farnham, 1995
M	B387UEX	Leyland Tiger TRCTL11/3R	Plaxton Paramount 3200	C57F	1985	Ex Rosemary, Terrington St Clement, 1992
	SJI4426	Scania K92CRB	Jonckheere Transcity	B47D	1986	Ex Your Bus, Alcester, 1994
B	FIL8614	Leyland Tiger TRCTL11/3RZ	Van Hool Alizée	C45FT	1987	Ex Travellers, 1989
B	FIL8615	Leyland Tiger TRCTL11/3RZ	Van Hool Alizée	C53F	1987	Ex Travellers, 1989
B	RJI7973	Kässbohrer Setra S215HD	Kässbohrer	C49FT	1987	Ex Landtourers, Farnham, 1995
B	SJI2764	Aüwaerter Neoplan N122/3	Aüwaerter Skyliner	CH50/27FT	1987	Ex ?, 1995
	D377JUM	Volkswagen LT55	Optare City Pacer	B25F	1987	Ex London Buses, 1992
	SJI4427	Scania N112DRB	Van Hool Astron	B44D	1988	Ex Terminus, Crawley, 1994
B	PJI4712	Toyota Coaster HB31R	Caetano Optimo	C18F	1988	Ex Spanish Speaking Services, 1992
B	SJI9319	Volvo B10M-61	Van Hool Alizée	C49FT	1988	Ex Shearings, 1993
B	SJI9320	Volvo B10M-61	Van Hool Alizée	C49FT	1988	Ex Shearings, 1993
B	SJI9321	Volvo B10M-61	Van Hool Alizée	C49FT	1989	Ex Shearings, 1992
M	F880TNH	Toyota Coaster HB31R	Caetano Optimo	C20F	1989	Ex The Kings Ferry, 1991
M	F94CBD	Volvo B10M-61	Jonckheere Deauville P599	C51FT	1989	Ex Hill's, Tredegar, 1992

Seen in Sudbury is SJI4426, a Scania K92 with a Jonckheere Trancity bus body This vehicle is distinctly one of the batch new to Scancoaches for LRT contracted service. Vehicles operated by Constable carry a white and blue livery. *David Cole*

B	222GRA	Kässbohrer Setra S215HDI	Kässbohrer Tornado	C49FT	1989	Ex Highliner, Felixstowe, 1992
B	226LRB	Kässbohrer Setra S215HR	Kässbohrer Rational	C49FT	1989	Ex Eve's Cs, Dunbar, 1995
M	G468JNH	Volvo B10M-61	Jonckheere Deauville P599	C50FT	1990	Ex Antler, Rugeley, 1992
M	G973LRP	Volvo B10M-61	Jonckheere Deauville P599	C51FT	1990	Ex Hilo, Sandy, 1993
B	PJI4713	Toyota Coaster HB31R	Caetano Optimo	C18F	1990	Ex Kingsman, Sheffield, 1992
B	FIL8617	Toyota Coaster HDB30R	Caetano Optimo II	C21F	1991	Ex Davies, Slough, 1994
	M759PVM	Mercedes-Benz 814D	Mellor	B31F	1995	

Livery: Sandy-brown with red, orange and black (Beestons); red (Mulleys and Cooks); white and blue (Constable).

Previous Registrations:

219GRA	WGV861X	PJI4084	HWC83N
221GRA	B646OAY	PJI4712	E174KNH
222GRA	F668DDO	PJI4713	G138KKW
226LRB	G182VBB	RJI7972	B486OPJ, 8760EL
DFK214	From new	RJI7973	D599BPA, LSU256
FHJ565	ODS464Y	SJI9319	E621UNE, WSV528, E489CDB
FIL4033	WGV866X	SJI9320	E620UNE, SPR124, E683CDB, PJI6392
FIL4034	B510GBD	SJI9321	E619UNE, XTW359, E684CDB, PJI6393
FIL4163	VGV446S	RUT684W	ODJ576W, VOI6874
FIL4164	A143RMJ	SJI2249	JJT435N
FIL4165	A144RMJ	SJI4423	FBJ3T
FIL4166	A145RMJ	SJI4424	YPL89T
FIL4169	WGV862X	SJI4425	YPL86T
FIL4345	RRT111W	SJI4426	C354SVV
FIL4741	WGV864X	SJI4427	E303FWV
FIL4742	WGV865X	SJI4429	JJT443N
FIL4743	HDX666V	SJI4430	MEL559P
FIL8613	A297RSU	SJI4431	MEL562P
FIL8614	D229HMT	SXF615	From new
FIL8615	D283HMT	TXI8762	XWK9X
FIL8617	H389CFT	WSV555	A623UGD
PJI3670	GLJ677N	YRP371	From new
PJI3671	GLJ678N		

Belle Coaches operate from several depots around Suffolk. The Bedford marque dominated for many years, and since its demise a variety of chassis types have been used. OJI4756 is seen with the flags of Parliament Square in the background. The vehicle is a Scania K112, carring Berkhof Esprite bodywork and was previously a Scania demonstrator. In contrast, OJI4758 is a rear-engined DAF with Plaxton Paramount 3500 coachwork, seen at Llanberis while operating a tour of north Wales.
Ralph Stevens

BELLE COACHES

BR Shreeve & Son Ltd, Belle Coachworks, Horn Hill, Lowestoft, Suffolk NR33 0PX

Depots : Belle Garage, Ravenmere, Beccles; Nine Acres, Aldingham, Leiston and Belle Coachworks, Horn Hill, Lowestoft .

PPG3R	Bedford YMT	Plaxton Supreme III	C53F	1977	Ex Towler, Brandon, 1982
OYV703R	Bedford YMT	Duple Dominant	C53F	1977	Ex Grey Green, 1981
VVD432S	Bedford YMT	Duple Dominant	C53F	1978	Ex Pan Atlas, East Acton, 1980
XYK760T	Bedford YLQ	Duple Dominant II	C41F	1978	Ex Grey Green, 1982
EGV719T	Bedford YMT	Plaxton Supreme III	C53F	1979	Ex Classic, Lowestoft, 1989
YYL776T	Bedford YMT	Duple Dominant II	C53F	1979	Ex Grey Green, 1983
YYL778T	Bedford YMT	Duple Dominant II	C53F	1979	Ex Grey Green, 1984
YYL783T	Bedford YMT	Duple Dominant II	C53F	1979	Ex Grey Green, 1983
YYL786T	Bedford YMT	Duple Dominant II	C53F	1979	Ex Grey Green, 1983
YYL795T	Bedford YLQ	Duple Dominant II	C41F	1979	Ex Grey Green, 1985
JFA450V	Bedford YMT	Plaxton Supreme IV	C53F	1979	Ex Cross Gates Coaches, 1987
CDO999V	Bedford YMT	Duple Dominant II	C53F	1980	Ex Wing, Sleaford, 1983
MDX668V	Bedford YMT	Duple Dominant II	C53F	1980	Ex Classic, Lowestoft, 1989
NPV308W	Bedford YMT	Duple Dominant II	C53F	1980	Ex Claremont, Worcester Park, 1987
NPV309W	Bedford YMT	Duple Dominant II	C53F	1980	Ex Claremont, Worcester Park, 1987
PRT700W	Bedford YMT	Duple Dominant II	C53F	1981	Ex Constable, Felixstowe, 1981
NJI9241	Bedford YNT	Plaxton Supreme VI Express	C53F	1982	Ex Taylor, York, 1986
OJI4627	Bedford YNT	Duple Dominant IV	C53F	1982	Ex Back, Witney, 1985
NJI9244	Bedford YMT	Plaxton Supreme IV	C53F	1983	Ex Crusader, Clacton, 1992
NJI9242	Bedford YNT	Plaxton Paramount 3200	C53F	1983	Ex Farnham Coaches, 1989
NJI9243	Bedford YNT	Plaxton Paramount 3200	C53F	1983	Ex Farnham Coaches, 1989
NJI9245	Bedford YNT	Plaxton Paramount 3200	C53F	1985	Ex Classic, Lowestoft, 1992
OJI4754	DAF SB2300DHS585	Plaxton Paramount 3200	C53F	1985	Ex Sweyne Coaches, Swinefleet, 1994
OJI4755	LAG G350Z	LAG Panoramic	C53F	1986	Ex 1st Battalion, Royal Green Jackets, 1991
OJI4756	Scania K112CRS	Berkhof Esprite 340	C54F	1985	Ex Scania demonstrator, 1988
D21XPF	LAG G355Z	LAG Panoramic	C49FT	1986	Ex Crusader, Clacton, 1991
D22XPF	LAG G355Z	LAG Panoramic	C49FT	1986	Ex Crusader, Clacton, 1991
OJI4758	DAF SB2300DHS585	Plaxton Paramount 3500 II	C49FT	1987	Ex Farnham Coaches, 1988
D613YCX	DAF SB2300DHS585	Plaxton Paramount 3500 III	C53F	1987	Ex Classic, Lowestoft, 1992
E83DRY	Bedford Venturer YNV	Duple 320	C57F	1987	Ex Classic, Lowestoft, 1992
E84DRY	Bedford Venturer YNV	Duple 320	C57F	1987	
E134KRP	LAG G355Z	LAG Panoramic	C48FT	1987	Ex Jalna, Church Gresley, 1991
E674NNV	LAG G355Z	LAG Panoramic	C49FT	1988	Ex Silver Coach Lines, Edinburgh, 1992
F218RJX	DAF SB3000DKV601	Van Hool Alizée	C51FT	1988	Ex Wharfedale Coaches, Yeadon, 1993
F466TJV	Scania K112CRB	Van Hool Alizée	C51F	1989	Ex Barnard, Kirton in Lindsey, 1993
F24WNH	LAG G355Z	LAG Panoramic	C49FT	1989	Ex Coach Stop, Leigh-on-Sea, 1994
G839VAY	Dennis Javelin 12SDA1907	Caetano Algarve	C53F	1989	Ex Lloyd, Nuneaton, 1994
G224HCP	DAF SB2305DHTD585	Duple 320	C57DL	1990	
G488KBD	LAG G355Z	LAG Panoramic	C49FT	1990	Ex Coach Stop, Leigh-on-Sea, 1994
J392BNG	Ford Transit VE6	Deansgate	M12	1991	
J20GSM	MAN 11.180	Berkhof Excellence 1000L	C35F	1991	Ex Mayne's, Buckie, 1993
K101VJU	Toyota Coaster HDB30R	Caetano Optimo II	C21F	1993	

Livery: Blue and cream

Previous Registrations:

NJI9241	TPM615X	NJI9245	B44LUT	OJI4755	C623UPG
NJI9242	BPJ673Y	OJI4627	WRY77X	OJI4756	C112JTM
NJI9243	BPJ674Y	OJI4754	B233RRU	OJI4758	538FCG, D992DPE
NJI9244	FUR895Y				

BISS BROTHERS

Biss Brothers Coaches Ltd, London Road, Spellbrook, Bishops Stortford,
Hertfordshire CM23 4AU

Part of the Lynton Travel Group

MCA676T	Leyland National 10351B/1R		B44F	1979	Ex Citibus, Middleton, 1994
KBH860V	Leyland Leopard PSU5C/4R	Plaxton Supreme IV	C57F	1980	
KBH861V	Leyland Leopard PSU5C/4R	Plaxton Supreme IV	C51F	1980	
125LUP	Mercedes-Benz 0303/15R	Jonckheere Jubilee P599	C51FT	1984	
556EHN	Bova FHM12.280	Bova Futura	C49FT	1985	
696BTV	Bova FHM12.280	Bova Futura	C49FT	1986	
E940CJN	Mercedes-Benz 709D	Reeve Burgess Beaver	C19F	1988	
E357NEG	Iveco Daily 49.10	Robin Hood City Nippy	DP19F	1988	Ex County, 1994
114UPH	Van Hool T815H	Van Hool Acron	C49FT	1988	
PUU970	Van Hool T815H	Van Hool Acron	C49FT	1990	
G643YVS	Mercedes-Benz 814D	Reeve Burgess Beaver	DP29F	1990	
J7BBC	Bova FHM12.290	Bova Futura	C49FT	1992	
J8BBC	Bova FHD12.290	Bova Futura	C49FT	1992	
L343FWF	Bova FHD12.340	Bova Futura	C49FT	1994	
M121SKY	Toyota Coaster HZB50R	Caetano Optimo III	C18F	1994	
M131SKY	Toyota Coaster HZB50R	Caetano Optimo III	C21F	1994	
M384WET	Bova FHD12.340	Bova Futura	C49FT	1995	
M61WER	Iveco TurboDaily 59-12	Marshall C31	DP25F	1995	

Livery: White and blue

Previous Registrations:

114UPH	E314MMM	556EHN	B558KRY	PUU970	G601VML
125LUP	A113SNH	696BTV	From new		

**The Bova Futura, built in Valkenswaard in The Netherlands, is currently imported through Optare
group. Most of the power units for this integral product are of MAN manufacture, with DAF and
Mercedes-Benz optional, DAF being the most common choice in the UK.   Biss' 696BTV is seen
passing through Tottenham Hale with a Mercedes-Benz badge giving a good indication of the power
unit fitted.** *Colin Lloyd*

BOON'S TOURS

HG & MD Boon, 29 Church Road, Boreham, Essex CM3 3BN

JSC883E	Leyland Atlantean PDR1/1	Alexander A	H43/31F	1967	Ex Lothian, 1980
SPW92N	Leyland Atlantean AN68/2R	Roe	H45/33D	1974	Ex Pegg, Caston, 1990
NNO63P	Leyland Atlantean AN68A/1R	Eastern Coach Works	H43/31F	1976	Ex Colchester, 1991
NNO66P	Leyland Atlantean AN68A/1R	Eastern Coach Works	H43/31F	1976	Ex Colchester, 1991
MVK538R	Leyland Atlantean AN68A/2R	Alexander AL	H48/34F	1976	Ex Colchester, 1990
GSU379	Kässbohrer Setra S215HR	Kässbohrer Rational	C49FT	1984	Ex Taylor, Frimley, 1991
TSU611	Kässbohrer Setra S215HD	Kässbohrer Tornado	C49FT	1990	Ex Tours Exclusive, 1991
RSU231	Kässbohrer Setra S215HD	Kässbohrer Tornado	C49FT	1992	
K550RJX	DAF SB3000DKVF601	Van Hool Alizée	C49FT	1992	
K11BOO	Scania K113TRB	Van Hool Alizée	C48FT	1993	
KSU369	Kässbohrer Setra S215HD	Kässbohrer Tornado	C48FT	1993	
SSU331	Kässbohrer Setra S215HD	Kässbohrer	C36FT	1994	
K129OCT	Kässbohrer Setra S215HD	Kässbohrer	C48FT	1994	
WSU225	Kässbohrer Setra S250	Kässbohrer	C49FT	1995	
M313VET	Scania K93CRB	Berkhof Excellence 1000L	C53F	1995	

Livery: Cream and red

Previous Registrations:

GSU379	A61EPH	RSU231	From new		TSU611	From new
KSU369	From new	SSU331	K124OCT		WSU225	M858YVW

Boon's Tours operate several Kässbohrer Setra coaches, including an example of the new S250 Special model, shown on the frontispiece. Also new for the 1995 season is M313VET, a Scania K93 with the lower height Berkhof Excellence body. *BBP*

BORDACOACH

GF & DS Stubbington, 4 Highview Road, Thundersley Common, Benfleet, Essex

Note: Bordabus and Dorayme Travel names are also used.

70	524FN	AEC Reliance 2U3RA	Plaxton Elite (1972)	C49F	1962	Ex East Kent, 1982
79	YPL91T	AEC Reliance 6U2R	Duple Dominant II Express	C53F	1979	Ex London Country, 1985
97	MED406P	AEC Reliance 6U3ZR	Duple Dominant	C57F	1976	Ex Baker, Weston-super-Mare, 1990
103	OJD448R	Leyland Fleetline FE30ALRSp	Park Royal	H44/24D	1977	Ex London Buses, 1992
109	BFR301R	Leyland Atlantean AN68A/2R	East Lancashire	H50/36F	1977	Ex Partridge, Hadleigh, 1994

Previous Registrations:
524FN   From new

Livery: White and blue, vehicles sometimes operate in as 'acquired livery'.

BUCKINGHAMSHIRE ROAD CAR

MK Metro Ltd, Snowdon Drive, Winterhill, Milton Keynes, Buckinghamshire, MK6 1AD

A subsidiary of Cambus Holdings Ltd

01-45

Mercedes-Benz L608D   Robin Hood*   B20F*   1986   *29 is Dormobile(1990) and B25F

01	D101VRP	10	D110VRP	19	D119VRP	28	D128VRP	37	D137VRP
02	D102VRP	11	D111VRP	20	D120VRP	29	D129VRP	38	D138VRP
03	D103VRP	12	D112VRP	21	D121VRP	30	D130VRP	39	D139VRP
04	D104VRP	13	D113VRP	22	D122VRP	31	D131VRP	40	D140VRP
05	D105VRP	14	D114VRP	23	D123VRP	32	D132VRP	41	D141VRP
06	D106VRP	15	D115VRP	24	D124VRP	33	D133VRP	42	D142VRP
07	D107VRP	16	D116VRP	25	D125VRP	34	D134VRP	43	D143VRP
08	D108VRP	17	D117VRP	26	D126VRP	35	D135VRP	44	D144VRP
09	D109VRP	18	D118VRP	27	D127VRP	36	D136VRP	45	D145VRP

47-64

Mercedes-Benz L608D   Alexander AM   DP19F*   1986   *55/6/64 are B20F

47	D147VRP	48	D148VRP	55	D155VRP	56	D156VRP	64	D164VRP

66-73

Mercedes-Benz 709D   Robin Hood   B25F   1988

66	E66MVV	68	E68MVV	70	E70MVV	72	E72MVV	73	E73MVV
67	E67MVV	69	E69MVV	71	E71MVV				

77	D177VRP	Mercedes-Benz L608D	Dormobile (1990)	B25F	1986
81	D181VRP	Mercedes-Benz L608D	Alexander AM	B20F	1986
83	D183VRP	Mercedes-Benz L608D	Alexander AM	B20F	1986
92	D192VRP	Mercedes-Benz L608D	Alexander AM	B20F	1986

93-99

Mercedes-Benz 709D   Dormobile Routemaker   B29F   1989-90

93	G93ERP	96	G96ERP	97	G97ERP	98	G98NBD	99	G99NBD
94	G94ERP							

Milton Keynes local services are mainly provided by Buckinghamshire Road Car who operate a fleet comprising mostly minibuses and Bristol VRs. Representative are 97, G97ERP, a Dormobile Routemaker-bodied Mercedes-Benz 709D and 3937, MCL937P, a Bristol VRT transferred from fellow group member Cambus in 1994. *Colin Lloyd*

100	G100NBD	Mercedes-Benz 709D	Dormobile Routemaker	B29F	1990	
201	J201JRP	Mercedes-Benz 709D	Plaxton Beaver	B27F	1991	
202	J202JRP	Mercedes-Benz 709D	Plaxton Beaver	B27F	1991	
203	J203JRP	Mercedes-Benz 709D	Plaxton Beaver	B27F	1991	
204	J204JRP	Mercedes-Benz 709D	Plaxton Beaver	B27F	1991	
359	F359GKN	Mercedes-Benz 811D	Dormobile Routemaker	B29F	1989	Ex Dormobile demonstrator, 1989
CT419	K419FAV	Mercedes-Benz 709D	Marshall C19	DP18FL	1993	
CT426	K426FAV	Mercedes-Benz 709D	Marshall C19	DP18FL	1993	
CT428	K428FAV	Mercedes-Benz 709D	Marshall C19	DP18FL	1993	
CT447	C447NNV	Renault-Dodge S56	Harrops Wellfair	M16L	1986	
CT448	C448NNV	Renault-Dodge S56	Harrops Wellfair	M16L	1986	
2618	PEX618W	Leyland National 2 NL116L11/1R		B49F	1980	Ex Cambus, 1995
2619	PEX619W	Leyland National 2 NL116L11/1R		B49F	1980	Ex Cambus, 1994
2622	PEX622W	Leyland National 2 NL116L11/1R		B49F	1980	Ex Cambus, 1994
3009	CBV9S	Bristol VRT/SL3/501(6LXB)	Eastern Coach Works	H43/31F	1977	Ex Ribble, 1993
3019	CBV19S	Bristol VRT/SL3/501(6LXB)	Eastern Coach Works	H43/31F	1977	Ex Ribble, 1993
3034	NJT34P	Bristol VRT/SL3/6LX	Eastern Coach Works	H43/31F	1976	Ex Wilts & Dorset, 1993
3136	NAH136P	Bristol VRT/SL3/6LXB	Eastern Coach Works	H43/31F	1976	Ex Cambus, 1993
3137	NAH137P	Bristol VRT/SL3/6LXB(501)	Eastern Coach Works	H43/31F	1976	Ex Cambus, 1993
3233	DNG233T	Bristol VRT/SL3/6LXB	Eastern Coach Works	H43/31F	1979	Ex Viscount, 1995
3282	MDM282P	Bristol VRT/SL3/6LXB	Eastern Coach Works	H43/31F	1975	Ex Happy Days, Woodseaves, 1993
3307	NRU307M	Bristol VRT/SL2/6LX	Eastern Coach Works	H43/31F	1974	Ex Wilts & Dorset, 1993
3310	NRU310M	Bristol VRT/SL2/6LX	Eastern Coach Works	H43/31F	1974	Ex Wilts & Dorset, 1993
3311	NRU311M	Bristol VRT/SL2/6LX	Eastern Coach Works	H43/31F	1974	Ex Wilts & Dorset, 1993
3353	YTU353S	Bristol VRT/SL3/501	Eastern Coach Works	H43/31F	1977	Ex Happy Days, Woodseaves, 1993
3436	OUD436M	Bristol VRT/SL3/6LX	Eastern Coach Works	H43/34F	1974	Ex Western National, 1993
3441	JJT441N	Bristol VRT/SL2/6LX	Eastern Coach Works	H43/31F	1975	Ex Wilts & Dorset, 1993
3556	MEL556P	Bristol VRT/SL3/6LXB	Eastern Coach Works	H43/31F	1976	Ex Wilts & Dorset, 1993
3559	MEL559P	Bristol VRT/SL3/6LXB	Eastern Coach Works	H43/31F	1976	Ex Viscount, 1995
3575	GNJ575N	Bristol VRT/SL2/6LX	Eastern Coach Works	H43/31F	1975	Ex Brighton & Hove, 1988
3711	GNG711N	Bristol VRT/SL3/6G	Eastern Coach Works	H43/31F	1975	Ex Cambus, 1993
3724	LOD724P	Bristol VRT/SL3/501	Eastern Coach Works	DPH31/29F	1975	Ex Southern National, 1993
3725	LOD725P	Bristol VRT/SL3/501	Eastern Coach Works	DPH31/29F	1975	Ex Southern National, 1993
3826	URB826S	Bristol VRT/SL3/501(6LXB)	Eastern Coach Works	H43/31F	1977	Ex Trent, 1992
3937	MCL937P	Bristol VRT/SL3/6LXB	Eastern Coach Works	H43/31F	1976	Ex Cambus, 1994
3942	URP942W	Bristol VRT/SL3/6LXB	Eastern Coach Works	H43/31F	1981	Ex United Counties, 1986

Livery: Green and cream (Buckinghamshire Road Car); White and yellow (City Bus)

Operators: City Bus: 01/7-11/3-26/8/30-45/7/8/92/5, Buckinghamshire: Remainder

Citybus livery is applied to several of the minibuses, including 18, D118VRP, seen on Midsummer Boulevard, Milton Keynes during mid-winter, 1994. A reorganisation of operations at Milton Keynes has seen the demise of the former Milton Keynes Citybus and Johnsons subsidiaries.
Colin Lloyd

BUFFALO

Bornyard Ltd & Grouptravs Ltd, Enterprise Way, Maulden Road Industrial Estate,
Flitwick, Bedfordshire, MK45 5BW

2	2583KP	Volvo B10M-61	Caetano Algarve	C53FT	1986	Ex Skill's, 1988
3	UXI7897	Volvo B10M-61	Duple Dominant IV	C53F	1983	Ex Bere Regis & District, 1992
4	VXI5357	Volvo B10M-61	Duple Dominant IV	C53F	1983	Ex Bere Regis & District, 1992
5	2997HL	Volvo B10M-61	Caetano Alpha	C53F	1983	
6	KAF577W	Volvo B58-56	Duple Dominant IV	C53F	1981	Ex Brown, Horley, 1988
7	9349KP	Volvo B58-61	Plaxton Supreme III	C57F	1978	Ex Fountain, Twickenham, 1981
9	LXI2743	Volvo B58-61	Plaxton Supreme III	C57F	1978	Ex Silver Fox, Renfrew, 1984
10	RNK749M	Bedford YRT	Plaxton Elite III	C53F	1973	Ex Isleworth Coaches, 1982
12	GTM155T	Bedford YMT	Duple Dominant II	C53F	1978	Ex Cedar, Bedford, 1992
15	WXI4357	Volvo B58-56	Plaxton Supreme III	C44F	1975	Ex Blunderbus, High Wycombe,
16	LUB514P	Volvo B58-56	Plaxton Supreme III	C53F	1975	Ex McColl, Balloch, 1992
17	7178KP	Dennis Javelin 8.5SDL1903	Duple 320	C35F	1988	Ex Brook, Werneth, 1995
21	H170DJF	Toyota Coaster HB31R	Caetano Optimo	C21F	1990	Ex Golden Boy, Roydon, 1995
24	JIL7424	Volvo B10M-61	Caetano Algarve II	C53F	1987	Ex Catteralls, Southam, 1995
30	WRY598	Auwaerter Neoplan N722/3	Plaxton Paramount 4000 II	CH53/18CT	1986	Ex Express Travel, 1995
55	L555GSM	Dennis Javelin 12SDA2131	Berkhof Excellence 1000	C51F	1994	Ex Mayne's, Buckie, 1995
57	L777GSM	Dennis Javelin 12SDA2131	Berkhof Excellence 1000	C51F	1994	Ex Mayne's, Buckie, 1995
62	GSL898N	Daimler Fleetline CRG6LX	Alexander AL	H49/34D	1975	Ex Independent, Horsforth, 1987
63	GHV979N	Daimler Fleetline CRL6	Park Royal	H45/32D	1975	Ex Ementon, Cranfield, 1988
64	THX493S	Leyland Fleetline FE30ALR	Park Royal	H44/24D	1977	Ex Morgan Staplehurst, 1994
65	THX533S	Leyland Fleetline FE30ALR	Park Royal	H44/27D	1978	Ex Morgan Staplehurst, 1994
66	THX605S	Leyland Fleetline FE30ALR	Park Royal	H44/27D	1978	Ex Midland Fox, 1995
67	OJD414R	Leyland Fleetline FE30ALR	Park Royal	H44/27D	1977	Ex Midland Fox, 1995
68	OJD468R	Leyland Fleetline FE30ALR	Park Royal	H44/24D	1975	Ex London Buses, 1991
69 w	TND439X	Dennis Dominantor DD136	Northern Counties	H43/33F	1981	Ex Go Whippet, Fenstanton, 1989
70 w	TND440X	Dennis Dominantor DD136	Northern Counties	H43/33F	1981	Ex Go Whippet, Fenstanton, 1989
71	OJD141R	Leyland Fleetline FE30AGR	Park Royal	H45/32F	1976	Ex Taylor, Sutton Scotney, 1994
72	OUC49R	Leyland Fleetline FE30AGR	MCW	H44/24D	1976	Ex Taylor, Sutton Scotney, 1994
74	WWJ771M	Daimler Fleetline CRG6LXB	Park Royal	O43/27D	1974	Ex South Yorkshire, 1986
77	K777KGM	Scania K93CRB	Plaxton Premiére 320	C53F	1994	Ex Mayne's, Buckie, 1995

Previous Registrations:

2583KP	C45OTV	LXI2743	DGD88T, 7178KP, HKX319T
2997HL	JNM55Y	UXI5357	ENF575Y
7178KP	E149AGG	UXI7897	ENF562Y
9349KP	CLC746T	WXI4357	LUB506P
DMJ305X	LCY302X, 7178KP	WRY598	C180KHG
JIL7424	D507WNV, 24PAE, D184DWP		

Livery: White, yellow and red

EAV810V of Buffalo is a Duple Dominant II Express now with bus seats in a coach shell. Based on a Volvo B58, it is seen in Luton destined for Hemel Hempstead. The sale of Buffalo's commercial services to The Shires returns the company to staple contract and private hire work.
Richard Godfrey

BUZZ

Buzz Co-operative Ltd, Denmar House, Riverway, Harlow, Essex, CM20 2DP

JPL185K	Leyland Atlantean PDR1A/1	Park Royal	H43/29D	1972	Ex preservation, 1993
F71SMC	Mercedes-Benz 609D	Reeve Burgess Beaver	DP25F	1988	
F72SMC	Mercedes-Benz 609D	Reeve Burgess Beaver	B20F	1988	
F73SMC	Mercedes-Benz 609D	Reeve Burgess Beaver	B20F	1988	
F74SMC	Mercedes-Benz 609D	Reeve Burgess Beaver	B20F	1988	
F75SMC	Mercedes-Benz 609D	Reeve Burgess Beaver	B20F	1988	
F76SMC	Mercedes-Benz 609D	Reeve Burgess Beaver	B20F	1988	
F77SMC	Mercedes-Benz 609D	Reeve Burgess Beaver	B20F	1988	
F78SMC	Mercedes-Benz 609D	Reeve Burgess Beaver	B20F	1988	
F79SMC	Mercedes-Benz 609D	Reeve Burgess Beaver	B20F	1988	
FIL7253	Leyland Tiger TRCTL11/3RZ	Plaxton Paramount 3500 II	C49FT	1986	Ex Ambassador, 1993
F365BUA	Mercedes-Benz 811D	Optare StarRider	DP30F	1988	Ex Optare demonstrator, 1989
F678AWW	Mercedes-Benz 811D	Optare StarRider	B27F	1988	Ex Optare demonstrator, 1989

Livery: White, yellow and grey

Previous Registrations:
FIL7253   C913BMG

The Buzz Co-operative operate minibus services around Harlow. Seen here is F79SMC showing the Reeve Burgess Beaver design. The destination blind reads Town station. *Keith Grimes*

CAMBUS / PREMIER TRAVEL

Cambus Ltd, 3-5 Dukes Court, Newmarket Road, Cambridge CB5 8DY
Premier Travel Services Ltd, Kilmaine Close, Kings Hedges Road,
Cambridge, CB4 2PH

Depots: Cowley Road, Cambridge; Kilmaine Close, Cambridge and Depot Road, Newmarket.

Subsidiaries of Cambus Holdings Ltd

W001	D632NOE	MCW MetroRider MF150/4	MCW	B25F	1987	On loan from West Midlands Travel	
W002	D648NOE	MCW MetroRider MF150/4	MCW	B25F	1987	On loan from West Midlands Travel	

155-169		Volvo B6-9M		Marshall C32		B32F	1993
155	L655MFL	**158**	L658MFL	**161**	L661MFL	**164**	L664MFL	**168**	L668MFL
156	L656MFL	**159**	L659MFL	**162**	L662MFL	**165**	L665MFL	**169**	L669MFL
157	L657MFL	**160**	L660MFL	**163**	L663MFL	**167**	L667MFL		

304	PEX620W	Leyland National 2 NL116AL11/1R		B49F	1981	Ex Viscount, 1990
305	PEX621W	Leyland National 2 NL116AL11/1R		B49F	1981	Ex Viscount, 1990
307	UVF623X	Leyland National 2 NL116AL11/1R		B49F	1981	Ex Eastern Counties, 1984
310	F167SMT	Leyland Lynx LX112L10ZR1S	Leyland Lynx	B49F	1989	Ex Miller, Foxton, 1992
311	F168SMT	Leyland Lynx LX112L10ZR1S	Leyland Lynx	B49F	1989	Ex Miller, Foxton, 1992
312	F171SMT	Leyland Lynx LX112L10ZR1S	Leyland Lynx	B49F	1989	Ex Miller, Foxton, 1992
389	F107NRT	Volvo B10M-61	Plaxton Paramount 3500 III	C49FT	1988	Ex Viscount, 1990
390	F108NRT	Volvo B10M-61	Plaxton Paramount 3500 III	C49FT	1988	Ex Viscount, 1990
391	HSV196	Volvo B10M-61	Plaxton Paramount 3500 III	C49FT	1988	Ex Viscount, 1990
400	ESU920	Scania K92CRB	Van Hool Alizée	C55F	1988	Ex Miller, Foxton, 1992
401	ESU913	Scania K92CRB	Van Hool Alizée	C53F	1988	Ex Miller, Foxton, 1992
402	H402DEG	Volvo B10M-60	Plaxton Paramount 3500 III	C51F	1990	
403	H403DEG	Volvo B10M-60	Plaxton Paramount 3500 III	C51F	1990	
404	HSV194	Volvo B10M-61	Plaxton Paramount 3500 III	C49FT	1988	Ex Wallace Arnold, 1991
405	HSV195	Volvo B10M-61	Plaxton Paramount 3500 III	C49FT	1988	Ex Wallace Arnold, 1991
406	H406GAV	Volvo B10M-60	Plaxton Paramount 3500 III	C51F	1991	
407	H407GAV	Volvo B10M-60	Plaxton Paramount 3500 III	C53F	1991	
408	J408TEW	Volvo B10M-60	Plaxton Paramount 3500 III	C53F	1992	
409	J409TEW	Volvo B10M-60	Plaxton Paramount 3500 III	C49FT	1992	

During 1993 Cambus took delivery of fourteen Volvo B6s with locally-built Marshall bodywork. Their C32 model is the 8.5 metre body; the C33 and C34 being the 9 and 10 metre lengths. Seen in Cambridge is 163, L663MFL.
J C Hillmer

Appropriately displaying the Millers of Cambridge fleetname, having been new to that operator is 400, ESU920, a Scania K92 with Van Hool Alizée coachwork. It is seen heading for Buckingham Palace during the 1995 summer. *BBP*

410	F947NER	Scania K112CRB	Plaxton Paramount 3500 III	C49FT	1988	Ex Miller, Foxton, 1993
411	F948NER	Scania K112CRB	Plaxton Paramount 3500 III	C49FT	1988	Ex Miller, Foxton, 1993
412	F252OFP	Volvo B10M-60	Plaxton Paramount 3500 III	C49FT	1989	On loan
413	J447HDS	Volvo B10M-60	Plaxton Premiére 350	C49FT	1992	Ex Park's, 1993
414	J448HDS	Volvo B10M-60	Plaxton Premiére 350	C49FT	1992	Ex Park's, 1993
421	K911RGE	Volvo B10M-60	Jonckheere Deauville P599	C49FT	1993	Ex Park's, 1994
422	K912RGE	Volvo B10M-60	Jonckheere Deauville P599	C49FT	1993	Ex Park's, 1994
424	K96OGA	Toyota Coaster HDB30R	Caetano Optimo II	C21F	1992	Ex Morrow, Glasgow, 1993
425	G525LWU	Volvo B10M-60	Plaxton Paramount 3500 III	C49FT	1990	Ex Wallace Arnold, 1994
426	G526LWU	Volvo B10M-60	Plaxton Paramount 3500 III	C49FT	1990	Ex Wallace Arnold, 1994
427	G527LWU	Volvo B10M-60	Plaxton Paramount 3500 III	C49FT	1990	Ex Wallace Arnold, 1994
428	K458PNR	Volvo B10M-60	Plaxton Premiére 350	C49FT	1993	Ex Supreme, Hadleigh, 1994
429	K457PNR	Volvo B10M-60	Plaxton Premiére 350	C49FT	1993	Ex Supreme, Hadleigh, 1994
430	G520LWU	Volvo B10M-60	Plaxton Paramount 3500 III	C49FT	1990	Ex Wallace Arnold, 1994

431-435

Volvo B10M-60 — Plaxton Paramount 3500 III — C48FT — 1991 — Ex Wallace Arnold, 1994
*431 is C49FT

431	H649UWR	432	H642UWR	433	H643UWR	434	H652UWR	435	H653UWR

437-444

Volvo B10M-60 — Plaxton Premiére 350 — C48FT — 1992 — Ex Wallace Arnold, 1994

737	J702CWT	439	J739CWT	441	J741CWT	443	J743CWT	444	J744CWT
738	J706CWT	440	J740CWT	442	J742CWT				

445-452

Volvo B10M-62 — Plaxton Expressliner II — C49FT — 1995

445	N445XVA	447	N447XVA	449	N449XVA	451	N451XVA	452	N452XVA
446	N446XVA	448	N448XVA	450	N450XVA				

Opposite: **Two vehicles from the Cambridge allocation are Bristol VRT 749, DBV28W, a low-height version recently acquired from Buckinghamshire Road Car, but new to Ribble, and 976, M976WWR, an Optare MetroRider and one of five delivered during 1995.** *Paul Wigan*

Premier Travel Services and Cambus' operations share a common fleet numbering system and vehicles do transfer between the two occasionally. The majority of coaches are Volvo, including two with Belgian-built Jonckheere Deauville bodywork. Seen working into London is 421, K911RGE, once part of the large Park's of Hamilton fleet. *Colin Lloyd*

481	A681KDV	Leyland Olympian ONLXB/1R	Eastern Coach Works	H45/32F	1983	Ex Southern National, 1995
483	A683KDV	Leyland Olympian ONLXB/1R	Eastern Coach Works	H45/32F	1983	Ex Southern National, 1995
500	E500LFL	Leyland Olympian ONLXCT/1RH	Optare	DPH43/27F	1988	
501	E501LFL	Leyland Olympian ONLXCT/1RH	Optare	DPH43/27F	1988	
503	UWW3X	Leyland Olympian ONLXB/1R	Roe	H47/29F	1982	Ex West Yorkshire PTE, 1987
504	UWW4X	Leyland Olympian ONLXB/1R	Roe	H47/29F	1982	Ex West Yorkshire PTE, 1987
505	UWW8X	Leyland Olympian ONLXB/1R	Roe	H47/29F	1982	Ex West Yorkshire PTE, 1987

512-517
Leyland Olympian ONLXB/1RZ Northern Counties H45/30F 1989

| 512 | F512NJE | 514 | F514NJE | 515 | F515NJE | 516 | F516NJE | 517 | F517NJE |
| 513 | F513NJE | | | | | | | | |

518	N518XER	Volvo Olympian YN2RV18Z4	Northern Counties Palatine	DPH45/31F	1995	
519	N519XER	Volvo Olympian YN2RV18Z4	Northern Counties Palatine	DPH45/31F	1995	
520	N520XER	Volvo Olympian YN2RV18Z4	Northern Counties Palatine	DPH45/31F	1995	
552	JAH552D	Bristol FLF6G	Eastern Coach Works	O38/32F	1966	Ex Viscount, 1990
703	NAH138P	Bristol VRT/SL3/501(6LXB)	Eastern Coach Works	H43/31F	1976	Ex Eastern Counties, 1984

709-718
Bristol VRT/SL3/6LXB Eastern Coach Works H43/31F 1976-77 Ex Viscount, 1992
715 ex Eastern Counties, 1984

| 709 | OPW179P | 712 | OPW182P | 716 | PEX386R | 717 | PVF353R | 718 | TEX405R |
| 710 | OPW180P | 715 | WPW200S | | | | | | |

719-729
Bristol VRT/SL3/6LXB Eastern Coach Works H43/31F 1978-79 Ex Eastern Counties, 1984
722 ex Viscount, 1991; 724 ex Green, Kirkintilloch, 1991

| 719 | YNG209S | 721 | YNG212S | 723 | BCL213T | 725 | DEX228T | 727 | DNG232T |
| 720 | YNG210S | 722 | YWY830S | 724 | FRP905T | 726 | DEX231T | 729 | DNG234T |

730-737
Bristol VRT/SL3/6LXB Eastern Coach Works H43/31F 1979-81 Ex York City & District, 1990

| 730 | FWR216T | 732 | FWR218T | 734 | NUM341V | 736 | SUB794W | 737 | SUB795W |
| 731 | FWR217T | 733 | JUB650V | 735 | PWY37W | | | | |

One of eight Bristol VRTs previously with **York City & District** is 730, FWR261T, photographed at Cambridge bus station as the vehicle sets out for Gamlingay in July 1995. *Paul Wigan*

738	RAH260W	Bristol VRT/SL3/6LXB	Eastern Coach Works	H43/31F	1980	Ex Eastern Counties, 1984
739	URP943W	Bristol VRT/SL3/501	Eastern Coach Works	H43/31F	1981	Ex Buckinghamshire Road Car, 1994

740-746   Bristol VRT/SL3/6LXB   Eastern Coach Works   H43/31F*   1980-81   Ex Eastern Counties, 1984
*741 is DPH42/24F

740	RAH265W	**742**	VEX295X	**744**	VEX296X	**745**	VEX303X	**746**	VEX304X
741	RAH268W	**743**	VEX300X						

747	STW24W	Bristol VRT/SL3/6LXB	Eastern Coach Works	H39/31F	1981	Ex Green, Kirkintilloch, 1991
748	STW30W	Bristol VRT/SL3/6LXC	Eastern Coach Works	H39/31F	1981	Ex Green, Kirkintilloch, 1991
749	DBV28W	Bristol VRT/SL3/6LXB	Eastern Coach Works	H43/31F	1980	Ex Buckinghamshire Roadcar, 1994
750	ONH927V	Bristol VRT/SL3/6LXB	Eastern Coach Works	H43/31F	1980	Ex Buckinghamshire Roadcar, 1994
751	VEX298X	Bristol VRT/SL3/6LXB	Eastern Coach Works	H43/31F	1981	Ex Eastern Counties, 1984
753	VEX289X	Bristol VRT/SL3/6LXB	Eastern Coach Works	H43/31F	1981	Ex Eastern Counties, 1984
755	VEX293X	Bristol VRT/SL3/6LXB	Eastern Coach Works	H43/31F	1981	Ex Eastern Counties, 1984
761	PTT92R	Bristol VRT/SL3/6LXB	Eastern Coach Works	H43/31F	1976	Ex Red Bus, 1986
762	XDV607S	Bristol VRT/SL3/6LXB	Eastern Coach Works	H43/31F	1978	Ex Red Bus, 1986
763	YVV896S	Bristol VRT/SL3/6LXB	Eastern Coach Works	H43/31F	1978	Ex Green, Kirkintilloch, 1991
764	WWY130S	Bristol VRT/SL3/6LXB	Eastern Coach Works	H43/31F	1978	Ex Viscount, 1992
899	E461TEW	Volkswagen LT55	Optare City Pacer	B25F	1987	
911	E911LVE	Volkswagen LT55	Optare City Pacer	B25F	1988	
912	E912LVE	Volkswagen LT55	Optare City Pacer	B25F	1988	
913	E913NEW	Volkswagen LT55	Optare City Pacer	B25F	1988	
922	E42RDW	Volkswagen LT55	Optare City Pacer	DP25F	1987	Ex Taff Ely, 1988
923	E43RDW	Volkswagen LT55	Optare City Pacer	DP25F	1987	Ex Taff Ely, 1988
924	E44RDW	Volkswagen LT55	Optare City Pacer	DP25F	1987	Ex Taff Ely, 1988
925	E45RDW	Volkswagen LT55	Optare City Pacer	DP25F	1987	Ex Taff Ely, 1988
926	E46RDW	Volkswagen LT55	Optare City Pacer	DP25F	1987	Ex National Welsh, 1989
927	E750VWT	Volkswagen LT55	Optare City Pacer	DP25F	1987.	Ex National Welsh, 1989

The Volkswagen LT55 based on the Optare City Pacer was initially popular in the late 1980s, though many have now moved from major operators, the Optare MetroRider being more reliable and available with larger capacity. One of those on loan to Cambus is numbered W001, D632NOE, which is seen in Cambridge on City Centre Shuttle duties. *Lee Whitehead*

960-974

Optare MetroRider — Optare — B29F — 1992-93

960	J960DWX	963	K963HUB	966	K966HUB	969	K969HUB	972	K972HUB
961	J961DWX	964	K964HUB	967	K967HUB	970	K970HUB	973	K973HUB
962	J962DWX	965	K965HUB	968	K968HUB	971	K971HUB	974	K974HUB

975-979

Optare MetroRider — Optare — B29F — 1995

975	M975WWR	976	M976WWR	977	M977WWR	978	M978WWR	979	M979VWY

990	K390TCE	Optare MetroRider	Optare	B29F	1993
2036	C336SFL	Ford Transit 190	Carlyle	DP16F	1986

Livery: White, Cambridge blue and dark blue; Cream and red (Millerbus); cream with light blue and dark blue (local coach), two-tone blue and grey (Premier).
National Express: 389/90, 404/5, 425/6, 445-52

Named vehicles:
329 *Chalkhill Blue;* 330 *Idonis Blue;* 332 *Holly Blue;* 387 *Monarch;* 388 *Valiant;* 389 *Imperial;* 391 *Emperor;* 392 *Regent**; 398 *Jim Darling;* 402 *Guardsman;* 403 *Bandsman;* 404 *Marksman;* 405 *Manxman;* 406 *Scotsman;* 407 *Clansman;* 408 *Huntsman;* 409 *Norseman;* 410 *Broadsman;* 411 *Fenman;* 412 *Gulliver;* 413 *Marco Polo;* 414 *Columbus.* *Not displayed in present livery.

Previous Registrations:
E461TEW	E814SUM, ESU913	ESU920	F950NER	HSV195	F905UNW
ESU913	F951NER	HSV194	E904UNW	HSV196	E315OEG

CAROLINE SEAGULL

Cobholm Hire Services Ltd, 59 Marine Parade
Great Yarmouth, Norfolk, NR30 2EJ

Depots: Queens Road, Great Yarmouth and Mill Road, Cobholm

LAH894A	AEC Reliance 2U3RA	Plaxton Elite III(1974)	C53F	1963	Ex East Kent, 1981
6539FN	AEC Reliance 2U3RA	Plaxton Elite III(1974)	C53F	1963	Ex East Kent, 1981
6545FN	AEC Reliance CHS2U3RA	Plaxton Supreme IV(1979)	C53F	1965	Ex East Kent, 1979
6546FN	AEC Reliance CHS2U3RA	Plaxton Supreme IV(1979)	C53F	1965	Ex East Kent, 1979
JSC890E	Leyland Atlantean PDR1/1	Alexander L	O43/31F	1967	Ex Partridge, Hadleigh, 1982
GNM235N	Bristol LHL6L	Plaxton Elite III	C51F	1974	Ex H & M, Chasetown, 1991
531FN	AEC Reliance 6U3ZR	Plaxton Supreme III	C55F	1977	Ex Isle Coaches, Owston Ferry, 1992
SHD293P	Bedford YMT	Plaxton Supreme III	C53F	1977	Ex Suffolk County Council, 1992
ODL175R	Bedford YMT	Duple Dominant	C51F	1977	Ex Southern Vectis, 1988
ODL176R	Bedford YMT	Duple Dominant	C51F	1977	Ex Southern Vectis, 1988
TDL127S	Bedford YMT	Duple Dominant	C51F	1978	Ex Southern Vectis, 1988
TDL420S	Bedford YMT	Duple Dominant	C51F	1978	Ex Southern Vectis, 1988
535FN	Ford R1114	Plaxton Supreme IV	C53F	1980	Ex Norfolk, Great Yarmouth, 1984
522FN	Ford R1114	Plaxton Supreme IV	C53F	1981	Ex Norfolk, Great Yarmouth, 1984
523FN	Ford R1114	Plaxton Supreme IV	C53F	1981	Ex Norfolk, Great Yarmouth, 1984
526FN	Ford R1114	Plaxton Supreme IV	C53F	1981	Ex Norfolk, Great Yarmouth, 1984
536FN	Ford R1114	Plaxton Supreme IV	C53F	1981	Ex Norfolk, Great Yarmouth, 1984
538FN	Ford R1114	Plaxton Supreme IV	C53F	1981	Ex Norfolk, Great Yarmouth, 1984
6543FN	Bedford YNT	Plaxton Paramount 3200	C53F	1983	
EPW928Y	Mercedes-Benz L307D	Reeve Burgess	M12	1983	
6547FN	Bedford YNT	Plaxton Paramount 3200	C53F	1983	
B97PLU	Bedford VAS5	Plaxton Supreme IV	C29F	1985	Ex Capital, West Drayton, 1992
6544FN	Scania K112CRS	Plaxton Paramount 3200 II	C51F	1985	Ex Rossendale, 1993
C445LGN	Bedford Venturer YNV	Duple Laser 2	C55F	1986	Ex Dhanoia, Orsett, 1995
537FN	Bedford Venturer YNV	Duple 340	C49FT	1987	
6541FN	Bedford Venturer YNV	Caetano Algarve	C53F	1988	
G469LVG	Dennis Javelin 12SDA1912	Plaxton Paramount 3200 III	C53F	1990	
G470LVG	Dennis Javelin 12SDA1907	Plaxton Paramount 3200 III	C53F	1990	
J652DVG	Toyota Coaster HDB30R	Caetano Optimo II	C21F	1992	

Livery: White, blue and orange

Previous Registrations:

522FN	TWX331W	537FN	D329LEX	6544FN	B547CHJ, NSU181, B162SEC
523FN	TWX333W	538FN	SVF512W	6545FN	DJG631C, FEX818T
526FN	TWX329W	6539FN	From new	6546FN	DJG628C, FEX817T
531FN	OKY66R	6541FN	E348TPW	6547FN	GEX631Y
535FN	LAH222V	6543FN	GEX632Y	LAH894A	6546FN
536FN	SVF511W				

New to Caroline Seagull was 6543FN, a Bedford YNT with Plaxton Paramount 3200 coachwork. The large number of -FN index marks reflect the operator's purchase of former East Kent AEC Reliances a handful of which remain in the fleet including two rebodied while with Caroline Seagull. *BBP*

CEDAR COACHES

E J Reid, Arkwright Road, Bedford, Bedfordshire, MK42 0LE

1	WRR396Y	Dennis Falcon V DDA403	East Lancashire	H50/38D	1982	Ex City of Nottingham, 1992
2	XRA397Y	Dennis Falcon V DDA403	East Lancashire	H50/38D	1983	Ex City of Nottingham, 1990
3	HHT57N	Leyland Atlantean AN68/1R	East Lancashire	H47/35F	1975	Ex Hale-Trent, Clevedon, 1983
4	VRS152L	Daimler Fleetline CRL6	Alexander AL	H45/29F	1973	Ex Grampian, 1983
6	GSL908N	Daimler Fleetline CRG6LXB	Alexander AL	H49/34D	1975	Ex Tayside, 1984
9	PYJ458L	Daimler Fleetline CRG6LX	Alexander AL	H49/34D	1971	Ex Enterprise & Silver Dawn, 1987
w	HOD55	Bedford OB	Duple Vista	C29F	1949	Ex Porter, Dummer, 1985
	OLN65P	Bedford J2SZ2	Caetano Sintra	C20F	1976	Ex Trollope, Salisbury, 1989
	NSJ3R	Seddon Pennine 7	Alexander AY	B53F	1976	Ex Western Scottish, 1987
	XTT5X	Dennis Lancet SD507	Wadham Stringer Vanguard	B52F	1982	Ex Tillingbourne, Cranleigh, 1988
	WSU368	Kässbohrer Setra S228DT	Kässbohrer Imperial	CH54/20DT	1984	Ex Travel De Courcey, Coventry, 1989
	713WAF	Aüwaerter Neoplan N116	Aüwaerter Cityliner	C53FT	1985	Ex Swallow, Rainham, 1993
	686CXV	Hestair Duple SDAK1404	Duple 425	C61F	1986	Ex Owen, Chapelhall, 1993
	D102SPP	Bedford YNT	Plaxton Paramount 3200 III	C53F	1987	
	E664KCX	DAF SB2305DHS585	Duple 340	C53FT	1988	Ex Fulcher, Cheadle Hulme, 1994
	G103YNK	Leyland Swift ST2B44C97TS	Elme	DP39F	1990	

Previous Registrations:

686CXV	D500NYS		HOD55	From new
713WAF	From new		WSU368	A263TYC

Livery: Red and cream

The functional Elme body design for the Leyland Swift is seen on Cedar's G103YNK as it passes through Bedford heading for Bolnhurst in June 1995. Cedar has an interestingly varied fleet for a smaller operator. *Malc McDonald*

CEDRIC'S

Cedric Garages (Wivenhoe) Ltd, Tudor House, The Avenue, Wivenhoe, Essex, CO7 9AH

1	E199UWT	Mercedes-Benz 811D	Optare StarRider	C29F	1988	
2	F313TLU	Mercedes-Benz 811D	Optare StarRider	C29F	1989	Ex Wings, Uxbridge, 1992
3	L3CED	Bova FHD12.340	Bova Futura	C49FT	1994	
4	LIW9272	Volvo B10M-50	Van Hool Alizée	C49FT	1990	Ex Harry Shaw, 1993
5	MXI8204	Volvo B10M-50	Jonckheere Deauville P599	C53FT	1991	Ex Harry Shaw, 1994
7	KIW7813	Volvo B10M-61	Ikarus Blue Danube	C49FT	1987	
8	HIL6244	Volvo B10M-61	Ikarus Blue Danube	C49FT	1988	Ex Direct, Birmingham, 1990
10w	LPF596P	Bristol VRT/SL3/6LXB	Eastern Coach Works	H41/31F	1976	Ex The Bee Line, 1992
11	WTU484W	Bristol VRT/SL3/6LXC	Eastern Coach Works	H43/31F	1981	Ex APT, Rayleigh, 1994
12	EIJ4016	Volvo B58-56	Caetano Alpha	C53F	1980	Ex JDW, Ipswich, 1982
14	KIW6416	Volvo B10M-61	Ikarus Blue Danube	C49FT	1987	Ex Boden, Dewsbury, 1991
15	HIL6245	Volvo B10M-61	Plaxton Paramount 3500 III	C48FT	1988	Ex Wallace Arnold, 1992
16	K878GOO	Iveco Daily 49-10	Dormobile	M16	1993	
17	WWY120S	Bristol VRT/SL3/6LXB	Eastern Coach Works	H43/31F	1977	Ex Stephenson, Rochford, 1993
18	TWS905T	Bristol VRT/SL3/6LXB	Eastern Coach Works	DPH39/28F	1978	Ex Badgerline, 1992
19	7463RU	Volvo B10M-61	Jonckheere Bermuda	C57F	1981	Ex Ayres, Dalkeith, 1986
20	KIW4391	Volvo B10M-61	Jonckheere Jubilee P50	C51FT	1985	Ex Len Wright, Isleworth, 1988
21	K908RGE	Volvo B10M-60	Jonckheere Deauville 45	C49FT	1993	Ex Park's, 1994
22	KIW4388	Volvo B10M-61	Jonckheere Jubilee P50	C49FT	1985	Ex Cantabrica, Watford, 1990
23	KIW4981	Volvo B10M-61	Jonckheere Jubilee P50	C57F	1985	Ex Budden, Woodfalls, 1990
24	NTC571R	Bristol VRT/SL3/6LXB	Eastern Coach Works	DPH39/28F	1977	Ex Badgerline, 1992
	PWR443W	Bristol VRT/SL3/6LXB	Eastern Coach Works	H43/31F	1981	Ex West Riding, 1993
	PWR446W	Bristol VRT/SL3/6LXB	Eastern Coach Works	H43/31F	1981	Ex West Riding, 1994
	HWJ933W	Bristol VRT/SL3/6LXB	Eastern Coach Works	H43/31F	1981	Ex RoadCar, 1995
	HWJ934W	Bristol VRT/SL3/6LXB	Eastern Coach Works	H43/31F	1981	Ex RoadCar, 1995
	M8CED	Bova FHD12.340	Bova Futura	C53F	1995	
	M15CED	Volvo B10M-62	Van Hool Alizée	C55F	1995	

Previous Registrations:

7463RU	XNV142W	HIL6245	E906UNW	KIW6416	D140SWL
EIJ4016	LRT841V	KIW4388	B493GBD	KIW7813	D773WHJ
F313TLU	F933AWW, WET590	KIW4391	B491GBD	LIW9272	G600CVC, 1KOV, G979FHP
HIL6244	E499UOP	KIW4981	C408LRP	MXI8204	H15URE

Livery: White, red orange and yellow (Coaches), red and yellow (buses).

Previously with West Riding, Bristol VRT PWR446W is now in Cedric's red and yellow livery. It carries a fixed school transport sign, introduced under recent transport regulations, as it passes along High Street, Colchester.
Richard Godfrey

CHALLENGER

Challenger Transport Ltd, 1 Orchard Walk, Lavendon, Luton, Bedfordshire MK46 4HF

Depot: Sundon Park Road, Leagrave, Luton

D54TLV	Freight Rover Sherpa	Carlyle	B18F	1986	Ex Midland, 1993
D127NON	Freight Rover Sherpa	Carlyle	B18F	1986	Ex Bee Line Buzz, 1991
D138NON	Freight Rover Sherpa	Carlyle	B18F	1986	Ex Bee Line Buzz, 1992
D157NON	Freight Rover Sherpa	Carlyle	B18F	1986	Ex Bee Line Buzz, 1992
D161NON	Freight Rover Sherpa	Carlyle	B18F	1986	Ex Bee Line Buzz, 1991
D162NON	Freight Rover Sherpa	Carlyle	B18F	1986	Ex Bee Line Buzz, 1991
D164NON	Freight Rover Sherpa	Carlyle	B18F	1986	Ex Bee Line Buzz, 1992
D169NON	Freight Rover Sherpa	Carlyle	B18F	1986	Ex Bee Line Buzz, 1991
D173NON	Freight Rover Sherpa	Carlyle	B18F	1986	Ex Bee Line Buzz, 1991
D175NON	Freight Rover Sherpa	Carlyle	B18F	1986	Ex Bee Line Buzz, 1991
D188NON	Freight Rover Sherpa	Carlyle	B18F	1986	Ex City Fleet, Aintree, 1992
D192NON	Freight Rover Sherpa	Carlyle	B18F	1986	Ex Bee Line Buzz, 1991
D197NON	Freight Rover Sherpa	Carlyle	B18F	1986	Ex Arrowline, Knutsford, 1992
D213OOJ	Freight Rover Sherpa	Carlyle	B18F	1986	Ex C-Line, 1993
D218OOJ	Freight Rover Sherpa	Carlyle	B18F	1986	Ex Bee Line Buzz, 1991
D226OOJ	Freight Rover Sherpa	Carlyle	B18F	1986	Ex Bolton Coachways, 1991
D228OOJ	Freight Rover Sherpa	Carlyle	B18F	1986	Ex C-Line, 1993
D245OOJ	Freight Rover Sherpa	Carlyle	B18F	1986	Ex Midland, 1993
D251OOJ	Freight Rover Sherpa	Carlyle	B18F	1986	Ex Bee Line Buzz, 1992
D820PUK	Freight Rover Sherpa	Carlyle Citybus	B18F	1987	Ex Dalybus, Eccles, 1993
D111WCC	Freight Rover Sherpa	Carlyle Citybus	B18F	1987	Ex Midland Red North, 1992
D112WCC	Freight Rover Sherpa	Carlyle Citybus	B18F	1987	Ex Midland Red North, 1992
D116WCC	Freight Rover Sherpa	Carlyle Citybus	B18F	1987	Ex Owen, Oswestry, 1992
D128WCC	Freight Rover Sherpa	Carlyle Citybus	B18F	1987	Ex Crosville Wales, 1992
D131WCC	Freight Rover Sherpa	Carlyle Citybus	B18F	1987	Ex Crosville Wales, 1992
D134WCC	Freight Rover Sherpa	Carlyle Citybus	B18F	1987	Ex Crosville Wales, 1992

Livery: Yellow, red and black

Typical of the Freight Rover Sherpa with Carlyle bodywork is D188NON, one of several in the Challenger fleet to have come from Bee Line Buzz, the south Manchester operation that commenced in 1986.
Colin Lloyd

CHAMBERS

H C Chambers & Son Ltd, Knowle House, High Street, Bures, Suffolk, CO8 5AB

A211JDX	Bedford YMT	Duple Dominant	B63F	1984	
B792MGV	Bedford YNT	Duple Laser	C53F/C29FL	1984	
B192BPP	Volvo B10M-61	Plaxton Paramount 3500	C16DL	1985	Ex Shaftesbury Society, Dovercourt, 1994
C668WRT	Bedford YMT	Duple Dominant	B63F	1986	
D172LTA	Renault-Dodge S56	Reeve Burgess	B23F	1986	Ex Sherratt, Swynnerton, 1994
D176LTA	Renault-Dodge S56	Reeve Burgess	B23F	1986	Ex Sherratt, Swynnerton, 1994
D642DRT	Bedford YMT	Duple Dominant	B63F	1987	
D211LWX	Volvo B10M-61	Duple 340	C53F/C31FL	1987	Ex Wallace Arnold, 1992
D212LWX	Volvo B10M-61	Duple 340	C50F/C20FL	1987	Ex Wallace Arnold, 1992
E87KGV	Leyland Lynx LX112L10ZR1R	Leyland Lynx	B52F	1988	
E633SEL	Volvo B10M-61	Van Hool Alizée	C49FT	1988	Ex Excelsior, 1993
E600WDV	Aüwaerter Neoplan N122/3	Aüwaerter Skyliner	CH59/18CT	1987	Ex Trathens, 1994
F246HNE	Peugeot-Talbot Pullman	Talbot	DP22F	1989	Ex Pine, Stalybridge, 1992
F779LNB	Peugeot-Talbot Pullman	Talbot	DP22F	1989	Ex Pine, Stalybridge, 1992
F976WEF	CVE Omni	CVE	B23F	1989	Ex Shamrock, Pontypridd, 1994
F243RRT	Leyland Olympian ONCL10/1RZ	Alexander RL	H47/32F	1989	
G760VRT	Leyland Olympian ONCL10/1RZ	Alexander RL	H47/32F	1989	
G208CHN	CVE Omni	CVE	B23F	1989	Ex Shamrock, Pontypridd, 1994
G855KKY	Mercedes-Benz 609D	Whittaker	C24F	1989	Ex Brown, Edenbridge, 1993
G864XDX	Leyland Olympian ONCL10/1RZ	Alexander RL	H47/32F	1989	
H204DVM	Van Hool T815H	Van Hool Alizée	C53F	1991	Ex Shearings, 1995

Livery: Red and cream (buses); red (coaches)

Previous Registrations:
B192BPP	B873BMT, NMC78S	E633SEL	E305OPR, XEL158

The newest of the double-deck trio with Chambers is G864XDX. All three are Cummins-engined Leyland Olympians each of which having Alexander's RL-type bodywork. The example illustrated is seen in Sudbury bus station while on service 27 to Colchester. *Richard Godfrey*

CHARLES COOK

J C Cook, 59 High Street, Biggleswade, Bedfordshire, SG18 0LH

Depot: Hitchin Street, Biggleswade

w	KJD12P	Leyland Fleetline FE30ALR	MCW	H44/29F	1976	Ex Taylor, Morley, 1992
	NVD328P	Leyland Leopard PSU3C/4R	Duple Dominant	C51F	1976	
w	OBN503R	Leyland Fleetline FE30AGR	Northern Counties	H43/32F	1977	Ex Rossendale, 1992
	238JUO	Leyland Royal Tiger B50	Van Hool Alizée	C49FT	1983	Ex Ford, Althorne, 1994
	C441HHL	Leyland Royal Tiger RTC	Leyland Doyen	C49FT	1985	
	F607PBH	Leyland DAF 400	Leyland DAF	M16	1989	Ex private owner, 1995

Previous Registrations:
238JUO   A989NNK, 959AYX

Livery: Red, gold and black

CLASSIC COACHES

D H Crowther, 1A Barbers Wood Close, Booker, High Wycombe, Bucks, HP12 4EW

Depot: Binders Industrial Estate, Cryers Hill and Dewsbury Bus Museum, Foundry Street, Ravensthorpe, West Yorkshire.

	GWT630	Albion Valkyrie CX13	Burlingham	C33F	1947	Ex preservation
	NHU2	Bristol LSX5G	Eastern Coach Works	B44F	1950	Ex preservation
	EHL336	Leyland Tiger PS2/12A	Roe	C35F	1952	Ex preservation
	JCY870	AEC Regal IV	Burlingham Seagull	C39C	1953	Ex preservation
*	JVH378	AEC Regent III	East Lancashire	H33/28R	1955	Ex preservation
	JHL983	AEC Reliance MU3RV	Roe Dalesman	C41C	1957	Ex preservation
	NDL869	AEC Reliance MU3RV	Duple Britannia	C41F	1957	Ex preservation
	NSV707	Leyland Titan PD2/30	Park Royal	L27/26RD	1957	Ex preservation
	5228NW	Leyland Titan PD3/5	Roe	H38/32R	1959	Ex preservation
	5280NW	Leyland Titan PD3/5	Roe	H38/32R	1959	Ex preservation
*	WWN191	AEC Reliance 2MU3RV	Harrington Cavalier	C41F	1960	Ex preservation
	570EFJ	AEC Reliance 2MU4RA	Harrington Cavalier	C40F	1962	Ex preservation
	572CNW	Daimler CVG6LX-30	Roe	H39/31F	1962	Ex preservation
	574CNW	Daimler CVG6LX-30	Roe	H39/31F	1962	Ex preservation
	264KTA	Bristol MW6G	Eastern Coach Works	C39F	1962	Ex preservation
	ABD253B	Bristol RELH6G	Eastern Coach Works	DP47F	1964	Ex preservation
*	HLP10C	AEC Reliance 2U3RA	Harrington Grenadier	C51F	1965	Ex preservation
*	ANW710C	AEC Reliance 2MU2RA	Roe	C37F	1965	Ex preservation
*	EDV505D	Bristol MW6G	Eastern Coach Works	C39F	1966	Ex preservation
	EDV546D	Bristol MW6G	Eastern Coach Works	C39F	1966	Ex preservation
*	HNW366D	Leyland Titan PD3A/2	Roe	H41/32RD	1966	Ex Black Prince, 1995
*	LDV847F	Bristol RELH6G	Eastern Coach Works	C45F	1968	Ex Sprinfield School, Marlow, 1995
	TBU30G	AEC Reliance 6MU3R	Plaxton Elite	C51F	1969	Ex preservation

Livery: mostly in colours of originator; * indicates operational PCV.

Previous Registrations:
NSV707   TWY7, NNW985A

Two of Leyland's Royal Tiger chassis are operated in the Charles Cook fleet. One carries a Van Hool body while C441HHL, seen heading for The Derby, is fitted with the integral Leyland Doyen body produced at Lillyhall. *Keith Grimes*

Classic Coaches operate special services using vintage vehicles brought together to form a collection which are also part of the Dewsbury Bus Museum. Seen on Buckinghamshire County Council service 78 is EDV505D, one of the fleet currently to full PCV status. Special summer Sunday services, using vintage buses, have grown in popularity in recent times. *Keith Grimes*

COACH SERVICES

Coach Services Ltd, 14/16 Croxton Road, Thetford, Norfolk, IP24 1AG

PNK167R	Bedford YMT	Plaxton Supreme III	C53F	1977	Ex Petch, Hopton, 1991
ELA389T	Bedford YMT	Duple Dominant	B63F	1979	Ex Clarke, Swaffham, 1989
DJA551T	Ford R1114	Plaxton Supreme IV	C53F	1979	Ex Martin, Woking, 1989
FVG667T	Ford R1114	Plaxton Supreme IV	C53F	1979	Ex Reynolds, Caister, 1990
EGV190T	Bedford YMT	Plaxton Supreme III Express	C53F	1979	Ex Petch, Hopton, 1991
100BGO	Ford R1114	Plaxton Supreme IV	C53F	1979	Ex Eagle, Basildon, 1989
GRT520V	Bedford YMT	Plaxton Supreme IV Express	C53F	1979	Ex Squirrell, Hitcham, 1992
NLH288	Ford R1114	Plaxton Supreme IV	C53F	1980	Ex Partridge, Hadleigh, 1987
FUJ904V	Bedford YMT	Duple Dominant II	C53F	1980	Ex Petch, Hopton, 1991
MMJ538V	Bedford YMT	Duple Dominant II	C53F	1980	Ex Petch, Hopton, 1991
MUD535W	Bedford YMT	Plaxton Supreme IV	C53F	1979	Ex YellowBus, Stoke Mandeville, 1993
KWB695W	Bedford YMT	Duple Dominant	B55F	1981	Ex Ramblers, Hastings, 1994
XNA337X	Ford R1114	Plaxton Supreme VI	C53F	1982	Ex Mayers, Manchester, 1984
PBB760	Bedford YNT	Plaxton Supreme VI	C53F	1982	Ex Cavalier, Ramsey, 1995
WOD142X	Bedford YNT	Duple Dominant IV	C53F	1982	Ex Petch, Hopton, 1991
UKY608Y	Bedford YNT	Duple Dominant	B55F	1983	Ex Bull, Rochdale, 1994
B345RVF	Bedford YNT	Duple Laser	C53F	1984	Ex Petch, Hopton, 1991
B23XKX	Bedford YNT	Plaxton Paramount 3200	C53F	1984	Ex Premier-Albanian, Watford, 1988
C815FMC	Bedford Venturer YNV	Duple Laser 2	C53F	1986	
C979HOX	MCW Metroliner DR130/31	MCW	CH55/16FT	1986	Ex Western National, 1995
D272HFX	Bedford Venturer YNV	Plaxton Paramount 3200 II	C53F	1986	Ex Excelsior, 1988
E832EUT	Bedford Venturer YNV	Plaxton Paramount 3200 III	C57F	1987	Ex Wainfleet, Nuneaton, 1991
F708ENE	Leyland Tiger TRCTL11/3RZA	Plaxton Paramount 3200 III	C53F	1989	Ex Shearings, 1992
F709ENE	Leyland Tiger TRCTL11/3RZA	Plaxton Paramount 3200 III	C53F	1989	Ex Shearings, 1992
F373MUT	Dennis Javelin 12SDA1907	Plaxton Paramount 3200 III	C53F	1989	Ex Leigh, Morden, 1993
F900RDX	Bova FHD12.290	Bova Futura	C53F	1989	Ex Petch, Hopton, 1991
G954GRP	LAG G355Z	LAG Panoramic	C49FT	1989	Ex Enterprise, Chatteris, 1994
1273LJ	DAF SB3000DKV601	Jonckheere Deauville P599	C49FT	1990	Ex Dunn-Line, Nottingham, 1994
N990BWJ	Toyota Coaster HZB50R	Caetano Optimo III	C21F	1995	

Previous Registrations:

100BGO	EBU854T	NLH288	HFX419V
1273LJ	G140MNH	PBB760	BGS304X

Livery: Cream and red

Coach Services Bova F900RDX is seen waiting time at Bury St Edmunds. A large part of this operators work is in support of the number of army and RAF bases situated in East Anglia as well as the more usual contract work around Breckland
BBP

COLCHESTER

Colchester Borough Transport Ltd, Magdalen Street
Colchester, Essex, CO1 2LD

A subsidiary of British Bus plc

9	BVP809V	Leyland National 2 NL116L11/1R			B49F	1980	Ex Midland Fox, 1994
10	BVP810V	Leyland National 2 NL116L11/1R			B49F	1980	Ex Midland Fox, 1994
12	BVP812V	Leyland National 2 NL116L11/1R			B49F	1980	Ex Midland Fox, 1994
19	EON829V	Leyland National 2 NL116L11/1R			B49F	1980	Ex Midland Fox, 1994
21	BVP821V	Leyland National 2 NL116L11/1R			B49F	1980	Ex Midland Fox, 1994
25	EON825V	Leyland National 2 NL116L11/1R			B49F	1980	Ex Midland Fox, 1994
26	EON826V	Leyland National 2 NL116L11/1R			B49F	1980	Ex Midland Fox, 1994
41	C41HHJ	Leyland Olympian ONLXCT/1RH	Eastern Coach Works		H47/31F	1985	
43	D43RWC	Leyland Olympian ONLXCT/1RH	Eastern Coach Works		H47/31F	1985	
45	F245MTW	Leyland Olympian ONCL10/1RZ	Leyland		DPH43/29F	1988	
48	H48MJN	Leyland Olympian ON2R50C13Z4	Leyland		H47/31F	1991	
49	H49MJN	Leyland Olympian ON2R50C13Z4	Leyland		H47/31F	1991	
55	JHK495N	Leyland Atlantean AN68/1R	Eastern Coach Works		O43/31F	1975	
63	RFR415P	Leyland Atlantean AN68/1R	Eastern Coach Works		H43/31F	1976	Ex London & Country, 1995
64	PUF131M	Leyland Atlantean AN68/1R	Park Royal		H43/30F	1974	Ex London & Country, 1994
65	MUA865P	Leyland Atlantean AN68/1R	Roe (1979)		H43/30F	1976	Ex London & Country, 1994
66	RFR416P	Leyland Atlantean AN68/1R	Eastern Coach Works		H43/31F	1976	Ex London & Country, 1994
67	TPU67R	Leyland Atlantean AN68A/1R	Eastern Coach Works		H43/31F	1977	
68	TPU68R	Leyland Atlantean AN68A/1R	Eastern Coach Works		H43/31F	1977	
69	TPU69R	Leyland Atlantean AN68A/1R	Eastern Coach Works		H43/31F	1977	Ex Midland, 1994
70	RFR421P	Leyland Atlantean AN68/1R	Eastern Coach Works		H43/31F	1976	Ex London & Country, 1994
71	TPU71R	Leyland Atlantean AN68A/1R	Eastern Coach Works		H43/31F	1977	
72	RFR419P	Leyland Atlantean AN68/1R	Eastern Coach Works		H43/31F	1976	Ex London & Country, 1994

73-90

		Leyland Atlantean AN68A/1R	Eastern Coach Works	H43/31F	1977-80

73	TPU73R	77	YNO77S	81	YNO81S	85	MEV85V	88	RVW88W
74	TPU74R	78	YNO78S	82	YNO82S	86	MEV86V	89	RVW89W
75	TPU75R	79w	YNO79S	83	MEV83V	87	MEV87V	90	RVW90W
76	TPU76R	80	YNO80S	84	MEV84V			

100	A250SVW	Leyland Tiger TRCTL11/3RP	Duple Caribbean	C57F	1984	Ex Southend, 1995
103	OHE274X	Leyland Tiger TRCTL11/3R	Duple Dominant IV	C53F	1982	Ex West Riding, 1987
104	OHE280X	Leyland Tiger TRCTL11/3R	Duple Dominant IV	C53F	1982	Ex West Riding, 1987

Livery: Cream and crimson

Previously with
London & Country,
Colchester's 70,
RFR421P, is a
Leyland Atlantean
with similar
bodywork to their
own examples. It is
seen in the town
during August, 1995.
Keith Grimes

COUNTY

County Bus & Coach Co Ltd, Fourth Avenue, Harlow, Essex, CM20 1DU

Depots and outstations: Langston Road, Debden; Gibbs Road, Edmonton; Fourth Avenue, Harlow; Pindar Road, Hoddesdon; Marsh Lane, Ware and Europa Park, West Thurrock, Grays.

A subsidiary of West Midlands Travel.

LR1-23   Leyland Olympian ONTL11/1R   Roe   H43/29F   1982

1	TPD101X	**4**	TPD104X	**9**	TPD109X	**11**	TPD111X	**17**	TPD117X
2	TPD102X	**5**	TPD105X	**10**	TPD110X	**15**	TPD115X	**23**	TPD123X
3	TPD103X	**7**	TPD107X						

BTL6	BAZ7385	Leyland Tiger TRCTL11/3RH	Berkhof Everest 370	C53F	1984	Ex London & Country, 1990
BTL10	BAZ7386	Leyland Tiger TRCTL11/3RH	Berkhof Everest 370	C53F	1984	Ex Speedlink, 1991
STL10	BAZ7384	Leyland Tiger TRCTL11/3RH	Plaxton Paramount 3500 II	C49FT	1985	Ex London & Country, 1992
TL10	TPC110X	Leyland Tiger TRCTL11/2R	Eastern Coach Works B51	C49F	1982	Ex Luton & District, 1991
TL13	TPC113X	Leyland Tiger TRCTL11/2R	Eastern Coach Works B51	C49F	1982	Ex Coppins & Wall, 1993
TL15	UJN634Y	Leyland Tiger TRCTL11/2R	Eastern Coach Works B51	C49F	1982	Ex Luton & District, 1991
TL17	KIW6511	Leyland Tiger TRCTL11/2R	Eastern Coach Works B51	C49F	1982	
TL20	UJN429Y	Leyland Tiger TRCTL11/2R	Eastern Coach Works B51	C49F	1982	
TL27	KIW8513	Leyland Tiger TRCTL11/2R	Eastern Coach Works B51	C49F	1982	
TL29	FBZ2514	Leyland Tiger TRCTL11/2R	Eastern Coach Works B51	C49F	1982	Ex Luton & District, 1991
TL30	WPH130Y	Leyland Tiger TRCTL11/2R	Eastern Coach Works B51	C49F	1982	Ex Luton & District, 1991
TL31	WPH131Y	Leyland Tiger TRCTL11/2R	Eastern Coach Works B51	C53F	1982	Ex Chartercoach, Gt Oakley, 1989
TL33	WPH133Y	Leyland Tiger TRCTL11/2R	Eastern Coach Works B51	C53F	1982	Ex Chartercoach, Gt Oakley, 1989
TDL37	530MUY	Leyland Tiger TRCTL11/3RH	Duple Caribbean	C55F	1984	Ex Premier Travel, 1989
MB45	D45OKH	Iveco Daily 49.10	Robin Hood City Nippy	DP19F	1987	Ex East Yorkshire, 1989
MB46	D46OKH	Iveco Daily 49.10	Robin Hood City Nippy	DP19F	1987	Ex East Yorkshire, 1989
MB47w	E347SWY	Iveco Daily 49.10	Robin Hood City Nippy	DP19F	1988	Ex Sovereign, 1989
MB48	E348SWY	Iveco Daily 49.10	Robin Hood City Nippy	DP19F	1988	Ex Sovereign, 1989
MB49w	E349SWY	Iveco Daily 49.10	Robin Hood City Nippy	DP19F	1988	Ex Sovereign, 1989
MB50w	E350SWY	Iveco Daily 49.10	Robin Hood City Nippy	DP19F	1988	Ex Sovereign, 1989
MB52	E352NEG	Iveco Daily 49.10	Robin Hood City Nippy	DP19F	1988	Ex Premier Travel, 1989
MB53	E353NEG	Iveco Daily 49.10	Robin Hood City Nippy	DP19F	1988	Ex Premier Travel, 1989
TDL53	C253SPC	Leyland Tiger TRCTL11/3RH	Duple 320	C53F	1986	Ex London & Country, 1993
TDL54	C254SPC	Leyland Tiger TRCTL11/3RH	Duple 320	C53F	1986	Ex London & Country, 1993
MB54	E354NEG	Iveco Daily 49.10	Robin Hood City Nippy	DP19F	1988	Ex Premier Travel, 1989
MB55	E355NEG	Iveco Daily 49.10	Robin Hood City Nippy	DP19F	1988	Ex Premier Travel, 1989

Opposite: **Sampson livery is carried by TDL37, 530MUY, seen in Waltham Cross while working a free bus service to North Weald Market.   CountyBus G919UPP shows the latest livery changes which include the WM motif of parent West Midlands Travel, now part of National Express plc.   MB919 is seen in Waltham Cross.** *Colin Lloyd*

Showing Townlink titles, County Bus TL31, WPH131Y, is one of the Leyland Tigers supplied with Eastern Coach Works bodies to the B51 design to meet National Bus specifications. It is seen passing through Parliament Square. *Colin Lloyd*

Sampson livery is worn by VPL501, L501MOO, a Volvo B10M with Plaxton Premiére 350 coachwork. *BBP*

Representing the Dennis Dart/Plaxton Pointer combination in the County fleet is DPL408, K408FHJ, seen at Harlow where the vehicle is based. *Colin Lloyd*

TDL60, C260SPC, is one of County's four Leyland Tigers with Duple 320 bodywork which were delivered new to London Country for the Green Line network. It is seen in St Albans, where it is lettered for the 724 service between Stansted and Heathrow airports. *Keith Grimes*

TDL55	C255SPC	Leyland Tiger TRCTL11/3RH	Duple 320		C49F	1986	Ex London & Country, 1993	
TDL60	C260SPC	Leyland Tiger TRCTL11/3RH	Duple 320		C49F	1986	Ex London & Country, 1993	
TP61	B261KPF	Leyland Tiger TRCTL11/2R	Plaxton Paramount 3200 IIE		C49F	1985	Ex Sovereign, 1990	
TDB61	F61SMC	Leyland Tiger TRBTL11/2RP	Duple 300		B55F	1988	Ex Sovereign, 1989	
TDB62	F62SMC	Leyland Tiger TRBTL11/2RP	Duple 300		B55F	1988	Ex Sovereign, 1989	
TDB63	F63SMC	Leyland Tiger TRBTL11/2RP	Duple 300		B55F	1988	Ex Sovereign, 1989	
TDL63	C263SPC	Leyland Tiger TRCTL11/3RH	Duple 320		C49F	1986	Ex London & Country, 1993	
VPB64	E564BNK	Volvo B10M-56	Plaxton Derwent II		B54F	1988	Ex Sampsons, Hoddesdon, 1989	
VPB65	E565BNK	Volvo B10M-56	Plaxton Derwent II		B54F	1988	Ex Sampsons, Hoddesdon, 1989	
TDL65	C265SPC	Leyland Tiger TRCTL11/3RH	Duple 320		C53F	1986		
TP70	OIB3520	Leyland Tiger TRCTL11/2R	Plaxton Paramount 3200 IIE		C49F	1985		
TP71	OIB3521	Leyland Tiger TRCTL11/2R	Plaxton Paramount 3200 IIE		C49F	1985		
TP72	OIB3522	Leyland Tiger TRCTL11/2R	Plaxton Paramount 3200 IIE		C49F	1985		
TP75	OIB3523	Leyland Tiger TRCTL11/2R	Plaxton Paramount 3200 IIE		C49F	1985		
M75	JBO75W	MCW Metrobus DR102/20	MCW		H46/31F	1981	Ex Newport, 1994	
M80	JBO80W	MCW Metrobus DR102/20	MCW		H46/31F	1981	Ex Newport, 1994	
AN110w	MPJ210L	Leyland Atlantean PDR1A/1Sp	MCW		O43/29D	1972	Ex Premier Travel, 1989	
MB115	F115JGS	Iveco Daily 49.10	Robin Hood City Nippy		B25F	1988	Ex Sampsons, Hoddesdon, 1988	
MB154	F154DKV	Iveco Daily 49.10	Reeve Burgess Beaver		B25F	1988	Ex Iveco demonstrator, 1989	
AN190	XPG190T	Leyland Atlantean AN68A/1R	Roe		H43/30F	1979	Ex Sovereign, 1989	
AN194	XPG194T	Leyland Atlantean AN68A/1R	Roe		H43/30F	1979	Ex Sovereign, 1989	
AN199	XPG199T	Leyland Atlantean AN68A/1R	Roe		H43/30F	1979	Ex Sovereign, 1989	
AN238	KPJ238W	Leyland Atlantean AN68B/1R	Roe		H43/30F	1980	Ex Luton & District, 1993	

AN244-256

Leyland Atlantean AN68B/1R — Roe — H43/30F — 1980

244	KPJ244W	247	KPJ247W	249	KPJ249W	251	KPJ251W	254	KPJ254W
245	KPJ245W	248	KPJ248W	250	KPJ250W	252	KPJ252W	256	KPJ256W
246	KPJ246W								

LX251-258

Leyland Lynx LX2R11C15Z4S — Leyland — B49F — 1990

251	H251GEV	253	H253GEV	255	H255GEV	257	H257GEV	258	H258GEV
252	H252GEV	254	H254GEV	256	H256GEV				

ELW266	M266VPU	Dennis Lance SLF 11SDA3201	Wight Endeavour	B40F	1994	
ELW267	M267VPU	Dennis Lance SLF 11SDA3201	Wight Endeavour	B40F	1994	
ELW268	M268VPU	Dennis Lance SLF 11SDA3201	Wight Endeavour	B40F	1994	
ELW269	M269VPU	Dennis Lance SLF 11SDA3201	Wight Endeavour	B40F	1994	
SN277	SPC277R	Leyland National 10351A/1R		B41F	1977	Ex Sovereign, 1989

DP301-313

Dennis Dart 9SDL3002* — Plaxton Pointer — B35F — 1991 — 309 rebodied 1992
*302-7/13 are 9SDL3011

301	J301WHJ	304	J304WHJ	307	J307WHJ	310	J310WHJ	312	J312WHJ
302	J302WHJ	305	J305WHJ	308	J308WHJ	311	J311WHJ	313	J313WHJ
303	J303WHJ	306	J306WHJ	309	J309WHJ				

DW314	J314XVX	Dennis Dart 9SDL3011	Wright Handy-bus	B35F	1992	
DW315	J315XVX	Dennis Dart 9SDL3011	Wright Handy-bus	B35F	1992	
DW316	J316XVX	Dennis Dart 9SDL3011	Wright Handy-bus	B35F	1992	
DW317	J317XVX	Dennis Dart 9SDL3011	Wright Handy-bus	B35F	1992	

DP318-323

Dennis Dart 9SDL3011 — Plaxton Pointer — B35F — 1992

318	K318CVX	320	K320CVX	321	K321CVX	322	K322CVX	323	K323CVX
319	K319CVX							

SN312	UPB312S	Leyland National 10351A/1R		B41F	1977	Ex Sovereign, 1989
SN319	UPB319S	Leyland National 10351A/1R		B41F	1977	Ex Sovereign, 1989
DWL401	J401XVX	Dennis Dart 9.8SDL3012	Wright Handy-bus	B40F	1992	
DWL402	J402XVX	Dennis Dart 9.8SDL3012	Wright Handy-bus	B40F	1992	
DWL403	J403XVX	Dennis Dart 9.8SDL3012	Wright Handy-bus	B40F	1992	
DWL404	J404XVX	Dennis Dart 9.8SDL3012	Wright Handy-bus	B40F	1992	

DPL405-414

Dennis Dart 9.8SDL3018 — Plaxton Pointer — B40F — 1993

405	K405FHJ	407	K407FHJ	409	K409FHJ	411	K411FHJ	413	K413FHJ
406	K406FHJ	408	K408FHJ	410	K410FHJ	412	K412FHJ	414	K414FHJ

Representing the new LeaValley livery on a double-deck is LR23, TPD123X, a Leyland Olympian with Roe high-bridge bodywork seen on service 310 as it passes through Enfield Town. *BBP*

DWL415	L415NHJ	Dennis Dart 9.8SDL3025	Wright Handy-bus	B40F	1994	
VPL501	L501MOO	Volvo B10M-60	Plaxton Premiere 350	C49FT	1993	
VPL503	H903AHS	Volvo B10M-60	Plaxton Paramount 3500 III	C53F	1991	Ex Park's, 1994
BP504	DDX741T	Bedford YLQ	Plaxton Supreme III	C45F	1978	Ex Davian, Enfield, 1991
BP507	SGS497W	Bedford YMT	Plaxton Supreme IV	C53F	1981	Ex Davian, Enfield, 1991
TPL510	OIB3510	Leyland Tiger TRCTL11/3RH	Plaxton Paramount 3200	C53F	1983	Ex Keighley & District, 1992
TPL518	E118KFV	Leyland Tiger TRCTL11/3ARZ(Vo)	Plaxton Paramount 3500 III	C51FT	1988	Ex Alan's Cs, Saffron Walden, 1993
LDL533	DSU733	Leyland Leopard PSU5A/4R	Duple 320 (1988)	C57F	1976	Ex Biss Brothers, 1994
VDL537	EBZ6531	Volvo B58-61	Duple Dominant II	C53F	1982	Ex Davian, Enfield, 1991
LP550w	KUB550V	Leyland Leopard PSU3E/4R	Plaxton Supreme IV Express	C49F	1979	Ex West Yorkshire, 1989
LP551w	KUB551V	Leyland Leopard PSU3E/4R	Plaxton Supreme IV Express	C49F	1980	Ex West Yorkshire, 1989
LD552	OMA504V	Leyland Leopard PSU3E/4R	Duple Dominant II Express	C49F	1980	Ex Citibus, Middleton, 1994
LD554	FYX814W	Leyland Leopard PSU3E/4R	Duple Dominant II Express	C49F	1980	Ex Davian, Enfield, 1991
LP555	WJM814T	Leyland Leopard PSU3E/4R	Plaxton Supreme IV Express	C46F	1979	Ex Golden Boy, Roydon, 1992
LP556	WJM816T	Leyland Leopard PSU3E/4R	Plaxton Supreme IV Express	C49F	1979	Ex Golden Boy, Roydon, 1992
AC570	H370GRY	Toyota Coaster HDB30R	Caetano Optimo II	C18F	1991	Ex Airport Coaches, 1993
BOV594	HDZ8354	Bova FHD12.280	Bova Futura	C49FT	1986	Ex Central, 1995
BOV595	G545JOG	Bova FHD12.290	Bova Futura	C46FT	1990	Ex Smiths, 1995
BOV596	JIW3696	Bova FHD12.290	Bova Futura	C47F	1988	Ex Smiths, 1995

MD601-612

		Mercedes-Benz 811D	Reeve Burgess Beaver	B28F	1991	

601	J601WHJ	**604**	J604WHJ	**607**	J607WHJ	**609**	J609WHJ	**611**	J611WHJ
602	J602WHJ	**605**	J605WHJ	**608**	J608WHJ	**610**	J610WHJ	**612**	J612WHJ
603	J603WHJ	**606**	J606WHJ						

MD613	L613LVX	Mercedes-Benz 811D	Dormobile Routemaker	B31F	1993	
MD614	L614LVX	Mercedes-Benz 811D	Dormobile Routemaker	B31F	1993	
MB700	E700EHJ	Iveco Daily 49.10	Dormobile Routemaker	DP25F	1988	Ex Sampson, Hoddesdon, 1989
MB701	E701EHJ	Iveco Daily 49.10	Dormobile Routemaker	B25F	1988	Ex Sampson, Hoddesdon, 1989
MB702w	D129DRV	Iveco Daily 49.10	Robin Hood City Nippy	B21F	1986	Ex Harrogate & District, 1994
MB706	E296VOM	Iveco Daily 49.10	Carlyle Dailybus 2	B23F	1988	Ex Southend, 1992

MB707-712

		Iveco TurboDaily 59.12	Dormobile Routemaker	B25F	1993	

707	K707FNO	**709**	K709FNO	**710**	K710FNO	**711**	K711FNO	**712**	K712FNO
708	K708FNO								

MBT713	L713OVX	Iveco TurboDaily 59.12	Marshall C31	B18FL	1994	
MBT714	L714OVX	Iveco TurboDaily 59.12	Marshall C31	B18FL	1994	
MBT715	L715OVX	Iveco TurboDaily 59.12	Marshall C31	B18FL	1994	
MBT716	L716OVX	Iveco TurboDaily 59.12	Marshall C31	B18FL	1994	

MB717-729

		Iveco TurboDaily 59.12	Marshall C31	B25F	1994	

717	L717OVX	**720**	M720UTW	**723**	L723PHK	**726**	M726UTW	**728**	M728UTW
718	L718OVX	**721**	M721UTW	**724**	L724PHK	**727**	M727UTW	**729**	M729UTW
719	M719UTW	**722**	L722OVX	**725**	M725UTW				

Introduced into the County fleet during 1994 was ELW269, M269VPU, a Dennis Lance SLF with Wright Endeavour bodywork. It was photographed at Romford Station on dedicated service 502. *Tony Wilson*

MB730-744

			Iveco TurboDaily 59.12		Marshall C31	B25F	1995		
730	M730AOO	733	M733AOO	736	M736AOO	739	N739AVW	742	N742AVW
731	M731AOO	734	M734AOO	737	M737AOO	740	N740AVW	743	N743ANW
732	M732AOO	735	M735AOO	738	M738AOO	741	N741AVW	744	N744AVW

MB743	E343SWY	Iveco Daily 49.10	Robin Hood City Nippy	B23F	1988	Ex Keighley & District, 1993	
MB745	E445TYG	Iveco Daily 49.10	Robin Hood City Nippy	B23F	1988	Ex Keighley & District, 1992	
MB748	E448TYG	Iveco Daily 49.10	Robin Hood City Nippy	DP25F	1988	Ex Keighley & District, 1993	
MB749	E449TYG	Iveco Daily 49.10	Robin Hood City Nippy	B23F	1988	Ex Keighley & District, 1992	
MB751	E451TYG	Iveco Daily 49.10	Robin Hood City Nippy	B23F	1988	Ex Keighley & District, 1992	
MB752	E452TYG	Iveco Daily 49.10	Robin Hood City Nippy	DP25F	1988	Ex Harrogate & District, 1993	
MB754w	D554HNW	Iveco Daily 49.10	Robin Hood City Nippy	B21F	1986	Ex Rover, Bromsgrove, 1993	
MB755	E455TYG	Iveco Daily 49.10	Robin Hood City Nippy	B23F	1988	Ex Harrogate & District, 1993	
MB795	F795JKX	Iveco Daily 49.10	Reeve Burgess Beaver	B21F	1988	Ex Sovereign, 1992	
MB796	F796JKX	Iveco Daily 49.10	Reeve Burgess Beaver	B21F	1988	Ex Sovereign, 1992	
MBT801	L801KNO	Peugeot-Talbot Freeway	TBP	B18FL	1993		
MBT802	L802KNO	Peugeot-Talbot Freeway	TBP	B18FL	1993		
MBT803	L803KNO	Peugeot-Talbot Freeway	TBP	B18FL	1993		
MBT804	L804KNO	Peugeot-Talbot Freeway	TBP	B18FL	1993		
MBT805	L805OVX	Peugeot-Talbot Freeway	TBP	B18FL	1993		

MB918-938

			Mercedes-Benz 709D		Reeve Burgess Beaver	B23F	1989-92		
918	G918UPP	926	G926WGS	930	G930WGS	933	J933WHJ	936	J936WHJ
919	G919UPP	927	G927WGS	931	G931WGS	934	J934WHJ	937	J937WHJ
924	G924WGS	928	G928WGS	932	G932WGS	935	J935WHJ	938	J938WHJ
925	G925WGS	929	G929WGS						

MB990	E290OMG	Mercedes-Benz 709D	Reeve Burgess Beaver	DP25F	1988	Ex Biss Brothers, 1994	

Liveries:
Cream and two-tone green; red (LRT Mobility) MBT713-6; blue and cream (Sampsons).

Green Line: TDL53-5/60/3/5, TP61/70-2/5, TPL510.

Sampsons: BTL6/10, STL10, TDL37, AN110, VPL501/3, BP504/7, TPL518, LDL533, VDL537, MC540, LD554, AC570, BOV594-6.

Buses carry one of three area logos depending on their allocation: Lea Valley (Edmonton and Ware); Thameside (West Thurrock) and Townlink (Harlow, and Debden).

Previous Registrations:

530MUY	A137RMJ	FBZ2514	WPH129Y	OIB3520	B270KPF
BAZ7384	C210PPE	HDZ8354	C904JOF, 245DOC, C566LOG	OIB3521	B271KPF
BAZ7385	B106KPF	JIW3696	E908UOH	OIB3522	B272KPF
BAZ7386	B110KPF	KIW6511	WPH117Y	OIB3523	B275KPF
DSU733	PNK160R, DSU470	KIW8513	WPH127Y	UJN429Y	WPH120Y
EBZ6531	HSF487X	OIB3510	EWW994Y	UJN634Y	WPH115Y,OIB3510

CRUSADER HOLIDAYS

Staines Crusader Coaches Ltd, 78-80 Pier Avenue, Clacton-on-Sea, Essex CO15 1NH

Depots: Ford Road, Clacton-on-Sea; Stephenson Road, Clacton-on-Sea and London Road, Copford.

4011LJ	Kässbohrer Setra S215HD	Kässbohrer	C48FT	1982	Ex The Kings Ferry, 1994
WCR819	Kässbohrer Setra S215HD	Kässbohrer	C49FT	1982	Ex The Kings Ferry, 1994
KSU473	Kässbohrer Setra S215HD	Kässbohrer	C49FT	1983	Ex The Kings Ferry, 1994
NSU113	Kässbohrer Setra S215HD	Kässbohrer	C49FT	1987	Ex The Kings Ferry, 1994
LSU113	Mercedes-Benz 0303/15RHD	Mercedes-Benz	C49FT	1987	Ex Dereham Coachways, 1994
114RVX	Van Hool TD824	Van Hool Astromega	CH55/16DT	1987	Ex Westbus, Hounslow 1993
E105GOO	Van Hool T815	Van Hool Alicron	C49FT	1988	
E106GOO	Van Hool T815	Van Hool Alicron	C49FT	1988	
E107GOO	Van Hool T815	Van Hool Alicron	C49FT	1988	
E108GOO	Van Hool T815	Van Hool Alicron	C49FT	1988	
G101CJN	Van Hool T815	Van Hool Alicron	C48FT	1990	
G102CJN	Van Hool T815	Van Hool Alicron	C48FT	1990	
G103CJN	Van Hool T815	Van Hool Alicron	C48FT	1990	
G104CJN	Van Hool T815	Van Hool Alicron	C48FT	1990	
L109PVW	EOS E180Z	EOS 90	C48FT	1994	
L110PVW	EOS E180Z	EOS 90	C48FT	1994	
L111PVW	EOS E180Z	EOS 90	C48FT	1994	
L112PVW	EOS E180Z	EOS 90	C48FT	1994	

Livery: White, red, orange, yellow and blue

Previous Registrations:

114RVX	D228HMT	KSU473	BPH267Y	NSU136	D158BPH
4011LJ	PKW323X	LSU113	D348CBC	WCR819	RAX21Y

On order: 5 Setra S250 coaches for 1996

Photographed at Albany Gardens, Clacton-on-Sea is WCR819, a Kässbohrer Setra S215HD displaying the Crusader Holidays livery. Five new Setra S250 models are on order which, with the associated Windmill operation, will run many luxury coaches for the 1996 season. *Geoff Mills*

DON'S

Don's Coaches (Dunmow) Ltd, Parsonage Downs, Great Dunmow, Essex CM6 2AT

NKY161	Bedford SBG	Yeates	C41F	1957	Ex preservation, 1988
ETC760B	Bedford VAS2	Plaxton Embassy II	C29F	1964	Ex Goodwin, Stockport, 1989
JGA189N	Leyland Atlantean AN68/1R	Alexander AL	H45/31F	1975	Ex Strathclyde, 1984
JUS774N	Leyland Atlantean AN68/1R	Alexander AL	H45/31F	1975	Ex Strathclyde, 1983
KSU850P	Leyland Atlantean AN68A/1R	Alexander AL	H45/31F	1975	Ex Strathclyde, 1983
YDS650S	Leyland Atlantean AN68A/1R	Alexander AL	H45/31F	1977	Ex Graham's, Paisley, 1990
TET748S	Leyland Fleetline FE30AGR	Roe	H43/33F	1977	Ex South Yorkshire's Transport, 1988
A62OJX	Leyland Leopard PSU5/2L	Plaxton Paramount 3200(1983)	C57F	1981	Ex Woods, Mirfield, 1985
TXI8756	Dennis Lancet SDA519	Jonckheere Piccolo P35	C37F	1985	Ex Ayres, Dalkeith, 1989
NIW4122	Dennis Javelin 12SDA1901	Duple 320	C57F	1987	Ex Nu-Venture, Aylesford, 1993
E758JAY	Dennis Javelin 12SDA1907	Duple 320	C57F	1988	Ex Morris Travel, Pencoed, 1992
PJI4655	Dennis Javelin 12SDA1908	Plaxton Paramount 3200 III	C49FT	1988	Ex Mitchell, Plean, 1993
E256PEL	Toyota Coaster HB31R	Caetano Optimo	C21F	1989	Ex Clegg & Brooking, Middle Wallop, 1992
H194TYC	Dennis Javelin 12SDA1907	Duple 320	C57F	1990	Ex Redwood, Hemyock, 1994

Livery:

Previous Registrations:

NIW4122	E951EPD	PJI4655	E508JWP	TXI8756	B135AAV

Don's of Dunmow operate four Leyland Atlanteans, mostly on their school contracts. All four were formerly in Scotland, with three operation with Strathclyde. The fourth previously worked with Grahams of Paisley and features the panoramic window version of Alexanders' AL body style. Seen in Dunmow is YDS 650S. *Geoff Mills*

EASTERN COUNTIES

Eastern Counties Omnibus Co Ltd, 79 Thorpe Road, Norwich, NR1 1UA

Depots: Cotton Lane, Bury St Edmunds; Wellington Road, Great Yarmouth; Star Lane, Ipswich; Vancouver Avenue, King's Lynn; St Michael's Road, Kings Lynn; Gas Works Road, Lowestoft; Roundtree Way Norwich and Vulcan Road, Norwich.

A subsidiary of FirstBus plc

OC1-5
Leyland Olympian ONLXB/1RZ | Northern Counties | H40/35F* | 1989 | *4 & 5 are DPH40/25F

1	F101AVG	2	F102AVG	3	F103AVG	4	F104AVG	5	F105AVG

JD6-10
Dennis Javelin 11SDL1933 | Duple 300 | DP48F | 1989

6	G706JAH	7	G707JAH	8	G708JAH	9	G709JAH	10	G710JAH

JP11-20
Dennis Javelin 11SDL1924 | Plaxton Derwent II | DP51F | 1990

11	H611RAH	13	H613RAH	15	H615RAH	17	H617RAH	19	H619RAH
12	H612RAH	14	H614RAH	16	H616RAH	18	H618RAH	20	H620RAH

OL21-25
Leyland Olympian ON2R50G13Z4 | Leyland | H45/31F | 1991

21	J621BVG	22	J622BVG	23	J623BVG	24	J624BVG	25	J625BVG

MD26-35
Mercedes-Benz 609D | Dormobile | B20F | 1992-93

26	K26HCL	28	K28HCL	30	J530FCL	32	K732JAH	34	K734JAH
27	K27HCL	29	K29HCL	31	K731JAH	33	K733JAH	35	K735JAH

LC36-40
Dennis Lance 11SDA3101 | Northern Counties Paladin | B49F | 1993

36	K736JAH	37	K737JAH	38	K738JAH	39	K739JAH	40	K740JAH

DP41	K741JAH	Dennis Dart 9SDL3011	Plaxton Pointer	B33F	1993
DP42	K742JAH	Dennis Dart 9SDL3011	Plaxton Pointer	B33F	1993
DP43	K743JAH	Dennis Dart 9SDL3011	Plaxton Pointer	B33F	1993
DP44	K744JAH	Dennis Dart 9SDL3011	Plaxton Pointer	B33F	1993

MG45-74
Mercedes-Benz 609D | Frank Guy | B20F | 1993-94

45	L245PAH	51	L251PAH	57	L257PAH	63	M363XEX	69	M369XEX
46	L246PAH	52	L252PAH	58	L258PAH	64	M364XEX	70	M370XEX
47	L247PAH	53	L253PAH	59	L259PAH	65	M365XEX	71	M371XEX
48	L248PAH	54	L254PAH	60	M360XEX	66	M366XEX	72	M372XEX
49	L249PAH	55	L255PAH	61	M361XEX	67	M367XEX	73	M373XEX
50	L250PAH	56	L256PAH	62	M362XEX	68	M368XEX	74	M374XEX

Eastern Counties' OC4, F104AVG, was initially numbered DD04 and it carried this number when it was photographed at Kings Lynn. This batch of Leyland Olympians carry Northern Counties bodywork and commenced a new numbering series in 1989. *Paul Wigan*

DP75-80 — Dennis Dart 9SDL3041 — Plaxton Pointer — B35F — 1994

75	M375YEX	77	M377YEX	78	M378YEX	79	M379YEX	80	M380YEX
76	M376YEX								

IC81	F702MBC	Iveco Daily 49-10	Carlyle Dailybus 2	B25F	1988	Ex Leicester City Bus, 1994
IC82	F705MBC	Iveco Daily 49-10	Carlyle Dailybus 2	B25F	1988	Ex Leicester City Bus, 1994
IC83	F710MBC	Iveco Daily 49-10	Carlyle Dailybus 2	B25F	1988	Ex Leicester City Bus, 1994

VP84-93 — Volvo B6-9.9M — Plaxton Pointer — B40F — 1994

84	M584ANG	86	M586ANG	88	M588ANG	90	M590ANG	92	M592ANG
85	M585ANG	87	M587ANG	89	M589ANG	91	M591ANG	93	M593ANG

IC94-104 — Iveco Daily 49-10 — Carlyle Dailybus 2 — B25F — 1988-89 Ex Leicester City Bus, 1994-95

94	F708MBC	97	F701MBC	99	F704MBC	101	F707MBC	103	F721PFP
95	F706MBC	98	F715PFP	100	F709NJF	102	F719PFP	104	F722PFP
96	F703MBC								

VR129-160 — Bristol VRT/SL2/6LX — Eastern Coach Works — H43/31F — 1974-75

129	RAH129M	138	SNG438M	143	GNG709N	151	JNG49N	158	JNG56N
130	RAH130M	139	SNG439M	147	GNG713N	153	JNG51N	159	JNG57N
134	RAH134M	141	TAH554N	148	GNG714N	154	JNG52N	160	JNG58N
136	SNG436M	142	GNG708N	149	GNG715N	156	JNG54N		

VR161	JNU137N	Bristol VRT/SL2/6LXB	Eastern Coach Works	H43/31F	1975	Ex Western National, 1992
VR162	MCL938P	Bristol VRT/SL3/6LXB	Eastern Coach Works	H43/31F	1976	
VR163	OUP683P	Bristol VRT/SL3/6LXB	Eastern Coach Works	H43/31F	1976	Ex Western National, 1992

VR164-171 — Bristol VRT/SL3/6LXB — Eastern Coach Works — H43/31F — 1976

164	MCL940P	168	MEX770P	169	MCL944P	170	MEX769P	171	MEX768P
165	MCL941P								

VL172	NAH135P	Bristol VRT/SL3/6LX(501)	Eastern Coach Works	H43/31F	1976	
VR176	NAH139P	Bristol VRT/SL3/6LXB	Eastern Coach Works	H43/31F	1976	
VR178	NAH141P	Bristol VRT/SL3/6LXB	Eastern Coach Works	H43/31F	1976	
VR179	OEL233P	Bristol VRT/SL3/501(6LXB)	Eastern Coach Works	H43/31F	1976	Ex Wilts & Dorset, 1993
VR180	OEL236P	Bristol VRT/SL3/501(6LXB)	Eastern Coach Works	H43/31F	1976	Ex Wilts & Dorset, 1993
VR181	OPW181P	Bristol VRT/SL3/6LXB	Eastern Coach Works	H43/31F	1976	
VL183	WDM345R	Bristol VRT/SL3/501	Eastern Coach Works	H43/31F	1977	Ex PMT, 1992
VR184	ODL657R	Bristol VRT/SL3/6LXB	Eastern Coach Works	H43/31F	1977	Ex Southern Vectis, 1991
VR185	ODL658R	Bristol VRT/SL3/6LXB	Eastern Coach Works	H43/31F	1977	Ex Southern Vectis, 1991
VR186	ODL659R	Bristol VRT/SL3/6LXB	Eastern Coach Works	H43/31F	1977	Ex Southern Vectis, 1991

VR187-211 — Bristol VRT/SL3/6LXB — Eastern Coach Works — H43/31F — 1976-78

187	PVF359R	192	TEX402R	197	TEX407R	203	XNG203S	206	XNG206S
188	PVF360R	193	TEX403R	198	TEX408R	204	XNG204S	207	XNG207S
189	RPW189R	194	TEX404R	199	WPW199S	205	XNG205S	211	YNG211S
191	TEX401R	196	TEX406R						

VL215	BRF691T	Bristol VRT/SL3/501	Eastern Coach Works	H43/31F	1978	Ex PMT, 1993

VR216-236 — Bristol VRT/SL3/6LXB — Eastern Coach Works — H43/31F — 1978-79

216	BCL216T	219	BVG219T	222	BVG222T	225	BVG225T	230	DEX230T
217	BCL217T	220	BVG220T	223	BVG223T	226	DEX226T	236	DNG236T
218	BVG218T	221	BVG221T	224	BVG224T	229	DEX229T		

VR237	GRA844V	Bristol VRT/SL3/6LXB	Eastern Coach Works	H43/31F	1980	Ex Trent, 1991

Overleaf, top: **Five Dennis Lance and four Dart buses were among vehicles added to the fleet in 1993, the former being fitted with bodywork by Northern Counties. Shown here is LC39, K739JAH while still numbered S39.** *Paul Wigan*

Overleaf, bottom: **Six further Dennis Darts were delivered during 1995, this time for the SuperRoute project. As such the vehicles are fitted with guide wheels for use on the guided busway at Kesgrave near Ipswich. Shown here is DP77, M376YEX.** *Phillip Stephenson*

The Eastern Bus Handbook

JD6 is one of five Dennis Javelins with Duple 300 bus bodies though fitted with high-back seating. Passing through Castle Meadow in Norwich it shows the attractive livery introduced by then parent GRT, now part of FirstBus plc.
Keith Grimes

An all-Leyland Olympian OL24, J624BVG, was built at Lillyhall. The frontal treatment is that used by Leyland for the last of the body styles to be built at the plant.
Cliff Beeton

VP93, M593ANG, is one of ten Volvo B6s delivered during 1994 having been diverted from Mainline after plans by that operator to start an operation in Ipswich were aborted. These were bodied by Plaxton with Pointer style bodies and the majority are now allocated to Ipswich where this picture was taken.
Phillip Stephenson

VR238-244

Bristol VRT/SL3/6LXB   Eastern Coach Works   H43/31F   1979

238	HAH238V	240	HAH240V	242	JAH242V	243	JAH243V	244	JAH244V
239	HAH239V	241	JAH241V						

VR245-250

Bristol VRT/SL3/6LXB   Eastern Coach Works   H43/31F   1979-80 Ex Trent, 1991

245	GRA841V	247	GRA843V	248	GRA845V	249	GRA847V	250	GRA846V
246	GRA842V								

VR251-282

Bristol VRT/SL3/6LXB   Eastern Coach Works   H43/31F   1980-81

251	PCL251W	256	PCL256W	262	RAH262W	270	RAH270W	275	TAH275W
252	PCL252W	257	PCL257W	263	RAH263W	271	TAH271W	276	TAH276W
253	PCL253W	258	RAH258W	266	RAH266W	272	TAH272W	277	VAH277X
254	PCL254W	259	RAH259W	267	RAH267W	273	TAH273W	281	VAH281X
255	PCL255W	261	RAH261W	269	RAH269W	274	TAH274W	282	VAH282X

VR283-302

Bristol VRT/SL3/6LXB   Eastern Coach Works   H43/31F*   1981-82 *284/5/7 are DPH41/25F

283	VEX283X	286	VEX286X	288	VEX288X	292	VEX292X	297	VEX297X
284	VEX284X	287	VEX287X	290	VEX290X	294	VEX294X	302	VEX302X
285	VEX285X								

VR303-310

Bristol VRT/SL3/6LXB   Eastern Coach Works   H43/31F*   1981   Ex Trent, 1991

303	PRC848X	305	PRC851X	307	PRC853X	309	PRC855X	310	PRC857X
304	PRC850X	306	PRC852X	308	PRC854X				

HVR331	KKE731N	Bristol VRT/SL2/6LX	Eastern Coach Works	H43/34F	1975	Ex Hastings & District, 1985
HVR332	KKE732N	Bristol VRT/SL2/6LX	Eastern Coach Works	H43/34F	1975	Ex Hastings & District, 1985
HVR333	KKE733N	Bristol VRT/SL2/6LX	Eastern Coach Works	H43/34F	1975	Ex Hastings & District, 1985
HVR334	KKE734N	Bristol VRT/SL2/6LX	Eastern Coach Works	H43/34F	1975	Ex Hastings & District, 1985
OT351w	OCK995K	Bristol VRT/SL2/6LX	Eastern Coach Works	O39/31F	1972	Ex Ribble, 1985
OT352	NCK980J	Bristol VRT/SL2/6LX	Eastern Coach Works	O39/31F	1971	Ex Ribble, 1985
OT353	JNG50N	Bristol VRT/SL2/6LX	Eastern Coach Works	O43/31F	1975	
VR378	OCK988K	Bristol VRT/SL2/6LX	Eastern Coach Works	H39/31F	1972	Ex Ribble, 1985
VR384	OCK994K	Bristol VRT/SL2/6LX	Eastern Coach Works	H39/31F	1972	Ex Ribble, 1985
VR385	OCK985K	Bristol VRT/SL2/6LX	Eastern Coach Works	H39/31F	1972	Ex Ribble, 1985
VR410	CJO470R	Bristol VRT/SL3/6LX	Eastern Coach Works	H43/31F	1977	Ex City of Oxford, 1984
VR411	CJO471R	Bristol VRT/SL3/6LX	Eastern Coach Works	H43/31F	1977	Ex City of Oxford, 1984
VR412	CJO472R	Bristol VRT/SL3/6LX	Eastern Coach Works	H43/31F	1977	Ex City of Oxford, 1984

RA421-426

Renault-Dodge S56   Alexander AM   B21F   1986   Ex SMT, 199..

421	D415ASF	423	D430ASF	424	D401ASF	425	D425ASF	426	D407ASF
422	D417ASF								

VR501	GAG48N	Bristol VRT/SL2/6LX	Eastern Coach Works	H43/31F	1974	Ex Rosemary, Terrington St Clement, 1993
VR502	YHN654M	Bristol VRT/SL2/6LX	Eastern Coach Works	H39/31F	1974	Ex Rosemary, Terrington St Clement, 1993
DD504	THX573S	Leyland Fleetline FE30ALRSp	Park Royal	H44/27D	1978	Ex Rosemary, Terrington St Clement, 1993
DD505	OJD195R	Leyland Fleetline FE30AGR	MCW	H45/32F	1977	Ex Rosemary, Terrington St Clement, 1993
DD506	THX531S	Leyland Fleetline FE30ALRSp	Park Royal	H44/27D	1978	Ex Rosemary, Terrington St Clement, 1993
DD507	WWH26L	Daimler Fleetline CRG6LX	Park Royal	H43/32F	1973	Ex Rosemary, Terrington St Clement, 1993
DD508	CKC312L	Daimler Fleetline CRG6LXB	MCW	H43/32F	1973	Ex Rosemary, Terrington St Clement, 1993
LP523	6920MX	Leyland Leopard PSU3B/4R	Plaxton Elite III Express	C51F	1974	Ex Rosemary, Terrington St Clement, 1993
BD525	EHE234V	Bedford YMT	Duple Dominant II	C53F	1980	Ex Rosemary, Terrington St Clement, 1993
LD527	GRF267V	Leyland Leopard PSU3E/4R	Duple Dominant	C53F	1979	Ex Sanders, Holt, 1993
TP528	7694VC	Leyland Tiger TRCTL11/3R	Plaxton Paramount 3200 III	C53F	1983	Ex Vanguard, 1993
TP529	6149KP	Leyland Tiger TRCTL11/3R	Plaxton Paramount 3200 III	C53F	1983	Ex Vanguard, 1993
LD530	YFV179R	Leyland Leopard PSU3E/4R	Duple Dominant	C51F	1977	Ex Powell, Lapford, 1993
LG567	PVF367R	Leyland National 11351A/1R	East Lancs Greenway (1995)	B52F	1976	
LG568	PVF368R	Leyland National 11351A/1R	East Lancs Greenway (1994)	B52F	1976	
LG569	PVF369R	Leyland National 11351A/1R	East Lancs Greenway (1995)	B52F	1976	
LG585	TVF620R	Leyland National 11351A/1R	East Lancs Greenway (1994)	B49F	1977	
LN586	WAH586S	Leyland National 11351A/1R		B52F	1977	
LG587	WAH587S	Leyland National 11351A/1R	East Lancs Greenway (199.)	B52F	1978	
LG588	WAH588S	Leyland National 11351A/1R	East Lancs Greenway (199.)	B52F	1978	
LN589	WAH589S	Leyland National 11351A/1R		B52F	1977	
LG590	WAH590S	Leyland National 11351A/1R	East Lancs Greenway (199.)	B52F	1978	

Several of the VRs now carry the cream-dominated livery, including VR285, VEX285X, seen here in Kings Lynn. The batch of vehicles represented here contains the penultimate VR built (and the last completed by ECW) in the form of VR294. *Paul Wigan*

Leyland Nationals from the Eastern Counties fleet are being refurbished under the Greenway programme with a dozen completed by late summer 1995. In addition to the revised body treatment by East Lancashire Coachbuilders, the vehicles are gaining Gardner power units, and the 'LG' fleet number prefix. Seen in Norwich is LG783, VFX981S, an example new to Hants & Dorset. *Malc McDonald*

Photographed at Newmarket was LD791, XWX181S, a Leyland Leopard with a Duple Dominant II body. This style, with deeper windscreens succeeded the Dominant I which was an express variant with roof-mounted destination equipment and shallow screens for National Bus customers.
Keith Grimes

LN591	WAH591S	Leyland National 11351A/1R			B52F	1977		
LN592	WAH592S	Leyland National 11351A/1R			B52F	1977		
LG593	WAH593S	Leyland National 11351A/1R	East Lancs Greenway (1993)		B52F	1977		
LN594	WAH594S	Leyland National 11351A/1R			B52F	1977		
LG598	WVF598S	Leyland National 11351A/1R	East Lancs Greenway (1993)		B52F	1978		
LG599	WVF599S	Leyland National 11351A/1R	East Lancs Greenway (1995)		B52F	1978		

LN601-617

Leyland National 2 NL116L11/1R			B49F	1980

601	KVG601V	604	KVG604V	608	KVG608V	613	PEX613W	616	PEX616W
602	KVG602V	606	KVG606V	609	KVG609V	614	PEX614W	617	PEX617W
603	KVG603V	607	KVG607V	610	PEX610W	615	PEX615W		

LN624-628

Leyland National 2 NL116AL11/1R   B49F   1981

624	UVF624X	625	UVF625X	626	UVF626X	627	UVF627X	628	UVF628X

SD637	C637BEX	Freight Rover Sherpa	Dormobile	B16F	1986
SD638	C638BEX	Freight Rover Sherpa	Dormobile	B16F	1986
SD652	C652BEX	Freight Rover Sherpa	Dormobile	B16F	1986
MH701	E701TNG	Mercedes-Benz 609D	Robin Hood	B20F	1988
MH702	E702TNG	Mercedes-Benz 609D	Robin Hood	B20F	1988

MA711-728

Mercedes-Benz L608D   Alexander AM   B20F   1986

711	C711BEX	715	C715BEX	719	C719BEX	723	C723BEX	726	C726BEX
712	C712BEX	716	C716BEX	720	C720BEX	724	C724BEX	727	C727BEX
713	C713BEX	717	C717BEX	721	C721BEX	725	C725BEX	728	C728BEX
714	C714BEX	718	C718BEX	722	C722BEX				

MB741-757   Mercedes-Benz L608D   Reeve Burgess   B20F   1986

741	C741BEX	745	C745BEX	749	C749BEX	752	C752BEX	755	C755BEX
742	C742BEX	746	C746BEX	750	C750BEX	753	C753BEX	756	C756BEX
743	C743BEX	747	C747BEX	751	C751BEX	754	C754BEX	757	C757BEX
744	C744BEX	748	C748BEX						

MB758	D758LEX	Mercedes-Benz 609D	Reeve Burgess	B20F	1987
MB759	D759LEX	Mercedes-Benz 609D	Reeve Burgess	B20F	1987

LN762-782   Leyland National 11351A/1R   B52F   1978   762/78/81/2 are B49F

781 is fitted with a Gardner 6HLX engine and a mark 2 National front.
LGs are East Lancs Greenway conversion (1994-95). Other are expected to follow

LN762u	XNG762S	LN766u	XNG766S	LN769	XNG769S	LN775	CCL775T	LG781	DPW781T
LN763	XNG763S	LN767	XNG767S	LN770	XNG770S	LN776	CCL776T	LG782	DPW782T
LG765	XNG765S	LG768	XNG768S	LN774	CCL774T	LN778	CCL778T		

LG783	VFX981S	Leyland National 11351A/1R	East Lancs Greenway (1994) B52F	1978	Ex Stagecoach South, 1993
LG784	UFX854S	Leyland National 11351A/1R	East Lancs Greenway (1994) B52F	1978	Ex Stagecoach South, 1993
LG785	YFY5M	Leyland National 11351A/1R	East Lancs Greenway (1994) B52F	1978	Ex Merseybus, 1993
LD789w	UVO121S	Leyland Leopard PSU3E/4R	Duple Dominant I	C49F	1977	Ex Trent, 1993
LD790w	URL856S	Leyland Leopard PSU3E/4R	Duple Dominant I	C53F	1978	Ex Trent, 1993
LD791	XWX181S	Leyland Leopard PSU3E/4R	Duple Dominant II	C51F	1978	Ex Powell, Lapford, 1994
LW792	OEX792W	Leyland Leopard PSU3E/4R	Willowbrook 003	C49F	1980	Ex Ambassador Travel, 1987
LW793	OEX793W	Leyland Leopard PSU3E/4R	Willowbrook 003	C49F	1980	Ex Ambassador Travel, 1987
LW794	OEX794W	Leyland Leopard PSU3E/4R	Willowbrook 003	C49F	1980	Ex Ambassador Travel, 1987
LD795	LLT345V	Leyland Leopard PSU3E/4R	Duple Dominant II	C51F	1980	Ex Lewis, Whitwick, 1993
LW796	OEX796W	Leyland Leopard PSU3E/4R	Willowbrook 003	C49F	1980	Ex Ambassador Travel, 1987
LD797	UVO124S	Leyland Leopard PSU3E/4R	Duple Dominant I	C49F	1977	Ex Trent, 1993
LD798	UVO122S	Leyland Leopard PSU3E/4R	Duple Dominant I	C49F	1977	Ex Trent, 1993
LD799	RRB116R	Leyland Leopard PSU3E/4R	Duple Dominant I	C49F	1977	Ex Trent, 1993
LW808	JCL808V	Leyland Leopard PSU3E/4R	Willowbrook 003	C49F	1980	Ex Ambassador Travel, 1987
LW809	JCL809V	Leyland Leopard PSU3E/4R	Willowbrook 003	C49F	1980	Ex Ambassador Travel, 1987
TD850	D779NUD	Ford Transit VE6	Dormobile	B16F	1986	Ex East Kent, 1988

TH851-856   Ford Transit VE6   Robin Hood   B16F   1987

851	E851PEX	853	E853PEX	854	E854PEX	855	E855PEX	856	E856PEX
852	E852PEX								

TH892-919   Ford Transit 190D   Robin Hood   B16F   1986

892	C892BEX	897	C897BEX	905	C905BEX	909	C909BEX	914	C914BEX
893	C893BEX	898	C898BEX	906	C906BEX	910	C910BEX	916	C916BEX
894	C894BEX	899u	C899BEX	907u	C907BEX	912	C912BEX	917	C917BEX
895	C895BEX	902	C902BEX	908	C908BEX	913	C913BEX	919	C919BEX
896	C896BEX	903	C903BEX						

TC952-961   Ford Transit 190D   Carlyle   B16F   1985

952	C952YAH	958	C958YAH	959	C959YAH	960	C960YAH	961u	C961YAH
957	C957YAH								

TD965-984   Ford Transit 190D   Dormobile   B16F   1985

965	C965YAH	970	C970YAH	979	C979YAH	981w	C981YAH	983w	C983YAH
966	C966YAH	972w	C972YAH	980w	C980YAH	982	C982YAH	984	C984YAH
967	C967YAH	975	C975YAH						

TD985	C725FKE	Ford Transit 190	Dormobile	B16F	1986	Ex East Kent, 1989
TD986	C726FKE	Ford Transit 190	Dormobile	B16F	1986	Ex East Kent, 1989
TD987	C727FKE	Ford Transit 190	Dormobile	B16F	1986	Ex East Kent, 1989

Livery: Ivory, red and orange

Previous Registrations:

6149KP	WWA300Y, 9258VC, GAC98Y	7694VC	FWH37Y
6920MX	RUP388M	URL856S	WRO447S, XRL965

When the mini-bus era commenced around ten years ago, National Bus procured chassis from Ford, Freight Rover and Mercedes Benz. The latter included the complete run-out of the L608D model before it was replaced by the 609 series and many are still to be found with diverse operators. Seen with Eastern National is 221, C221HJN. *Phillip Stephenson*

New vehicles for the FirstBus subsidiaries carry forward the vehicle investment programme although current deliveries continue from those orders placed separately by GRT and Badgerline. A recent arrival with Eastern National is Dennis Dart 829, N829APU, seen in Chelmsford. *Keith Grimes*

EASTERN NATIONAL

Eastern National Ltd, 48-49 New Writtle Street, Chelmsford, Essex, CM2 0SD

Depots and outstations: Anchor Street, Bishops Stortford; Fairfield Road, Braintree; Duke Street, Chelmsford; Telford Road, Clacton-on-Sea; Haven Road, Colchester; Queen Street, Colchester; Dunmow; Station Road, Harwich; High Street, Maldon and Walton-on-the-Naze.

A subsidiary of FirstBus Plc

202-223   Mercedes-Benz L608D   Reeve Burgess   B20F   1985-86

202	C202HJN	205	C205HJN	208w	C208HJN	215	C215HJN	220w	C220HJN
203	C203HJN	206w	C206HJN	210	C210HJN	217	C217HJN	223w	C223HJN
204	C204HJN	207w	C207HJN	212	C212HJN				

228-236   Mercedes-Benz L608D   Reeve Burgess   B20F   1986   Ex City Line, 1993

228	C482BHY	230	C485BHY	232	C489BHY	234	C494BHY	236	C496BHY
229	C484BHY	231	C486BHY	233	C493BHY	235	C495BHY		

237-246   Mercedes-Benz L608D   Reeve Burgess   B20F*   1985-86 Ex Western National, 1993
*242-6 are B19F

237	C678ECV	239	C685ECV	241	C688ECV	243	C697ECV	245u	C700ECV
238	C684ECV	240	C687ECV	242	C695ECV	244	C698ECV	246	C964GCV

247	D534KGL	Mercedes-Benz L608D	Robin Hood	B20F	1986	Ex Western National, 1994
248	C107HGL	Mercedes-Benz L608D	Reeve Burgess	B20F	1986	Ex Western National, 1994
249u	C231HCV	Mercedes-Benz L608D	Robin Hood	B20F	1986	Ex Western National, 1994
250	C232HCV	Mercedes-Benz L608D	Robin Hood	B20F	1986	Ex Western National, 1994
251	C990GCV	Mercedes-Benz L608D	Robin Hood	B20F	1986	Ex Western National, 1994
252	C230HCV	Mercedes-Benz L608D	Robin Hood	B20F	1986	Ex Western National, 1994

601-617   Mercedes-Benz 709D   Reeve Burgess Beaver   B23F   1991

601	H601OVW	605	H605OVW	609	H609OVW	612	J612UTW	615	J615UTW
602	H602OVW	606	H606OVW	610	J610UTW	613	J613UTW	616	J616UTW
603	H603OVW	607	H607OVW	611	J611UTW	614	J614UTW	617	J617UTW
604	H604OVW	608	H608OVW						

618-630   Mercedes-Benz 709D   Plaxton Beaver   B23F   1991

618	J618UTW	621	J621UTW	624	J624UTW	627	J627UTW	629	J629UTW
619	J619UTW	622	J622UTW	625	J625UTW	628	J628UTW	630	J630UTW
620	J620UTW	623	J623UTW	626	J626UTW				

631-656   Mercedes-Benz 709D   Plaxton Beaver   B23F   1993-94

631	K631GVX	637	K637GVX	642	K642GVX	647	L647MEV	652	L652MEV
632	K632GVX	638	K638GVX	643	K643GVX	648	L648MEV	653	L653MEV
633	K633GVX	639	K639GVX	644	K644GVX	649	L649MEV	654	L654MEV
634	K634GVX	640	K640GVX	645	K645GVX	650	L650MEV	655	L655MEV
635	K635GVX	641	K641GVX	646	K646GVX	651	L651MEV	656	L656MEV
636	K636GVX								

657-676   Mercedes-Benz 709D   Plaxton Beaver   B23F   1995

657	M657VJN	661	M661VJN	665	M665VJN	669	M669VJN	673	M673VJN
658	M658VJN	662	M662VJN	666	M166VJN	670	M670VJN	674	M674VJN
659	M659VJN	663	M663VJN	667	M667VJN	671	M671VJN	675	M675VJN
660	M660VJN	664	M664VJN	668	M668VJN	672	M672VJN	676	M676VJN

677	L21AHA	Mercedes-Benz 709D	Plaxton Beaver	B23F	1993	Ex Frontline, 1995

801-822

Dennis Dart 9SDL3034 — Plaxton Pointer — B34F — 1993-94

801	L801MEV	806	L806OPU	811	L811OPU	815	L815OPU	819	L819OPU
802	L802MEV	807	L807OPU	812	L812OPU	816	L816OPU	820	L820OPU
803	L803OPU	808	L808OPU	813	L813OPU	817	L817OPU	821	L821OPU
804	L804OPU	809	L809OPU	814	L814OPU	818	L818OPU	822	L822OPU
805	L805OPU	810	L810OPU						

823-830

Dennis Dart 9.8SDL3054 — Plaxton Pointer — B39F — 1995

823	N823APU	825	N825APU	827	N827APU	829	N829APU	830	N830APU
824	N824APU	826	N826APU	828	N828APU				

1001-1007

Leyland Tiger TRBTL11/2R — Duple Dominant — DP47F — 1983-84 Ex Yorkshire Rider, 1995

1001	EWR651Y	1003	EWR653Y	1005	A663KUM	1006	A665KUM	1007	A668KUM
1002	EWR652Y	1004	A660KUM						

1111-1125

Leyland Tiger TRCTL11/3R — Alexander TE — C53F — 1983

1111w	HHJ372Y	1114w	HHJ375Y	1120w	HHJ381Y	1121	HHJ382Y	1125w	A694OHJ
1112w	HHJ373Y	1115w	HHJ376Y						

1128	B696WAR	Leyland Tiger TRCTL11/3R	Plaxton Paramount 3500 II	C51F	1985
1129	B697WAR	Leyland Tiger TRCTL11/3R	Plaxton Paramount 3500 II	C51F	1985
1130	C130HJN	Leyland Tiger TRCTL11/3R	Plaxton Paramount 3200 II E	C53F	1986
1131	EWW946Y	Leyland Tiger TRCTL11/3R	Plaxton Paramount 3200 E	C53F	1983 Ex Yorkshire Rider, 1995

1401-1429

Leyland Lynx LX112L10ZR/1R — Leyland Lynx — B49F* — 1988 — 1427-9 are B47F

1401	E401HWC	1407	F407LTW	1414	F414MNO	1425	F425MJN	1428	F428MJN
1402	F402LTW	1408	F408LTW	1415	F415MWC	1426	F426MJN	1429	F429MJN
1403	F403LTW	1413	F413MNO	1416	F416MWC	1427	F427MJN		

1832-1924

Leyland National 11351A/1R — B49F — 1978-79

1832	VAR898S	1860w	YEV318S	1865u	YEV323S	1874	BNO664T	1914w	JHJ140V
1833u	VAR899S	1861	YEV319S	1867	YEV325S	1885	BNO675T	1916	JHJ142V
1844w	WJN564S	1862	YEV320S	1870u	YEV328S	1890	BNO680T	1921	JHJ147V
1850	YEV308S	1863	YEV321S	1872	ANO271S	1899	DAR121T	1924	JHJ150V
1851	YEV309S								

1933u	MHJ729V	Leyland National 2 NL116L11/1R		B49F	1980
1935u	MHJ731V	Leyland National 2 NL116L11/1R		B49F	1980
1940w	KEP829X	Leyland National 2 NL116L11/1R		B49F	1980 Ex SWT, 1990
2383	WNO479	Bristol KSW5G	Eastern Coach Works	O33/28R	1953
2384	WNO480	Bristol KSW5G	Eastern Coach Works	O33/28R	1953

3069-3094

Bristol VRT/SL3/6LXB — Eastern Coach Works — H39/31F — 1980-81

3069	KOO787V	3076	KOO794V	3079	STW23W	3084	STW28W	3093	STW37W
3071	KOO789V	3077	STW21W	3083	STW27W	3092	STW36W	3094	STW38W
3072	KOO790V	3078	STW22W						

3103	UAR593W	Bristol VRT/SL3/6LXB	Eastern Coach Works	H43/31F	1981
3106	UAR596W	Bristol VRT/SL3/6LXB	Eastern Coach Works	H43/34F	1981
3109	UAR599W	Bristol VRT/SL3/6LXB	Eastern Coach Works	H43/31F	1981
3112	XHK217X	Bristol VRT/SL3/6LXB	Eastern Coach Works	H43/34F	1981
3127	XHK232X	Bristol VRT/SL3/6LXB	Eastern Coach Works	H43/31F	1981
3219	VTH941T	Bristol VRT/SL3/501	Eastern Coach Works	H43/31F	1978 Ex Brewers, 1990
3220	WTH949T	Bristol VRT/SL3/501	Eastern Coach Works	H43/31F	1979 Ex Brewers, 1990
3221	WTH958T	Bristol VRT/SL3/501	Eastern Coach Works	H43/31F	1979 Ex Brewers, 1990
3222	BEP963V	Bristol VRT/SL3/501	Eastern Coach Works	H43/31F	1980 Ex Brewers, 1990
3223	MFA721V	Bristol VRT/SL3/501	Eastern Coach Works	DPH39/28F	1980 Ex PMT, 1994

Opposite, top: **Leyland Lynx continue to perform sterling service and though the model is discontinued several of their features have been passed on to the successor, the Volvo B10B. One of the early examples is 1401, E401HWC, seen here in service with Eastern National at Chelmsford.** *Paul Wigan*

Opposite, bottom: **The Dennis Dart is supplied to many of the Badgerline fleets to meet their mid-size single-deck requirement. Here, 809, L809OPU, is seen heading for Greenstead. Badgerline became part of FirstBus in June 1995 and since then the badger motif has been removed from vehicles, being replaced by a circle with and 'f' that appears also to be a roadway and junction.** *Phillip Stephenson*

Transferred to Eastern National from Yorkshire Rider in 1995 were seven Leyland Tigers with Duple Dominant bus bodywork. Photographed in Chelmsford when heading for Bishops Stortford was 103, EWR653Y. These appear to have replaced a similar number of Alexander-bodied Tigers which were on coach chassis, the new arrivals being on the rarer bus version. *Keith Grimes*

3224-3233

Bristol VRT/SL3/6LXB   Eastern Coach Works   H43/31F   1977-81 Ex Yorkshire Rider, 1994-95
3226 was rebodied 1979

| 3224 | AYG848S | 3226 | DWU298T | 3228 | LWU469V | 3230 | SUB789W | 3232 | JWT760V |
| 3225 | AYG850S | 3227 | LUA716V | 3229 | PWY44W | 3231 | SWW302R | 3233 | LUA717V |

| 3500 | WNO546L | Bristol VRT/SL2/6LX | Eastern Coach Works | 039/31F | 1973 |
| 3501 | NPU974M | Bristol VRT/SL2/6LX | Eastern Coach Works | 039/31F | 1973 |

4007-4021

Leyland Olympian ONLXB/1R   Eastern Coach Works   DPH42/30F   1986   4010/12 ex Thamesway, 1995/92

4007	C407HJN	4012	C412HJN	4015	C415HJN	4017	C417HJN	4019	C419HJN
4008	C408HJN	4013	C413HJN	4016	C416HJN	4018	C418HJN	4021	C421HJN
4010	C410HJN	4014	C414HJN						

4501	B689BPU	Leyland Olympian ONTL11/2RHSp	Eastern Coach Works	CH45/28F	1985
4503	B691BPU	Leyland Olympian ONTL11/2RHSp	Eastern Coach Works	CH45/28F	1985
4510	D510PPU	Leyland Olympian ONTL11/2RHSp	Eastern Coach Works	CH45/28F	1986
4511	D511PPU	Leyland Olympian ONTL11/2RHSp	Eastern Coach Works	CH45/24F	1986
4512	D512PPU	Leyland Olympian ONTL11/2RHSp	Eastern Coach Works	CH45/24F	1986

Livery: Green and yellow.

Bury St Edmunds is the location for this picture of 1129, B697WAR. A Leyland Tiger with Plaxton Paramount 3500 bodywork it may regularly be found on excursion work and is one of only four coaches in the fleet. *Keith Grimes*

The last version of Leyland Olympian-based bodywork from Eastern Coach Works, and one aimed to attract NBC double-deck coach orders, is seen on Eastern National 4510, D510PPU, one of three similar 1986 registered vehicles remaining in the fleet. It is seen in Victoria Street while performing a commuter service. *Colin Lloyd*

EMBLINGS

J & B Embling, Bridge Garage, Guyhirn, Cambridgeshire, PE13 4ED

	Reg	Chassis	Body	Seating	Year	Notes
	EJR791	Leyland Royal Tiger PSU1/15	Plaxton Panorama I(1966)	C43F	1952	Ex Hogg, Sheffield, 1992
	MEB626	Trojan	Trojan	M13	1961	
	OFL113J	Daimler Fleetline CRG6LX	Alexander L	H48/32D	1971	Ex Partridge, Hadleigh, 1984
	UUF110J	Bristol VRT/SL2/6G	Eastern Coach Works	H39/31F	1971	Ex Brighton & Hove, 1987
w	UUF112J	Bristol VRT/SL2/6G	Eastern Coach Works	H39/31F	1971	Ex Southdown, 1987
	UUF115J	Bristol VRT/SL2/6G	Eastern Coach Works	H39/31F	1971	Ex Brighton & Hove, 1987
	WXI9252	Leyland Leopard PSU3B/4R	Duple Dominant Express	C53F	1973	Ex Fowler, Holbeach Drove, 1991
	3196DD	Bristol VRT/SL2/6G	Eastern Coach Works	H43/34F	1974	Ex Rover, Horsley, 1990
	HTU154N	Bristol VRT/SL2/6G	Eastern Coach Works	H43/31F	1975	Ex Crosville, 1988
	JVE370P	AEC Reliance 6U3ZR	Plaxton Supreme III Express	C49F	1975	Ex Fowler, Holbeach Drove, 1994
	PRE205R	Bedford VAS5	Plaxton Supreme III	C29F	1976	Ex Kirkpatricks of Deeside, 1994
w	SVA7S	Ford R1114	Plaxton Supreme III Express	C53F	1978	
	CAV312V	Ford Transit	S & N	M12	1979	
	CEW205V	Ford R1114	Plaxton Supreme IV Express	C53F	1979	
	RGV684W	Bedford YMT	Duple Dominant II	C53F	1980	Ex Haines, Frampton West, 1991
	YXI9255	Ford R1014	Plaxton Supreme IV	C35F	1980	Ex Hunter, Hucknall, 1993
	JIL5655	DAF SB2300DHS585	Jonckheere Jubilee	C51FT	1983	Ex West Kingsdown Coaches, 1994
	JIL2760	Peugeot-Talbot Express	Dixon Lomas	M12	1984	Ex Cowlbeck, Wisbech, 1993
	HIL4585	Bedford Venturer YNV	Plaxton Paramount 3200 II	C53F	1985	Ex Perrett, Shipton Oliffe, 1993
	JIL5660	DAF MB230DKVL615	Duple 340	C50F	1986	Ex Bennett, Chieveley, 1994
	JIL7539	DAF MB230DKVL615	Plaxton Paramount 3?00 III	C53F	19??	Ex ??
	F705ENE	Leyland Tiger TRCTL11/3ARZM	Plaxton Paramount 3200 III	C53F	1989	Ex Jewitt, Humshaugh, 1994
	G697VAV	Bova FHD12.290	Bova Futura	C49FT	1990	
	H271CEW	Scania K113CRB	Van Hool Alizée	C49FT	1990	
	H854DAV	Scania K113CRB	Van Hool Alizée	C49FT	1990	

Livery: White, red and blue

Previous Registrations:

3196DD	GUD750N, YWD687, KAD397N	JIL7539	??
EJR791	From new	MEB626	From new
HIL4585	C153UDD	OFL113J	PRG132J, 3196DD
JIL2760	B374SND	WXI9252	JKE107L, 805AFC, LFL304L
JIL5655	A111SNH, A2WKC	YXI9255	GJU854V
JIL5660	C126DWR		

Photographed in the centre of Wisbech, Emblings Coaches CEW205V is a Ford R1114 with Plaxton Supreme IV Express bodywork. The type was most popular with rural operators who had operated Ford and Bedford variants for many years. *Paul Wigan*

ENTERPRISE

Enterprise Safety Coaches Ltd, Black Horse Lane, Chatteris,
Cambridgeshire, PE16 6RB

w	BFS18L	Leyland Atlantean AN68/1R	Alexander AL	H45/30D	1973	Ex Lothian, 1989
	BFS19L	Leyland Atlantean AN68/1R	Alexander AL	H45/30D	1973	Ex Lothian, 1989
w	BFS21L	Leyland Atlantean AN68/1R	Alexander AL	H45/30D	1973	Ex Lothian, 1989
	VBH602S	Ford Transit 160	Dormobile	M16	1977	Ex Juniper, Chatteris, 1985
	SHL882S	Bedford YMT	Plaxton Supreme III	C53F	1978	Ex Angel, Tottenham, 1984
	THX225S	Leyland National 10351A/2R		B48F	1978	Ex London Buses, 1991
	THX513S	Leyland Fleetline FE30ALR	Park Royal	H44/24D	1977	Ex London Buses, 1992
	THX625S	Leyland Fleetline FE30ALR	Park Royal	H44/27D	1978	Ex London Buses, 1992
	YWF512T	Bedford YMT	Duple Dominant II	C53F	1978	Ex Vision Travel, Ipswich, 1994
	RJR869Y	Ford R1114	Duple Dominant IV	C53F	1982	Ex Melton Bus & Coach, Queeniborough, 1994
	RNY313Y	Leyland Tiger TRCTL11/2R	Plaxton Paramount 3200 E	C49F	1983	Ex Hill's, Tredegar, 1991
	B134YSL	DAF MB200DKVL600	Plaxton Paramount 3500 II	C49F	1984	Ex Earnside Coaches, Glenfarg, 1994
	C333HHB	DAF SBR2305DHS570	Jonckheere Jubilee P99	CH55/16CT	1986	Ex Thomas, Clydach Vale, 1989
	D369JUM	Volkswagen LT55	Optare City Pacer	B25F	1987	Ex Goodlad, Chelmsford, 1994
	E23FLD	Freight Rover Sherpa	Chassis Developments	M16	1987	Ex Goodlad, Chelmsford, 1994
	E816UKW	Freight Rover Sherpa	Whittaker	M16	1987	
	E519PWR	Volkswagen LT55	Optare City Pacer	B25F	1987	Ex Morgan, Staplehurst, 1994
	PJI8333	Bova FHD12.290	Bova Futura	C49FT	1987	Ex Colins Coaches, Shepshed, 1994
	G818YJF	Bova FHD12.290	Bova Futura	C53FT	1990	
	G828YJF	Bova FHD12.290	Bova Futura	C53FT	1990	
	H2LWJ	LAG E180Z	LAG EOS	C53FT	1990	Ex Crown, Cramlington, 1993
	J2EST	Hestair Duple SDA1512	Duple 425	C55F	1991	
	L121OWF	Bova FHD12.340	Bova Futura	C53FT	1994	

Livery: Olive green and grey

Previous registrations:

113TYB	?	H2LWJ	H749UCU	PJI8333	F35GHL

**Two Leyland B20 Fleetlines in the current Enterprise fleet were purchased during 1992, both have
Park Royal bodies and came from London Buses. Now in a livery of grey and green is THX513S seen
at Huntingdon.** *Richard Godfrey*

FARGO COACHLINES

LJ Smith, Allviews, School Road, Rayne, Braintree, Essex CM7 8SS

Reg	Chassis	Body	Seating	Year	Notes
MBE616R	Leyland Fleetline FE30AGR	Roe	H45/33F	1977	Ex Stephenson, Rochford, 1994
FNJ993V	Bedford YLQ	Duple Dominant II	C45F	1980	Ex WHM, Hutton, 1989
KHB35W	Ford R1114	Plaxton Supreme IV Express	C53F	1981	Ex Bebb, Llantwit Fardre, 1986
Q394MPU	Dodge S66	Rootes	B27F	1982	Ex USAF, 1993
HIJ6931	Mercedes-Benz 0303/15R	Mercedes-Benz	C49FT	1984	Ex Kinch, Barrow-on-Soar, 1990
784EYB	Mercedes-Benz 0303/15R	Mercedes-Benz	C49FT	1985	Ex Prentice, West Calder, 1992
C707OPN	Ford Transit 160	Ford	M12	1985	Ex private owner, 1994
C238HNO	Mercedes-Benz L608D	Smith	C19F	1986	
FAR601T	Bedford YMP	Plaxton Paramount 3200 II	C29F	1986	Ex Premier Travel, 1989
E218OEG	Ford Transit VE6	Ford	M11	1988	Ex private owner, 1994
E872EHK	Mercedes-Benz 811D	Optare StarRider	DP29F	1988	
E353DHK	Ford Transit VE6	Ford	M8	1988	
F81WBD	Freight Rover Sherpa	Chassis Developments	M16	1988	
F82WBD	Freight Rover Sherpa	Chassis Developments	M16	1988	
H982KVX	Ford Transit VE6	Ford	M11	1991	
H144NVW	Ford Transit VE6	Ford	M8	1991	
L634ANX	Leyland DAF 400	Jubilee	M16	1993	
L637ANX	Leyland DAF 400	Jubilee	M16L	1993	
L668WFT	Leyland DAF 400	Jubilee	M16	1993	
M374HOX	Renault Master T35D	Jubilee	M9L	1994	
M306VET	Scania K113TRB	Irizar Century	C49FT	1995	
M307VET	Scania K113TRB	Irizar Century	C49FT	1995	
M308VET	Scania K113CRB	Van Hool Alizée	C49FT	1995	
M309VET	Scania K113CRB	Van Hool Alizée	C49FT	1995	
M310VET	Scania K113CRB	Van Hool Alizée	C49FT	1995	

Livery: Yellow, orange, red and white

Previous Registrations:

784EYB	From new	FAR601T	C333PEW	HIJ6931	B152MJU

The two-axle Scania with Irizar Century coachwork has attracted much attention since it was first launched at the 1993 NEC Bus and Coach show. A tri-axle version was introduced in 1995 and the Brighton Rally was the location for this picture of Fargo Coachlines, M306VET.
Ivor Norman

FELIX

Felix Taxi Co, 8 Windmill Hill, Long Melford, Suffolk, CO10 9AD

DBU889	Bedford OB	Duple Vista	C27F	1947	Ex Dangerfield, Stroud, 1988
SHR780N	Bedford SB5	Plaxton Panorama IV	C41F	1974	Ex Williams, Bampton, 1993
WYV820T	Bedford YLQ	Duple Dominant II	C45F	1979	Ex Belle Coaches, Lowestoft, 1994
A197RUR	Mercedes-Benz L608D	Plaxton Mini Supreme	C25F	1984	Ex Croxford, Farnham, 1988
E221LER	Mercedes-Benz L207D	Felix	M7	1988	
E743OEW	Mercedes-Benz L207D	Felix	M11	1988	
E856GFV	Mercedes-Benz 609D	Elme	C16F	1987	
WET880	Mercedes-Benz 811D	Optare StarRider	C21FT	1988	Ex Wings, Uxbridge, 1994
F301RMH	Mercedes-Benz 709D	Reeve Burgess Beaver	B25F	1988	
H475KSG	Iveco Daily 49.10	Carlyle Dailybus 2	B25F	1990	Ex Neal's, Isleham, 1994
J220HDS	Mercedes-Benz 811D	Dormobile Routemaker	B33F	1992	
K392BVS	Mercedes-Benz 711D	Plaxton Beaver	C25F	1993	
L198SCM	Mercedes-Benz 814L	North West Coach Sales	DP29F	1994	

Livery: White, red and black.

Previous Registrations:

WET880	F600TLB		
		WYV820T	248D193

The Mercedes-Benz 814L is a forward control version of the more popular 814. This example has a body built by North West Coach Sales who have recently ceased trading. L198SCM is seen in Bury St Edmunds. *Paul Wigan*

A bright yellow and green livery adorns the Flying Banana fleet of minibuses to be found in Great Yarmouth. Heading for the hospital is D70TLV, an example new to North Western and one of a dwindling number of Sherpas in the fleet. *David Longbottom*

The integral Van Hool Astromega remains an uncommon sight in Britain, though several are still used on continental feeder or shuttle routes. JEV245Y is operated by Fords Coaches of Althorne and is seen passing through Parliament Square, London. This vehicle was a startling addition to the Southend fleet when new and operated on their London commuter services. *BBP*

FLYING BANANA

Halesworth Transit Ltd, Unit 12, Yarmouth Business Park, Suffolk Road, Gt Yarmouth, Norfolk, NR31 0PY

B201GNL	Ford Transit 190D	Alexander AM	B16F	1985	Ex Go-Ahead Northern, 1991
B204GNL	Ford Transit 190D	Alexander AM	B16F	1985	Ex Go-Ahead Northern, 1991
B420NJF	Ford Transit 190D	Rootes	B16F	1985	Ex Midland Fox, 1991
C307CRH	Ford Transit 190D	Carlyle	B16F	1985	Ex Clyde Coast, 1994
C316URF	Ford Transit 190D	Dormobile	B16F	1985	Ex Midland, 1994
C38WBF	Ford Transit 190D	Dormobile	B16F	1986	Ex Midland, 1994
C57WBF	Ford Transit 190D	Dormobile	B16F	1986	Ex Midland, 1994
C430BHY	Ford Transit 190D	Dormobile	B16F	1986	Ex City Line, 1989
C431BHY	Ford Transit 190D	Dormobile	B16F	1986	Ex City Line, 1989
C114HUH	Ford Transit 190D	Robin Hood	B16F	1986	Ex Clyde Coast, 1994
C535TJF	Ford Transit 190D	Rootes	B16F	1986	Ex Midland Fox, 1991
D43DNH	Iveco Daily 49.10	Robin Hood City Nippy	B19F	1987	Ex People Mover, Bridgend, 1994
D179LTA	Renault-Dodge S56	Reeve Burgess	B23F	1987	Ex Sherratt, Cold Meece, 1992
D70TLV	Freight Rover Sherpa	Carlyle	B20F	1987	Ex Brian Isaac, Morriston, 1993
E237VOM	Freight Rover Sherpa	Carlyle Citybus 2	B16F	1988	Ex Strathclyde, 1990
H533KSG	Iveco Daily 49.10	Carlyle Dailybus 2	B25F	1991	Ex Collison, Stonehouse, 1994
K340HNG	Leyland DAF 400	Minibus Options	B20F	1992	
M384KVR	Mercedes-Benz 709D	Alexander AM Sprint	B27F	1995	

Livery: Yellow and green.

FORDS COACHES

A A W Ford, The Garage, Fambridge Road, Althorne, Essex, CM3 6BZ

PRG124J	Daimler Fleetline CRG6LX	Alexander L	H48/35F	1971	Ex Moffat & Williamson, 1984
PRG127J	Daimler Fleetline CRG6LX	Alexander L	H48/35F	1971	Ex Moffat & Williamson, 1984
PRG134J	Daimler Fleetline CRG6LX	Alexander L	H48/32D	1971	Ex Partridge, Hadleigh, 1984
PKE806M	Bristol VRT/SL2/6G	Eastern Coach Works	H43/31F	1973	Ex Cedric, Wivenhoe, 1994
820KPO	Bedford YRT	Plaxton Elite III	C53F	1975	Ex Porter, Great Totham, 1988
ONR79R	Bedford YRQ	Plaxton Elite III	C45F	1976	Ex Wells, Maldon, 1984
WGR66R	Bedford YRQ	Plaxton Supreme III	C45F	1977	Ex Weardale, Frosterley, 1981
AUD460R	Bristol VRT/SL3/6LXB	Eastern Coach Works	H43/31F	1977	Ex Carter, Colchester, 1990
TDT32S	Bedford YMT	Duple Dominant II	C53F	1977	Ex Morris, Borehamwood, 1978
VNM900S	Bedford YLQ	Plaxton Supreme III	C45F	1977	Ex Porter, Great Totham, 1994
XNV882S	Bristol VRT/SL3/6LXB	Eastern Coach Works	H43/31F	1978	Ex Thamesway, 1991
LJI477	Bedford YRT	Willowbrook Warrior(1986)	B55F	1978	Ex Cave, Solihull, 1992
CKX392T	Bedford YMT	Duple Dominant II	C53F	1979	Ex Morris, Borehamwood, 1980
EYH693V	Bedford YMT	Plaxton Supreme IV	C53F	1980	Ex Barnes, Clacton-on-Sea, 1987
CHK312X	Bedford YNT	Plaxton Supreme IV	C53F	1982	
GEX790Y	Bova EL26/581	Bova Europa	C53F	1983	Ex Bird's, Hunstanton, 1985
JEV245Y	Van Hool T824	Van Hool Astromega	C57/27F	1983	Ex Southend, 1990
A128NAR	Volvo B10M-61	Van Hool Alizée	C48FT	1983	
C658KVW	Bedford Venturer YNV	Van Hool Alizée	C53F	1986	
C995ERO	Bedford YNT	Plaxton Paramount 3200 II	C53F	1986	Ex Dinsey, Luton, 1988
C141KFL	DAF SB2300DHS585	Jonckheere Jubilee P599	C53FT	1985	Ex Fenn, March, 1989
D66ONS	Bedford Venturer YNV	Duple 320	C57F	1986	Ex Squirrell, Hitcham, 1990
G854VAY	Dennis Javelin 12SDA1907	Caetano Algarve	C53FT	1989	Ex APT, Rayleigh, 1992
H830YGA	Mercedes-Benz 609D	Scott	C21F	1990	Ex Gem Liner, Stockton, 1992
H411CJF	DAF MB230DKVL615	Caetano Algarve II	C49FT	1990	Ex Welsh, Pontefract, 1995
M486HBC	Dennis Javelin 12SDA2136	Caetano Algarve II	C53FT	1994	

Livery: Green and red (contract fleet); white, red and orange (coach fleet).

Previous Registrations:

820KPO	LAY474P	LJI477	XNM830SONR79R	KUT589P

GALLOWAY

Galloway European Coachlines Ltd, Denters Hill, Stowmarket Road, Mendlesham, Suffolk, IP14 5RR

R = Rex Motor Services, Thorndon.

	Registration	Chassis	Body	Seating	Year	Notes
	RCH501R	Bedford YMT	Plaxton Supreme III Express	C53F	1976	Ex Eastern Counties, 1989
	OHE934R	Bedford YMT	Plaxton Supreme III	C53F	1977	Ex Davids Coaches, Elmswell, 1995
	GOI1294	Bedford YMT	Plaxton Supreme III	C53F	1978	Ex Bebb, Llantwit Fardre, 1982
R	XPV657S	Ford R1114	Plaxton Supreme III Express	C53F	1978	Ex Simonds, Botesdale, 1989
	AFJ759T	Bristol VRT/SL3/6LXB	Eastern Coach Works	H43/31F	1979	Ex Nottingham Omnibus, 1994
	DHE699V	Bedford YMT	Plaxton Supreme IV	C53F	1979	Ex Wells, Thorndon, 1990
	KDH832V	Bedford YMT	Plaxton Supreme IV	C53F	1979	Ex Squirrell, Hitcham, 1993
	EPC906V	DAF MB200DKTL600	Plaxton Supreme IV	C53F	1979	Ex Bluebird, Weymouth, 1995
R	2513PP	Ford R1114	Plaxton Supreme IV	C53F	1979	Ex Bennett, Newbury, 1988
	BBM53A	Bedford YMT	Plaxton Supreme IV	C53F	1980	Ex Sampson, Cheshunt, 1990
	1440PP	DAF MB200DKTL600	Plaxton Supreme IV	C57F	1980	Ex Majestic, Shareshill, 1985
	TPA666X	Bedford YNT	Plaxton Supreme IV	C53F	1981	Ex Beckett, Little Horwood, 1988
	6037PP	Leyland Tiger TRCTL11/3R	Plaxton Supreme IV	C53F	1981	Ex ??, 1995
R	A504HUT	Bedford YNT	Duple Laser	C53F	1984	Ex Bexleyheath Transport, 1989
	4092PP	DAF SB2305DHTD585	Plaxton Paramount 3200	C53F	1985	Ex Smith, Alcester, 1989
	C46DUR	DAF SB2305DHTD585	Plaxton Paramount 3200 II	C53F	1985	Ex Dinsey, Luton, 1988
	2086PP	Bova FLD12.250	Bova Futura	C53F	1986	Ex Supreme, Coventry, 1988
	5048PP	DAF SB2305DHS585	Van Hool Alizée	C53F	1987	Ex Landtourers, Farnham, 1995
R	E226WKW	Freight Rover Sherpa	Whittaker	M16	1987	
R	E233WKW	Mercedes-Benz 609D	Whittaker	C24F	1988	
R	F863FWB	Mercedes-Benz 609D	Whittaker	C24F	1989	
	1482PP	DAF SB2305DHTD585	Plaxton Paramount 3200 III	C53F	1989	
	5516PP	DAF SB3000DKV585	Van Hool Alizée	C53F	1989	Ex London Coaches, 1992
	1754PP	Bova FHD12.290	Bova Futura	C49FT	1989	
R	G434ART	Mercedes-Benz 609D	Whittaker	C24F	1990	
	J811KHD	DAF SB3000DKV601	Van Hool Alizée	C49FT	1992	Ex Amberline, 1994
	5611PP	DAF SB3000DKV601	Van Hool Alizée	C49FT	1992	Ex Redwing, Camberwell, 1994
	K110TCP	DAF SB3000DKVF601	Van Hool Alizée	C49FT	1993	
	K120TCP	DAF SB3000DKVF601	Van Hool Alizée	C51FT	1993	
	M830RCP	DAF SB3000DKVF601	Van Hool Alizée	C51FT	1995	
	N665JGV	DAF SB220LC550	Ikarus CitiBus	B49F	1995	

Livery: Cream, yellow and orange

Previous Registrations:

1440PP	NRO229V, 7476PP	2513PP	PNB785W	5611PP	J815KHD
1482PP	F764RRT	4092PP	B885AJX	BBM53A	KBH850V
1754PP	G494WDX	5048PP	D863EFS, GSU371, D344ONW	GOI1294	YUE593S
2086PP	C126AHP	5516PP	F254RJX		

Galloway have used different applications of white and yellow in their livery. Here we see two DAF coaches, above is 1482PP, a SB2305 variant with Plaxton Paramount 3200 bodywork while below is K120TCP, a SB3000 bodied by Van Hool and fitted with continental doorway. Both were photographed while operating relief National Express work. *Colin Lloyd*

GOLDEN BOY

Jetsie Ltd, Low Hill Garage, Roydon, Essex CM19 5JT

401	YOI2642	Leyland Leopard PSU3D/4R	Plaxton Supreme III	C49F	1976	Ex H & M Coaches, 1991
402	YOI7757	Volvo B10M-61	Van Hool Alizée	C53F	1986	Ex Shearings, 1992
403	YOI5475	Leyland Leopard PSU5C/4R	Plaxton Supreme IV	C50F	1980	Ex Mulligan, Harlow, 1992
405	YOI7725	Leyland Tiger TRCTL11/2R	Plaxton Supreme V Express	C53F	1982	Ex Capitol, Cwmbran, 1992
407	D459POO	Renault Extra	Renault	M12	1987	Ex Macs, Roydon, 1994
409	YOI7353	Volvo B10M-61	Van Hool Alizée	C53F	1985	Ex Shearings, 1991
410	WJM810T	Leyland Leopard PSU3E/4R	Plaxton Supreme IV Express	C46F	1979	Ex Alder Valley South, 1987
412	WJM812T	Leyland Leopard PSU3E/4R	Plaxton Supreme IV Express	C46F	1979	Ex Alder Valley South, 1987
413	YOI2805	Leyland Tiger TRCTL11/3R	Plaxton Paramount 3200 E	C57F	1983	Ex Merlyn's, Skewen, 1990
416	YOI7079	Mercedes-Benz L307D	Reeve Burgess	M12	1983	Ex Graves, Hertford, 1991
417	YOI7373	Leyland Tiger TRCTL11/3R	Plaxton Viewmaster IV	C53F	1982	
418	YOI949	Van Hool T815	Van Hool Alizée	C53F	1989	
419	YOI5997	Leyland Leopard PSU5/4R	Plaxton Elite III	C50F	1974	Ex Bonner, Ongar, 1992
421	YOI7374	Leyland Tiger TRCTL11/3R	Duple Dominant II	C53F	1980	Ex Sampson, Hoddesdon, 1988
424	YOI7575	Leyland Tiger TRCTL11/3R	Plaxton Viewmaster IV	C40FT	1983	Ex Green, Brierley Hill, 1987
435	YOI7744	Leyland Leopard PSU3E/4R	Plaxton Supreme IV	C53F	1979	Ex HB Coaches, Wood Green, 1992
436	YOI2517	AEC Reliance 6U2R	Duple Dominant II Express	C53F	1978	Ex Bonner, Ongar, 1992
458	YOI7145	Iveco 79F14	Caetano Viana	C19F	1985	Ex Linkline, Harlesden, 1986
4	YOI8271	Bedford YMT	Plaxton Supreme IV	C53F	1980	Ex Chivers, Wallington, 1995
4	C163JTW	Ebro-Nissan	Coachcraft	C23F	1985	Ex Macs, Roydon, 1995
4	F722SML	Mercedes-Benz 811D	Reeve Burgess Beaver	DP33F	1989	Ex Neal's, Isleham, 1994
4	YOI1214	Mercedes-Benz 811D	Reeve Burgess Beaver	DP29F	1989	Ex NPT Coaches, South Normanton, 1993
4	BAZ8576	Volvo B10M-60	Van Hool Alizée	C49FT	1990	Ex Shearings, 1995
4	M365UCT	Mercedes-Benz 814D	Autobus Classique 2	C33F	1995	

Previous Registrations:

BAZ8576	G876VNA	YOI5475	KBH840V	YOI7374	MNK428V
YOI949	F580RML	YOI5997	GNM225N	YOI7575	A80NHK
YOI1214	F264RPH, A10NPT	YOI7079	KAR986Y	YOI7725	NDW138X
YOI2517	XPK51T	YOI7145	C358LVV	YOI7744	HGA637T, HGA748T
YOI2642	RYG537R	YOI7353	B473UNB	YOI7757	C333DND
YOI2805	DBJ369Y	YOI7373	DNK581Y	YOI8271	BBB546V

Named vehicles: 401 *Miss Cara*, 402 *Miss Geraldine*, 403 *Miss Maria*, 405 *Miss Elaine*, 409 *Miss Shelagh*, 410 *Miss Gemma*, 412 *Miss Kelly*, 413 *Miss Bernadette*, 417 *Miss Mary*, 418 *Miss Angela*, 421 *Miss Patricia*, 424 *Miss Annie*, 435 *Miss Leanne*, 436 *Miss Karen*, 458 *Miss Jacqueline*.

Livery: Gold, burgundy and black

GRAHAM'S

G M & R A Ellis, 180 High Street, Kelvedon, Essex CO5 9JD

ACP832V	Ford R1114	Plaxton Supreme IV	C53F	1980	Ex Holden Bay, Bury, 1984
XKX640X	Ford R1114	Plaxton Supreme IV	C53F	1981	Ex Blue Diamond, Harlow, 1985
B423CMC	Mercedes-Benz L608D	Reeve Burgess	C19F	1985	
MBZ3733	Leyland Tiger TRCTL11/3R	Van Hool Alizée	C52F	1983	Ex Lodge, High Easter, 1995
E786MEU	Ford Transit VE6	Steedrive	M13	1988	
F977APW	Mercedes-Benz 609D	Reeve Burgess Beaver	C19F	1988	Ex Dereham Coachways, 1993
G228PGU	Fiat Ducato	Jubilee	M11L	1990	Ex van, 1993
G805RNC	Scania K93CRB	Plaxton Paramount 3200 III	C53F	1990	Ex Lowland, 1995
G885VNA	Scania K93CRB	Plaxton Paramount 3200 III	C53F	1990	Ex Shearings, 1995
M345UVX	Mercedes-Benz 811D	Plaxton Beaver	B31F	1994	

Livery: White and blue

Previous Registrations:
MBZ3733   NYS57Y, 46AEW, UJNxxxY

The single deck integral from Van Hool is the T815 seen here with the Alizée body option - the other available types being the Alicron and Acron. Shown in Golden Boy Coaches' gold and burgundy livery, YOI949 is seen working a tour to the capital. *BBP*

One of a pair of DAF SB2305's on the Grahams fleet is F652OHD. Both were acquired from Brown of East Grinstead in 1992 though both examples have recently been replaced by Scanias. *Keith Grimes*

Great Yarmouth's double-deck requirement is now mostly met by ten Bristol VRs, typical of which is 26, PVG26W. Three former London Buses Metrobuses and two Volvo Citybuses have recently been sold. *Malc McDonald*

One of the earliest operators to take the Dennis Dart, Great Yarmouth have three examples bodied by Duple, the first manufacturer to produce bodies on the new chassis. Seen here is 56, G456KNG. *Malc McDonald*

The 1993 intake of Darts were of the longer, 9.8 metre version and bodied by East Lancashire. Seen while heading out to Newtown is 63, K63KEX. *Paul Wigan*

68

GREAT YARMOUTH TRANSPORT

Great Yarmouth Transport Ltd, Caister Road, Great Yarmouth,
Norfolk, NR30 4DF

1	4750WY	Volvo B10M-61	Plaxton Paramount 3200	C51F	1983	Ex Wallace Arnold, 1988
2	6220WY	Volvo B10M-61	Plaxton Paramount 3200	C51F	1983	Ex Wallace Arnold, 1988
3	C517DND	Volvo B10M-61	Plaxton Paramount 3200 II	C53F	1986	Ex Shearings, 1993

24-36

Bristol VRT/SL3/6LXB   Eastern Coach Works   H43/31F*   1977-81   *35-36 are H43/34F

24	PVG24W	26	PVG26W	28	CVF28T	30	CVF30T	35	RVF35R
25	PVG25W	27	PVG27W	29	CVF29T	31	CVF31T	36	RVF36R

40	E40OAH	Volvo Citybus B10M-50	East Lancashire	DPH45/33F	1987	
41	E41OAH	Volvo Citybus B10M-50	East Lancashire	DPH45/33F	1987	
42	E42OAH	MCW MetroRider MF151/9	MCW	DP25F	1987	
43	E43OAH	MCW MetroRider MF151/9	MCW	DP25F	1987	
44	E44OAH	MCW MetroRider MF151/9	MCW	DP25F	1987	
45	E45OAH	MCW MetroRider MF151/9	MCW	DP25F	1987	
46	E46RVG	MCW MetroRider MF159/1	MCW	B33F	1988	
47	E47RVG	MCW MetroRider MF159/1	MCW	B33F	1988	
48	E48RVG	MCW MetroRider MF159/1	MCW	B33F	1988	
49	E49RVG	MCW MetroRider MF159/1	MCW	B33F	1988	
50	G833RDS	Mercedes-Benz 811D	Reeve Burgess Beaver	B31F	1990	Ex Timeline, Leigh, 1995
51	G453SGB	Mercedes-Benz 811D	Reeve Burgess Beaver	B31F	1990	Ex Timeline, Leigh, 1995
52	G52GEX	Mercedes-Benz 811D	Reeve Burgess Beaver	DP33F	1989	
53	G53GEX	Mercedes-Benz 811D	Reeve Burgess Beaver	DP33F	1989	
54	G54GEX	Mercedes-Benz 811D	Reeve Burgess Beaver	B33F	1989	
55	G55GEX	Mercedes-Benz 811D	Reeve Burgess Beaver	B33F	1989	
56	G456KNG	Dennis Dart 9SDL3002	Duple Dartline	B39F	1990	
57	G457KNG	Dennis Dart 9SDL3002	Duple Dartline	B39F	1990	
58	G458KNG	Dennis Dart 9SDL3002	Duple Dartline	B39F	1990	
59	G834RDS	Mercedes-Benz 811D	Reeve Burgess Beaver	B33F	1990	Ex Pattersons, Birmingham, 1995
60	G395OWB	Mercedes-Benz 811D	Whittaker Europa	B26F	1990	Ex Pattersons, Birmingham, 1995
61	J404WDA	Mercedes-Benz 811D	Whittaker Europa	B31F	1992	Ex Pattersons, Birmingham, 1995
62	K62KEX	Dennis Dart 9.8SDL3025	East Lancashire	DP43F	1993	
63	K63KEX	Dennis Dart 9.8SDL3025	East Lancashire	DP43F	1993	
64	D604AFR	MCW MetroRider MF151/4	MCW	B23F	1987	Ex Blackburn, 1994
65	D605AFR	MCW MetroRider MF151/4	MCW	B23F	1987	Ex Blackburn, 1994
66	D606AFR	MCW MetroRider MF151/4	MCW	B23F	1987	Ex Blackburn, 1994
67	D610AFR	MCW MetroRider MF151/5	MCW	DP23F	1987	Ex Blackburn, 1994
68	M68XVF	Mercedes-Benz 811D	Marshall C16	B33F	1994	
69	M69XVF	Mercedes-Benz 811D	Marshall C16	B33F	1994	

79-87

AEC Swift 3MP2R   Eastern Coach Works   B43D   1973

79	WEX679M	81	WEX681M	83	WEX683M	86	WEX686M	87	WEX687M
80	WEX680M	82	WEX682M	85	WEX685M				

Livery: Blue and cream

Previous Registrations:

4750WY	FUA385Y	6220WY	FUA386Y

HALLMARK

Hallmark Cars Ltd, Hallmark House, Chase Street, Luton, Bedfordshire LU1 3QZ

Depots: Grimstock Hill, Lichfield Road, Coleshill, Warwickshire; 57 Albion Road, Hounslow, Middlesex and Chase Street, Luton.

B251DNV	Volkswagen LT31	Devon Conversions	M11	1985	
MSK286	Volvo B10M-61	Van Hool Alizée	C28FT	1986	Ex Sworder, Walkern, 1991
E836FRP	Volkswagen LT31	Devon Conversions	M8	1987	
E837FRP	Volkswagen LT31	Devon Conversions	M8	1987	
E992JOO	Toyota Coaster HB31R	Caetano Optimo	C18F	1988	
F96CBD	MAN 16.290	Jonckheere Deauville	C50F	1989	
HC8936	MAN 16.290	Jonckheere Deauville	C32FT	1989	
MSK287	MAN 16.290	Jonckheere Deauville	C23FT	1989	
G757VNR	Toyota Coaster HB31R	Caetano Optimo	C18F	1989	Ex People to Places, Coleshill, 1994
TSU610	Kässbohrer Setra S215HD	Kässbohrer Tornado	C49FT	1990	
G603YUT	Toyota Coaster HB31R	Caetano Optimo	C18F	1990	
G167XJF	Toyota Coaster HB31R	Caetano Optimo	C18F	1990	
H10BCK	Toyota Coaster HDB30R	Caetano Optimo II	C18F	1991	Ex People to Places, Coleshill, 1994
H101NVW	Ford Transit	Asquith	C16F	1991	Ex People to Places, Coleshill, 1994
H403ERP	MAN 10.180	Jonckheere Deauville	C34FT	1991	
H385HRY	MAN 10.180	Jonckheere Deauville	C34FT	1992	Ex People to Places, Coleshill, 1994
J63GCX	DAF SB3000DKV601	Van Hool Alizée	C51FT	1992	
J788KHD	DAF SB2700HS585	Van Hool Alizée	C51FT	1992	
J811KHD	DAF SB3000DKV601	Van Hool Alizée	C55F	1992	
J465NJU	Toyota Coaster HDB30R	Caetano Optimo II	C18F	1992	
K31VRY	Toyota Coaster HDB30R	Caetano Optimo II	C18F	1993	
K32VRY	Toyota Coaster HDB30R	Caetano Optimo II	C18F	1993	
K886BRW	Toyota Coaster HDB30R	Caetano Optimo II	C21F	1992	Ex Supreme, Coventry, 1994
K226WNH	MAN 16.290	Jonckheere Deauville 45	C51F	1993	
K227WNH	MAN 16.290	Jonckheere Deauville 45	C51F	1993	
K521RJX	DAF SB3000DKV601	Van Hool Alizée	C51FT	1993	
K525RJX	DAF SB3000DKV601	Van Hool Alizée	C51FT	1993	
L526EHD	DAF MB230LTRH615	Van Hool Alizée	C51FT	1994	
L530EHD	EOS E180Z	EOS 90	C49FT	1994	
L531EHD	EOS E180Z	EOS 90	C49FT	1994	
L707CNR	Toyota Coaster HZB50R	Caetano Optimo III	C18F	1994	
L129GBA	LDV 400	Concept	M16	1994	
L130GBA	LDV 400	Concept	M16	1994	
M15HMC	Aüwaerter Neoplan N116/3	Aüwaerter Cityliner	C48FT	1995	
M16HMC	Aüwaerter Neoplan N116/3	Aüwaerter Cityliner	C48FT	1995	
M601RCP	EOS E180Z	EOS 90	C49FT	1995	
M602RCP	EOS E180Z	EOS 90	C49FT	1995	
M603RCP	EOS E180Z	EOS 90	C51FT	1995	
M604RCP	EOS E180Z	EOS 90	C49FT	1995	
M612RCP	DAF SB220LC550	Ikarus CitiBus	B48F	1995	
M613RCP	DAF SB3000WS601	Van Hool Alizée	C49FT	1995	
M614RCP	DAF SB3000WS601	Van Hool Alizée	C49FT	1995	
M615RCP	DAF SB3000WS601	Van Hool Alizée	C49FT	1995	
M616RCP	DAF SB3000WS601	Van Hool Alizée	C49FT	1995	
M617RCP	DAF SB3000WS601	Van Hool Alizée	C51FT	1995	
M618RCP	DAF SB3000WS601	Van Hool Alizée	C51FT	1995	
M619RCP	DAF SB3000WS601	Van Hool Alizée	C51FT	1995	
M802RCP	DAF MB230LT615	Van Hool Alizée	C51FT	1994	
M803RCP	DAF MB230LT615	Van Hool Alizée	C53F	1994	
M804RCP	DAF MB230LT615	Van Hool Alizée	C51FT	1994	
M805RCP	DAF MB230LT615	Van Hool Alizée	C51FT	1994	
M806RCP	DAF SB220LC550	Ikarus CitiBus	B48F	1994	
M839RCP	Mercedes-Benz 711D	Autobus Classique II	C33F	1995	
M841LFT	Toyota Coaster HZB50R	Caetano Optimo III	C18F	1995	
M842LFT	Toyota Coaster HZB50R	Caetano Optimo III	C18F	1995	

Previous Registrations:

H385HRY	H404ERP, H4PSW	MSK286	C238GBH		TSU610	From new
HC8936	F99CBD	MSK287	G840GNV			

The last design to emanate from the erstwhile LAG coachbuilders was the EOS' launched in 1989. Shortly afterwards the company was sold to Van Hool who continue to produce vehicles under the EOS name at the original factory in the Netherlands. Seen at Wembley shortly after delivery to Hallmark is M602RCP. *Colin Lloyd*

MSK286 is one of the executive coaches in the Hallmark fleet with just 28 seats and tables together with servery and other facilities. Based on a Volvo B10M chassis, the Van Hool body looks somewhat regal as it arrives at Wembley in May 1995. *BBP*

HARRIS BUS

Frank Harris (Coaches) Ltd, Manor Road, West Thurrock, Essex, RM16 1EH
Harris Bus Company Ltd, Manor Road, West Thurrock, Essex, RM16 1EH

w	PBD40R	Bristol VRT/SL3/6LXB	Alexander AL	H45/27D	1977	Ex Northampton, 1990
w	PBD43R	Bristol VRT/SL3/6LXB	Alexander AL	H45/27D	1977	Ex Northampton, 1990
	VRP37S	Bristol VRT/SL3/6LXB	Alexander AL	H45/27D	1977	Ex Northampton, 1990
	VRP39S	Bristol VRT/SL3/6LXB	Alexander AL	H45/27D	1977	Ex Northampton, 1990
	VVV65S	Bristol VRT/SL3/6LXB	Alexander AL	H45/27D	1977	Ex Northampton, 1992
	OCO117S	Leyland Atlantean AN68/1R	Roe	H43/28F	1978	Ex Southampton Citybus, 1993
w	OCO118S	Leyland Atlantean AN68/1R	Roe	H43/28F	1978	Ex Southampton Citybus, 1993
w	STK122T	Leyland Atlantean AN68/1R	Roe	H43/28F	1979	Ex Southampton Citybus, 1993
w	STK123T	Leyland Atlantean AN68/1R	Roe	H43/28F	1979	Ex Southampton Citybus, 1993
	WRJ447X	Volvo B55-10 MkIII	Northern Counties	H43/35F	1982	Ex Lancaster, 1993
	WRJ448X	Volvo B55-10 MkIII	Northern Counties	H43/35F	1982	Ex Lancaster, 1993
	6306FH	DAF SB2300DKSB585	Van Hool Alizée	C48FT	1985	
	9242FH	Scania K112TRS	Plaxton Paramount 4000 II	CH54/18CT	1985	
	2942FH	Bova FHD12.280	Bova Futura	C53FT	1986	
	D301PEV	Volvo B10M-46	Plaxton Bustler	B38F	1986	
	D302PEV	Volvo B10M-46	Plaxton Bustler	B38F	1986	
	D303PEV	Volvo B10M-46	Plaxton Bustler	B38F	1986	
	D304PEV	Volvo B10M-46	Plaxton Bustler	B38F	1986	
	E305EVW	MCW MetroRider MF150/89	MCW	B25F	1988	
	E306EVW	MCW MetroRider MF150/89	MCW	B24F	1988	
	E859AKN	Peugeot-Talbot Freeway	Talbot	B18FL	1988	Ex Kent CC, 1994
	5970FH	DAF SB3000DKV601	Van Hool Alizée	C49FT	1988	
	7968FH	DAF SB3000DKV601	Van Hool Alizée	C49FT	1988	
	F310OVW	MCW MetroRider MF150/112	MCW	B24F	1988	
	F849LHS	Ford Transit VE6	Dormobile	M16	1989	
	F312PEV	Scania N113DRB	Alexander RH	H47/31F	1989	
	F314RHK	Scania N113DRB	Alexander RH	H47/31F	1989	
	1245FH	DAF SB3000DKV601	Van Hool Alizée	C49FT	1989	
	FHV504	DAF SB3000DKV601	Van Hool Alizée	C49FT	1989	
	H477LHJ	Leyland DAF 200	Leyland DAF	M12	1991	Ex Tunnel Truck, West Thurrock, 1991
	J91WWC	Kässbohrer Setra S215HD	Kässbohrer Tornado	C49FT	1991	
	J92YAR	Kässbohrer Setra S215HD	Kässbohrer Tornado	C49FT	1991	
	J76VTG	Kässbohrer Setra S215HD	Kässbohrer Tornado	C49FT	1991	
	J582WVX	Mercedes-Benz 709D	Alexander AM	B25F	1991	
	J583WVX	Mercedes-Benz 709D	Alexander AM	B25F	1991	
	J51GCX	DAF SB220LC550	Ikarus CitiBus	B49F	1992	Ex Strathclyde, 1994
	J52GCX	DAF SB220LC550	Ikarus CitiBus	B49F	1992	Ex Strathclyde, 1994
	K622WOV	Peugeot-Talbot Freeway	TBP	B18FL	1992	
	K623WOV	Peugeot-Talbot Freeway	TBP	B18FL	1992	
	K95GEV	DAF SB3000DKVF601	Van Hool Alizée	C48FT	1993	
	K96GEV	DAF SB3000DKVF601	Van Hool Alizée	C48FT	1993	
	K97GEV	DAF SB3000DKVF601	Van Hool Alizée	C48FT	1993	
	K122OCT	Kässbohrer Setra S215HD	Kässbohrer Tornado	C49FT	1993	
	K123OCT	Kässbohrer Setra S215HD	Kässbohrer Tornado	C49FT	1993	
	L93OAR	Aüwaerter Neoplan N122/3	Aüwaerter Skyliner	CH54/16CT	1994	
	L97PTW	Toyota HZB50R	Caetano Optimo III	C21F	1994	
	L98PTW	Toyota HZB50R	Caetano Optimo III	C21F	1994	
	L475GOV	Peugeot-Talbot Freeway	TBP	B18FL	1994	
	L476GOV	Peugeot-Talbot Freeway	TBP	B18FL	1994	
	M52WEV	LDV 400	LDV	M16	1995	
	M501XWC	DAF SB3000WS601	Van Hool Alizée	C49FT	1995	
	M502XWC	DAF SB3000WS601	Van Hool Alizée	C49FT	1995	
	M503XWC	DAF SB3000WS601	Van Hool Alizée	C49FT	1995	
	M504XWC	Aüwaerter Neoplan N122/3	Aüwaerter Skyliner	CH54/16DT	1995	
	N	Mercedes-Benz 709D	Wadham Stringer Wessex 2B	F	1995	
	N	Mercedes-Benz 709D	Wadham Stringer Wessex 2B	F	1995	

Livery: White and blue (buses); two-tone green (coaches)

Previous Registrations:

1245FH	F98RAR	6306FH	B89CNO	9242FH	C400JOO
2942FH	C90LVX	7968FH	E95EVW	FHV504	F99RAR
5970FH	E96EVW				

Photographed before it gained a private index mark Van Hool-bodied F98RAR is now 1245FH in the Frank Harris Coaches fleet. It is seen at Lloyd's bowling alley in Enfield. *Keith Grimes*

Brought south from Lancaster in 1993 was a pair of Volvo B55 double-deck buses with Northern Counties bodywork. New to Greater Manchester, they formed part of the evaluation fleet and are essentially Volvo-badged Ailsas. Now in Harris Bus blue and white livery, WRJ448X was photographed in Gravesend. *BBP*

One of the latest arrivals with Frank Harris Coaches fleet is M503XWC seen here in Eurolines contract livery. *Colin Lloyd*

HEDINGHAM OMNIBUSES

Hedingham & District Omnibuses Ltd, Wethersfield Road, Sible Hedingham, Essex, CO9 3LB

Depots: Springfield Ind Est, Burnham-on-Crouch; Telford Road Industrial Estate, Clacton-on-Sea; Ingestre Street, Harwich; Wethersfield Road, Sible Hedingham; High Street, Kelvedon; Church Lane, Little Tey; Meeking Road, Sudbury; Railway Station Yard, Walton-on-the-Naze.

L81	YNO481L	Bedford YRT	Marshall Camair	B53F	1973	
L84	RGV284N	Leyland Leopard PSU3B/4R	Willowbrook	B55F	1974	
L85	GPV685N	Bedford YRQ	Willowbrook 001	B47F	1975	
L86	KHJ786P	Bedford YRQ	Willowbrook 001	B47F	1975	
L87	PHK387R	Bedford YRQ	Duple Dominant	B47F	1976	
L88	REV188R	Bedford YLQ	Duple Dominant	B47F	1976	
L89	CEV89T	Bedford YLQ	Duple Dominant	B47F	1978	
L94	GVW894T	Bedford YMT	Plaxton Supreme IV Express	C53F	1979	
L95	JAR495V	Bedford YLQ	Duple Dominant	B47F	1979	
L96	NFX446P	Bedford YMT	Plaxton Supreme III	C53F	1976	Ex National Travel SW, 1979
L98	SPU898W	Bedford YMQ	Duple Dominant	B47F	1980	
L100	UNO100W	Bedford YMT	Plaxton Supreme IV Express	C53F	1981	
L103	BAR103X	Leyland Leopard PSU3E/4R	Plaxton Bustler	B55F	1982	
L105	BEV105X	Leyland Leopard PSU3E/4R	Plaxton Supreme IV Express	C53F	1982	
L111	UVX4S	Bristol LH6L	Eastern Coach Works	B43F	1977	Ex Eastern National, 1982
L112	UVX5S	Bristol LH6L	Eastern Coach Works	B43F	1977	Ex Eastern National, 1982
L113	UVX6S	Bristol LH6L	Eastern Coach Works	B43F	1977	Ex Eastern National, 1982
L114	UVX7S	Bristol LH6L	Eastern Coach Works	B43F	1977	Ex Eastern National, 1982
L115	FEV115Y	Leyland Leopard PSU3E/4R	Plaxton Supreme IV	C53F	1982	
L116	HAR116Y	Bedford YNT	Plaxton Paramount 3200 E	C53F	1983	
L121	DBH452X	Leyland Leopard PSU5C/4R	Plaxton Supreme IV	C53F	1981	Ex Flight's, 1983
L122	A122PAR	Leyland Tiger TRCTL11/2R	Plaxton Paramount 3200 E	C53F	1983	
L124	B124BOO	Leyland Tiger TRCTL11/2R	Plaxton Paramount 3200	C53F	1985	
L125	BNO700T	Bedford YMT	Duple Dominant II Express	C53F	1979	Ex Eastern National, 1984
L126	BNO703T	Bedford YMT	Duple Dominant II Express	C53F	1979	Ex Eastern National, 1984
L133	BHK710X	Bedford YNT	Plaxton Supreme IV Express	C53F	1982	Ex Jennings, Ashen, 1984
L135	KGS489Y	Leyland Tiger TRCTL11/3R	Plaxton Paramount 3500	C53F	1983	Ex Travellers, Hounslow, 1985
L136	D136XVW	Bedford YMP	Plaxton Derwent II	B47F	1987	
L137	D137XVW	Bedford YMP	Plaxton Derwent II	B47F	1987	
L138	B273AMG	Leyland Tiger TRCTL11/3R	Plaxton Paramount 3200	C57F	1984	Ex Goldenport, London, 1987
L139	FCY287W	Bedford YMQ	Duple Dominant	B43F	1981	Ex South Wales, 1987
L140	FCY288W	Bedford YMQ	Duple Dominant	B43F	1981	Ex South Wales, 1987
L141	FCY289W	Bedford YMQ	Duple Dominant	B43F	1981	Ex South Wales, 1987
L146	FCY285W	Bedford YMQ	Duple Dominant	B43F	1981	Ex South Wales, 1987
L147	NCD553M	Bristol VRT/SL2/6LX	Eastern Coach Works	H43/31F	1973	Ex Southdown, 1988
L148	WPH135Y	Leyland Tiger TRCTL11/2R	East Lancs EL2000 (1993)	B55F	1982	Ex Kentish Bus, 1988
L149	E79HVX	Iveco Daily 49.10	Carlyle Dailybus	B25F	1988	
L150	F150LTW	Leyland Lynx LX112L10ZR1	Leyland Lynx	B51F	1988	
L151	F151NPU	Leyland Swift LBM6T/2R	Wadham Stringer Vanguard II	B39F	1988	
L152	D576VBV	Freight Rover Sherpa	Dormobile	B16F	1987	Ex Ribble, 1988
L153	D345WPE	Ford Transit 190	Carlyle	B16F	1987	Ex Alder Valley, 1988
L155	D232HMT	Leyland Tiger TRCTL11/3RZ	Van Hool Alizée	C53F	1986	Ex Travellers, Hounslow, 1988
L156	NPU979M	Bristol VRT/SL2/6LX	Eastern Coach Works	H39/31F	1974	Ex Eastern National, 1989
L158	VOD590S	Bristol VRT/SL3/6LXB	Eastern Coach Works	H43/31F	1978	Ex South Midland, 1989
L159	TBW451P	Bristol VRT/SL3/6LXB	Eastern Coach Works	H43/31F	1978	Ex South Midland, 1989
L160	H160HJN	Leyland Olympian ONCL10/1RZA	Alexander RL	H47/32F	1990	
L161	SNJ591R	Bristol VRT/SL3/6LX	Eastern Coach Works	H43/31F	1977	Ex Brighton & Hove, 1990
L162	MOD569P	Bristol VRT/SL3/6LX	Eastern Coach Works	H43/32F	1975	Ex United, 1990
L163	MGR672P	Bristol VRT/SL3/6LX	Eastern Coach Works	H43/31F	1975	Ex United, 1990
L164	SUP685R	Bristol VRT/SL3/6LX	Eastern Coach Works	H43/31F	1976	Ex United, 1990
L165	LRA801P	Bristol VRT/SL3/501(6LX)	Eastern Coach Works	H43/34F	1975	Ex Trent, 1990

Opposite, top: **Hedingham are now one of the larger fleets in the eastern area of England having purchased many local operators in the past few years including Norfolk's, Partridge Coaches and Freemans. Seen at Sudbury is L148, WPH135Y, a Leyland Tiger with a new East Lancashire body that was built in 1993, replacing an Eastern Coach Works product.**
Opposite, bottom: **One of the latest buses with Hedingham is L211, M211WHJ, a Dennis Lance SLF with Wright bodywork. It is seen in Witham heading for Maldon employed normally on Essex County Council-sponsored accessible services.** *Richard Godfrey*

L203, BRC839T is one of a pair of Bristol VRs acquired from Trent in 1993. Seen in Colchester while on lay-over, it is one of many double-deck buses which are used for schools contracts. *Paul Wigan*

L166	MRB802P	Bristol VRT/SL3/6LX	Eastern Coach Works	H43/34F	1976	Ex Trent, 1990
L167	JWT757V	Bristol VRT/SL3/6LXB	Eastern Coach Works	H43/31F	1979	Ex Keighley & District, 1990
L168	PWY43W	Bristol VRT/SL3/6LXB	Eastern Coach Works	H43/31F	1981	Ex Keighley & District, 1990
L169	JKV414V	Bedford YMT	Plaxton Supreme IV	C53F	1979	Ex Kemp, Clacton, 1991
L170	WOO903W	Bedford YMT	Plaxton Supreme IV	C53F	1981	Ex Kemp, Clacton, 1991
L175	A331VHB	Leyland Tiger TRCTL11/3R	Jonckheere Jubilee P50	C49FT	1983	Ex Kemp, Clacton, 1991
L178	DWU294T	Bristol VRT/SL3/6LXB	Eastern Coach Works	H43/31F	1979	Ex Keighley & District, 1991
L180	UBJ847R	AEC Reliance 6U3ZR	Plaxton Supreme III	C55F	1977	Ex Norfolk, Nayland, 1991
L181	GPV212T	AEC Reliance 6U3ZR	Plaxton Supreme III Express	C53F	1978	Ex Norfolk, Nayland, 1991
L183	CFM345S	Leyland National 11351A/1R (6HLX)		B49F	1978	Ex Norfolk, Nayland, 1991
L184	CFM347S	Leyland National 11351A/1R (6HLX)		B49F	1978	Ex Norfolk, Nayland, 1991
L185	LMA413T	Leyland National 11351A/1R (6HLX)		B49F	1979	Ex Norfolk, Nayland, 1991
L186	CBV305S	Leyland Atlantean AN68A/2R	East Lancashire	H50/36F	1977	Ex Norfolk, Nayland, 1991
L187	CBV306S	Leyland Atlantean AN68A/2R	East Lancashire	H50/36F	1977	Ex Norfolk, Nayland, 1991
L188	CBV307S	Leyland Atlantean AN68A/2R	East Lancashire	H50/36F	1977	Ex Norfolk, Nayland, 1991
L189	CBV308S	Leyland Atlantean AN68A/2R	East Lancashire	H50/36F	1977	Ex Norfolk, Nayland, 1991
L190	CBV309S	Leyland Atlantean AN68A/2R	East Lancashire	H50/36F	1977	Ex Norfolk, Nayland, 1991
L192	A709KRT	Van Hool T815H	Van Hool Acron	C49FT	1984	Ex Norfolk, Nayland, 1991
L193	D600MVR	Leyland Tiger TRCTL11/3RZ	Plaxton Paramount 3200 III	C53F	1986	Ex Shearings, 1991
L194	JWV271W	Bristol VRT/SL3/680	Eastern Coach Works	H43/31F	1981	Ex Brighton & Hove, 1991
L195	D584MVR	Leyland Tiger TRCTL11/3RZ	Plaxton Paramount 3200 III	C53F	1986	Ex Shearings, 1992
L196	H48NDU	Leyland Lynx LX2R11C15Z4R	Leyland Lynx II	B51F	1990	Ex Volvo demonstrator, 1992
L197	GGM108W	Bristol VRT/SL3/6LXB	Eastern Coach Works	H43/31F	1980	Ex City of Oxford, 1992
L198	K198EVW	Dennis Dart 9.8SDL3017	Alexander Dash	B43F	1992	
L199	HJB464W	Bristol VRT/SL3/6LXB	Eastern Coach Works	H43/31F	1980	Ex City of Oxford, 1992
L200	J295TWK	Leyland Lynx LX2R11C14Z4S	Leyland Lynx II	B51F	1991	Ex Volvo demonstrator, 1992
L201	F781GNA	Leyland Tiger TRCTL11/3RZ	Plaxton Paramount 3200 III	C53F	1989	Ex Shearings, 1993
L202	BRC836T	Bristol VRT/SL3/6LXB	Eastern Coach Works	H43/31F	1979	Ex Trent, 1993
L203	BRC839T	Bristol VRT/SL3/6LXB	Eastern Coach Works	H43/31F	1979	Ex Trent, 1993
L204	AUD461R	Bristol VRT/SL3/6LXB	Eastern Coach Works	H43/31F	1979	Ex Midland Fox, 1993
L205	E668UNE	Leyland Tiger TRCTL11/3RZ	Plaxton Paramount 3200 III	C53F	1988	Ex Shearings, 1994
L206	J724KBC	Leyland Lynx LX2R11V18Z4S	Leyland Lynx II	B51F	1992	Ex Westbus, Ashford, 1994
L207	L207RNO	Volvo B6-9.9M	Alexander Dash	B41F	1994	
L208	L208RNO	Volvo B6-9.9M	Alexander Dash	B41F	1994	
L209	H645UWR	Volvo B10M-60	Plaxton Paramount 3500 III	C53F	1991	Ex Wallace Arnold, 1994
L210	M210VEV	Dennis Dart 9SDL3031	Plaxton Pointer	B34F	1994	
L211	M211WHJ	Dennis Lance SLF 11SDA3201	Wright Endeavour	B40F	1995	
L212	M212WHJ	Dennis Lance SLF 11SDA3201	Wright Endeavour	B40F	1995	

L201, F781GNA, in the Hedingham fleet is one of four coaches formerly in Shearings' touring fleet. A Leyland Tiger with Plaxton Paramount 3200 bodywork it is seen in fine fettle in Bury St Edmunds. *Paul Wigan*

L213	THM630M	Daimler Fleetline CRL6	MCW	H44/33F	1974	Ex Partridge Coaches, Hadleigh, 1994
L214	MDW584P	Bedford YRQ	Duple Dominant	C45F	1976	Ex Partridge Coaches, Hadleigh, 1994
L215	MKK458P	Bedford YRT	Plaxton Supreme III	C53F	1976	Ex Partridge Coaches, Hadleigh, 1994
L216	759KFC	Bedford YRT	Plaxton Supreme III	C53F	1976	Ex Partridge Coaches, Hadleigh, 1994
L217	OJD126R	Leyland Fleetline FE30ALR	Park Royal	H45/32F	1976	Ex Partridge Coaches, Hadleigh, 1994
L218	UAT274R	Leyland Leopard PSU3/3RT	Plaxton Supreme III(1977)	C53F	1964	Ex Partridge Coaches, Hadleigh, 1994
L219	THX324S	Daimler Fleetline FE30ALRSp	MCW	H44/32F	1978	Ex Partridge Coaches, Hadleigh, 1994
L220	DNK431T	Ford R1114	Duple Dominant II	C53F	1979	Ex Partridge Coaches, Hadleigh, 1994
L221	229LRB	Leyland Leopard PSU5C/4R	Plaxton Supreme IV	C57F	1979	Ex Partridge Coaches, Hadleigh, 1994
L222	HAX94W	Bedford YMT	Duple Dominant II	C53F	1980	Ex Partridge Coaches, Hadleigh, 1994
L224	A486FPV	Bedford YNT	Duple Laser	C53F	1983	Ex Partridge Coaches, Hadleigh, 1994
L225	A487FPV	Bedford YNT	Duple Laser	C53F	1983	Ex Partridge Coaches, Hadleigh, 1994
L226	129SDV	Leyland Tiger TRCTL11/3R	Duple Laser	C57F	1985	Ex Partridge Coaches, Hadleigh, 1994
L229	F464NRT	Leyland Tiger TRCTL11/3RZ	Duple 320	C61F	1988	Ex Partridge Coaches, Hadleigh, 1994
L230	F145SPV	Leyland Tiger TRCTL11/3RZM	Plaxton Paramount 3200 III	C57F	1989	Ex Partridge Coaches, Hadleigh, 1994
L231	F146SPV	Leyland Tiger TRCTL11/3RZM	Plaxton Paramount 3200 III	C57F	1989	Ex Partridge Coaches, Hadleigh, 1994
L232	F147SPV	Leyland Tiger TRCTL11/3RZM	Plaxton Paramount 3200 III	C57F	1989	Ex Partridge Coaches, Hadleigh, 1994
L233	F148SPV	Leyland Tiger TRCTL11/3RZM	Plaxton Paramount 3200 III	C57F	1989	Ex Partridge Coaches, Hadleigh, 1994
L234	J245MFP	Dennis Javelin 12SDA1929	Plaxton Paramount 3200 III	C51FT	1991	Ex Partridge Coaches, Hadleigh, 1994
L235	WJM831T	Bristol VRT/SL3/6LXB	Eastern Coach Works	H43/31F	1979	Ex The Bee Line, 1995
L236	CJH143V	Bristol VRT/SL3/6LXB	Eastern Coach Works	H43/31F	1980	Ex The Bee Line, 1995
L237	GGM84W	Bristol VRT/SL3/6LXB	Eastern Coach Works	H43/31F	1980	Ex The Bee Line, 1995
L239	BCJ733V	Ford R1114	Duple Dominant II	C53F	1979	Ex Freeman, Great Cornard, 1994
L240	XPW877X	Leyland Leopard PSU3G/4R	Eastern Coach Works B51	C47F	1982	Ex Carter, Colchester, 1995

Livery: Cream and red

Previous Registrations:

A709KRT	A104TVW, 90NOR	GPV212T	BPV300T, 229LRB
129SDV	B288OGV	UBJ847R	OKY65R, 301XRA
229LRB	VWS976T, 162EKH, VAS589T	UAT274R	TRN754
759KFC	MNW731P		

IPSWICH BUSES

Ipswich Buses Ltd, Constantine Road, Ipswich, Suffolk, IP1 2DL

| 9 | MRT9P | Leyland Atlantean AN68/1R | Roe | | O43/26D | 1976 | |

18-35   Leyland Atlantean AN68A/1R   Roe   H43/29D   1976-77

18	RDX18R	22	SDX22R	26w	SDX26R	30	SDX30R	33	SDX33R
19	RDX19R	23	SDX23R	27	SDX27R	31	SDX31R	34	SDX34R
20	RDX20R	24	SDX24R	29	SDX29R	32	SDX32R	35	SDX35R
21	SDX21R	25	SDX25R						

40	M640EPV	Volvo Olympian YN2RV18V3	East Lancashire	H49/31D	1995	
41	M41EPV	Volvo Olympian YN2RV18V3	East Lancashire	H49/31D	1995	
42	M42EPV	Volvo Olympian YN2RV18V3	East Lancashire	H49/31D	1995	
75	LDX75G	Leyland Atlantean PDR2/1	Eastern Coach Works	O43/31F	1970	On loan
81	F81ODX	Dennis Dominator DDA907	East Lancashire	H45/26D	1988	
82	B82NDX	Dennis Dominator DDA907	East Lancashire	H43/27D	1985	

100-105   Dennis Falcon HC SDA406   East Lancashire   B44D   1983

100	YDX100Y	101	YDX101Y	103	YDX103Y	104	YDX104Y	105	YDX105Y

| 106 | C106SDX | Dennis Falcon HC SDA416 | East Lancashire | B44D | 1985 |

107-113   Dennis Falcon HC SDA416   Northern Counties   B45F   1985-86

107	C107SDX	109	C109SDX	111	C111SDX	112	C112SDX	113	C113SDX
108	C108SDX	110	C110SDX						

114-124   Dennis Falcon HC SDA419*   East Lancashire   B44D   1988-89 *118-24 are SDA420

114	E114KDX	117	E117KDX	119	G119VDX	121	G121VDX	123	G123VDX
115	E115KDX	118	G118VDX	120	G120VDX	122	G122VDX	124	G124VDX
116	E116KDX								

144	B114LDX	Bristol B21	Alexander N	B49D	1985	
145	B115LDX	Bristol B21	Alexander N	B49D	1985	
146	B116LDX	Bristol B21	Alexander N	DP47D	1985	
147	B117LDX	Bristol B21	Alexander N	DP47D	1985	
148	WOI607	Bristol B21	Alexander N	B44D	1985	Ex Belfast Citybus, 1991
149	TDX124W	Bristol B21	Alexander N	B53F	1980	Ex Ulsterbus, 1991
150	XRT931X	Bristol B21	Alexander N	B53F	1981	Ex Ulsterbus, 1991
151	TDX120W	Bristol B21	Alexander N	B53F	1982	Ex Ulsterbus, 1991
152	XRT932X	Bristol B21	Alexander N	B53F	1982	Ex Ulsterbus, 1991
153	XRT947X	Bristol B21	Alexander N	B53F	1982	Ex Ulsterbus, 1991
160	J160LPV	Dennis Lance 11SDA3101	East Lancashire	B45D	1992	
161	L161ADX	Dennis Lance SDA3113	East Lancashire	B41D	1994	
162	L162ADX	Dennis Lance SDA3113	East Lancashire	B41D	1994	
169	L169ADX	Dennis Lance SDA3113	Optare Sigma	B41D	1994	
170	TBB283S	Bedford YMT	Plaxton Supreme III	C53F	1978	Ex Bickers, Coddenham, 1986
180	H180HPV	DAF SB220LC550	Optare Delta	B45D	1991	
181	L181ADX	DAF SB220LC550	Optare Delta	B44D	1994	
182	L182ADX	DAF SB220LC550	Optare Delta	B44D	1994	
183	L183APV	DAF SB220LC550	Optare Delta	B44D	1994	
184	L184APV	DAF SB220LC550	Optare Delta	B44D	1994	

Opposite: **Ipswich's 1994 deliveries of Dennis Lance feature differing body types. The upper picture shows 162, L162ADX, with East Lancashire bodywork. The lower picture of 169, L169ADX, shows the Optare Sigma body. Ipswich are one of the few operators still specifying dual-door bodywork.**
Richard Godfrey/Paul Wigan

The Bristol B21 was often referred to as a Leyland National chassis and indeed there were many common components. Seen here is 150, XRT931X, a B21 with Alexander N-type bodywork which was new to Ulsterbus and one of six from Northern Ireland which joined Ipswich's own quartet in 1991. *David Cole*

Newly delivered in 1995 were three Volvo Olympians with East Lancashire dual-door bodywork. Representing the type is 41, M41EPV, seen outside the Constantine Road depot. *Richard Godfrey*

An interesting comparison can be made with the Alexander N-type body in the picture of 150 opposite. Here is illustrated a dual-door version 145, B115LDX, also a B21 but built new for Ipswich. It is seen in St Matthew's Street, Ipswich. *Richard Godfrey*

213	M213EDX	Optare MetroRider	Optare	B29F	1994	
214	M214EDX	Optare MetroRider	Optare	B29F	1994	
215	M215EDX	Optare MetroRider	Optare	B29F	1994	
216	M216EDX	Optare MetroRider	Optare	B29F	1994	
217	L832MWT	Optare MetroRider	Optare	DP31F	1993	Ex Optare demonstrator, 1994
218	J218NRT	Optare MetroRider	Optare	B31F	1992	
219	K219PPV	Optare MetroRider	Optare	B31F	1992	
220	F220PPV	MCW MetroRider MF155	MCW	DP31F	1989	

| *221-228* | | Optare MetroRider | | Optare | | B23F | 1990-91 | |

221	G221VDX	223	G223VDX	225	H225EDX	227	H227EDX	228	J228JDX
222	G222VDX	224	G224VDX	226	H226EDX				

229	K100LCT	Optare MetroRider	Optare	DP31F	1992	Ex Lancaster, 1993

Livery: Green and cream

Previous Registrations:

TDX120W	WOI3002	XRT931X	WOI3005	XRT947X	WOI3004
TDX124W	WOI3001	XRT932X	WOI3003		

Named vehicles:
9 *Eastern Belle*; 18 *Memory*; 19 *Mimosa*; 20 *Northdown*; 21 *Orion*; 22 *Perseus*; 23 *Phoenician*; 24 *Pride of Ipswich*; 25 *Reminder*; 26 *Reporter*; 27 *Saxon*; 29 *Sunbeam*; 30 *Thalatta*; 31 *Tollesbury*; 32 *Triton*; 33 *Vanguard*; 34 *Veronica*; 35 *Xylonite*; 40 *Beatrice Maud*; 41 *May*; 42 *Vigilant*; 75 *Eastbourne Queen*; 81 *British Oak*; 82 *Margaret Catchpole*; 100 *Agincourt*; 101 *Alaric*; 103 *Albion*; 104 *Alma*; 105 *Anglia*; 106 *Ardwina*; 107 *Beric*; 108 *Centaur*; 109 *Cygnet*; 110 *Ena*; 111 *Kindly Light*; 112 *Leading Light*; 113 *Mystery*; 114 *Avocet*; 115 *Eldred Wattains*; 116 *Excelsior*; 117 *Felix*; 118 *Lady Daphne*; 119 *Lady Jean*; 120 *Marjorie*; 121 *Nautilus*; 122 *Orinoco*; 123 *Pudge*; 124 *Venture*; 143 *Haste Away*; 144 *Great Western*; 145 *Great Eastern*; 146 *Godspeed*; 147 *Bristolian*; 148 *Maid of Connaught*; 149 *Hibernia*; 150 *Shamrock*; 151 *Esmeralda*; 152 *Kathleen*; 153 *Muriel*; 160 *Barbara Jean*; 161 *Adie*; 162 *Doris*; 169 *King John*; 180 *New Spirit of Ipswich*; 181 *Peter Bruff*; 182 *Leonard Squirrell*; 183 HN *'Jimmy' James*; 213 *Ariel*; 214 *Miranda*; 215 *Oberon*; 216 *Umbriel*; 218 *Apollo*; 219 *Thisbe*; 220 *Hyperion*; 221 *Dione*; 222 *Mimas*; 223 *Rhea*; 224 *Tethys*; 225 *Eros*; 226 *Pallas*; 227 *Vesta*; 228 *Icarus*; 229 *Lancastrian*.

J B S

J Brown, 75 Putnoe Street, Bedford, MK41 8JB

Depot : Lodge Farm, Barford Road, Blunham

URF666S	Bristol VRT/SL3/501	Eastern Coach Works	H43/31F	1978	Ex Southend, 1992
VHB672S	Bristol VRT/SL3/501	Eastern Coach Works	H43/31F	1978	Ex Southend, 1992
VOI5888	Volvo B58-61	Duple Dominant	C53F	1978	Ex Coakley, New Stevenston, 1994
1230HN	Bedford YMT	Plaxton Supreme IV	C53F	1979	Ex Day, Kilnhurst, 1994
8552PE	Volvo B58-61	Plaxton Supreme IV	C53F	1980	Ex Marshall's Cs, Leighton Buzzard, 1992
LDZ3142	Volvo B10M-61	Jonckheere Bermuda	C50FT	1982	Ex Skill's, 1995
TXI2440	DAF MB200DKTL600	Caetano Algarve	C53F	1983	Ex Simpson, Rosehearty, 1992
C324YPW	Ford R1115	Plaxton Paramount 3200 II	C53F	1985	Ex Daisy, Broughton, 1995
M961ENH	Iveco TurboDaily 59-12	Marshall C31	B27F	1994	

Livery : Blue

Previous Registrations:

1230HN	YAN815T		TXI2440	UTN951Y
8552PE	UNP784V		VOI5888	RVY937T
LDZ3142	ADV158Y, 9338AD, UDW652Y			

JBS' operate from Lodge Farm, Blunham where this picture of 8552PE, a Volvo B58 with Plaxton Supreme bodywork, and VHB672S, a Bristol VRT are seen. The Volvo was new to Price of Halesowen where it bore the index mark UNP784V. *Geoff Mills*

JACKSONS

M J Jackson, Bicknacre House, Leighams Road, Bicknacre,
Essex, CM3 4NF

1	NSU182	Volvo B10M-61	Berkhof Esprite 350	C53F	1983	Ex Snow, Great Wakering, 1995
2	MJI3376	Bova EL26/581	Bova Europa	C50F	1982	Ex Harris Coach, Grays, 1990
4	MJI2374	Aüwaerter Neoplan N122/3	Aüwaerter Skyliner	CH47/11CT	1986	Ex APT, Rayleigh, 1992
5	BDZ5198	DAF SB2300DHS585	Plaxton Paramount 3200 II	C49FT	1982	Ex Angel, Edmonton, 1991
6	F78VWK	Dennis Javelin 12SDA1907	Plaxton Paramount 3200 III	C53F	1989	Ex Wainfleet, Nuneaton, 1995
7	F303RMH	Mercedes-Benz L307D	Reeve Burgess	M12	1988	
8	F67NLH	Mercedes-Benz L407D	Coachcraft	M15	1988	
9	F321SMD	Mercedes-Benz 811D	Optare StarRider	C29F	1988	Ex WHM, Little Waltham, 1993
10	B897AGJ	Mercedes-Benz 307D	Devon Conversions	M10	1984	Ex Kent Transmissions, Sidcup, 1990
	OSR192R	Bristol VRT/SL3/6LXB	Alexander AL	H43/34D	1977	Ex City of Nottingham, 1994
	OSR194R	Bristol VRT/SL3/6LXB	Alexander AL	H43/34D	1977	Ex City of Nottingham, 1994
	C245OFE	Mercedes-Benz L608D	Reeve Burgess	B20F	1986	Ex RoadCar, 1995
	D609PJN	Ford Transit 190	Ford	M10	1986	Ex Levey Contractors, Billericay, 1992
	L738NWU	Mercedes-Benz 609D	Autobus Classique	C23F	1993	

Livery: Cream, purple and yellow

Previous Registrations:

BDZ5198	C335UFP		MJI3376	8947FH,AOO101X
MJI2374	28903PK		NSU182	KNO222Y

Photographed prior to its withdrawal, Jackson's D202NON is a Freight Rover Sherpa with Carlyle bodywork. It is seen entering Basildon bus station on local service 237. *Keith Grimes*

Kenzie's attractive new livery of silver with orange as an addition to their two-tone blue is seen on two Volvo B10Ms at the UK coach rally in Brighton. Above is M61WEB, an example with Van Hool Alizée bodywork which can be compared to M63WEB which features the latest Plaxton Excalibur product. *Keith Grimes*

KENZIE'S

Kenzies Coaches Ltd, Mead House, Shepreth, Cambridgeshire, SG8 6QH

p	JBY804	Bedford OB	Duple Vista	C29F	1951	Ex Barber, Mitcham, 1963
p	GUP743C	Bedford VAL14	Plaxton Panorama	C52F	1965	Ex Carr, New Silksworth, 1980
	PJE999J	Bedford YRQ	Plaxton Elite III	C45F	1971	
	LER666P	Bedford YLQ	Duple Dominant	C41F	1976	
	PEB2R	Bedford YMT	Plaxton Supreme III	C45F	1977	
	XVE8T	Volvo B58-61	Plaxton Supreme IV	C57F	1979	
	YJE3T	Bedford YMT	Plaxton Supreme IV	C53F	1979	
	CVE7V	Bedford YLQ	Duple Dominant II	C45F	1980	
	CVE12V	Volvo B58-61	Plaxton Supreme IV	C50F	1980	
	HFL14W	Bedford YMQ	Plaxton Supreme IV	C45F	1981	
	LEW16W	Volvo B10M-61	Plaxton Supreme IV	C53F	1981	
	62CBK	Kässbohrer Setra S215HD	Kässbohrer	C49FT	1982	
	C25KAV	Volvo B10M-61	Van Hool Alizée	C57F	1985	
	C28RFL	Volvo B9M	Van Hool Alizée	C41F	1986	
	D30BEW	Volvo B10M-61	Van Hool Alizée	C57F	1987	
	D31CFL	Mercedes-Benz 609D	Reeve Burgess	C19F	1987	
	E34MCE	Volvo B10M-61	Van Hool Alizée	C52D	1988	
	F36DAV	Volvo B10M-60	Van Hool Alizée	C52DT	1989	
	F39EEG	Volvo B10M-60	Van Hool Alizée	C51FT	1989	
	G40SAV	Volvo B10M-60	Van Hool Alizée	C57F	1990	
	J42PAV	Volvo B10M-60	Van Hool Alizée	C48F	1992	
	J43UFL	Volvo B10M-60	Van Hool Alizée	C52F	1992	
	J45UFL	Volvo B10M-60	Van Hool Alizée	C53F	1992	
	J46UFL	Volvo B10M-60	Van Hool Alizée	C53F	1992	
	K49TER	Volvo B10M-60	Van Hool Alizée	C53F	1993	
	K51TER	Volvo B10M-60	Van Hool Alizée	C48FT	1993	
	K52TER	Volvo B10M-60	Van Hool Alizée	C53F	1993	
	K53TER	Volvo B10M-62	Van Hool Alizée	C53F	1993	
	L54REW	Volvo B10M-62	Van Hool Alizée	C53F	1994	
	L56REW	Volvo B10M-62	Van Hool Alizée	C49FT	1994	
	L57REW	Volvo B10M-62	Van Hool Alizée	C53F	1994	
	L58TEW	EOS E180Z	EOS 90	C48FT	1994	
	M59WEB	EOS E180Z	EOS 90	C49FT	1995	
	M61WEB	Volvo B10M-62	Van Hool Alizée	C53F	1995	
	M62WEB	Volvo B10M-62	Plaxton Excalibur	C48F	1995	
	M63WEB	Volvo B10M-62	Plaxton Excalibur	C49FT	1995	
	M64WEB	Volvo B10M-62	Van Hool Alizée	C53F	1995	
	M65WEB	Volvo B10M-62	Van Hool Alizée	C53F	1995	
	M67WEB	Volvo B10M-62	Van Hool Alizée	C53F	1995	

Livery: Turquoise, red and silver.

Previous Registrations:

62CBK	VAV1X	JBY804	From new

The more established Kenzie's livery is displayed on LEW16W, an early example of the Volvo B10M which has a Plaxton Supreme IV body. The vehicle is seen passing through Parliament Square during the 1995 summer. *BBP*

85

Two examples of the Van Hool Alizée coach built some ten years apart are shown here and illustrate the continuity and the subtle changes made over the period this product has been on the market. Above is 436VVT, built on a Leyland Tiger while the picture below shows the current styling demonstrated on a Scania K113, M7SLC. With a product expected to last some 20 years it is important that styling is not dated quickly by fashion and most agree the Alizée has succeeded in that. *Ivor Norman*

LAMBERTS

Lamberts Coaches (Beccles) Ltd, Unit 7, Ellough Ind Est, Beccles, Suffolk, NR34 7TD

DWP3S	AEC Reliance 6U3ZR	Plaxton Supreme III	C53F	1977	Ex ?, 1995
VNT7S	Bedford YMT	Duple Dominant II	C53F	1977	Ex Nadder Valley, Tisbury, 1991
BFL503V	Bedford YMT	Plaxton Supreme IV	C53F	1979	Ex Matthews, Shouldham, 1980
FIL2296	Bedford YMT	Plaxton Supreme IV	C53F	1980	Ex Tate, Potten End, 1986
TVN330X	Bedford YNT	Plaxton Supreme VI	C53F	1982	Ex Cropper, Leeds, 1992
SIB4671	Aüwaerter Neoplan N122/3	Aüwaerter Skyliner	CH57/20CT	1982	Ex Amberline, 1992
FIL2294	DAF SB2300DHS585	Berkhof Esprite 350	C53F	1983	Ex Crusader, Clacton, 1987
856GKH	Bova FHD12.280	Bova Futura	C53F	1984	Ex Easton's, Hevingham, 1995
E581TYG	Iveco 35.10	Coachcraft	M15	1988	Ex Hermitage, Darfield, 1995
M441CVG	Volvo B6-9.9M	Plaxton Pointer	B40F	1995	
M832CVG	Volvo B6-9.9M	Plaxton Pointer	B40F	1995	

Livery: White and two-tone blue

Previous Registrations:

856GKH	A585GPE	FIL2296	MWU186V
FIL2294	JVW159Y	SIB4671	MVL608Y, 5142SC, OES628Y

LODGE'S

J W Lodge & Sons Ltd, The Garage, High Easter, Chelmsford, Essex, CM1 4QS

MJB481	Bedford SBG	Duple Super Vega	C41F	1956	Ex Abbeyways, Halifax, 1994
YMJ555S	Bedford YMT	Duple Dominant II Express	C53F	1978	
XNM820S	Bedford YMT	Duple Dominant II	C53F	1978	Ex Armchair, Brentford, 1979
FSU637	Van Hool T815	Van Hool Alizée	C53F	1984	Ex Ferris, Senghenydd, 1994
AAL551A	Leyland Tiger TRCTL11/3R	Van Hool Alizée	C53F	1984	Ex Eddie Brown, Helperby, 1994
436VVT	Leyland Tiger TRCTL11/3RZ(Vo)	Van Hool Alizée	C53FT	1985	Ex Eddie Brown, Helperby, 1994
MBZ7136	Bova FHD12.280	Bova Futura	C45FT	1985	Ex Janick Travel, Mansfield, 1995
C130GHS	MAN MT8-136	Reeve Burgess Riviera	C32F	1985	Ex Den Caney, Birmingham, 1995
D764TDV	Bedford YMP	Plaxton Paramount 3200 III	C35F	1987	Ex Wheadon, Cardiff, 1995
E432KRT	Van Hool T815H	Van Hool Alicron	C49FT	1988	Ex Leiston Motor Hire, 1993
E663YDT	Scania K112CRB	Van Hool Alizée	C53FT	1988	Ex Wessex, 1993
46AEW	Scania K112CRB	Van Hool Alizée	C53FT	1988	Ex Wessex, 1993
G964WNR	Toyota Coaster HB31R	Caetano Optimo	C21F	1989	Ex Billies, Mexborough, 1994
M7SLC	Scania K113CRB	Van Hool Alizée	C51F	1995	

Livery: Cream, red and blue.

Previous Registrations:

46AEW	E665YDT	AAL551A	A164MNE	MBZ7136	B62DMB
436VVT	B551VWT	FSU637	A779VFM	MJB481	From new

LUCKYBUS

Lucketts Garage (Watford) Ltd, Unit 2, Olds Approach, Tolpits Lane,
Watford, Hertfordshire, WD1 8TD

AEG121Y	Bedford YNT	Plaxton Supreme V	C49DTL	1982	Ex Skill's, 1990
JIL8238	Mercedes-Benz 307D	Whittaker	M12	1983	Ex Hague, Platts Common, 1994
LIL2288	Mercedes-Benz 307D	Reeve Burgess	M12	1984	Ex Hague, Platts Common, 1994
C525EWR	Volkswagen LT55	Optare City Pacer	B25F	1986	Ex Ward, Watford, 1990
D203RGH	Volkswagen LT55	Optare City Pacer	B25F	1987	Ex Ward, Watford, 1990
D989JYG	Volkswagen LT55	Optare City Pacer	DP20FL	1986	Ex Ward, Watford, 1990
D121EFH	Bedford Venturer YNV	Duple 320	C57FL	1987	Ex Swanbrook, Cheltenham, 1993
D447FSP	Volvo B10M-61	Duple 320	C52F	1987	Ex Express Travel, 1994
G171BLH	Dennis Javelin 12SDA1919	Duple 320	C57F	1990	
L100BUS	Dennis Dart 9.8SDL3035	Plaxton Pointer	B39F	1993	
L200BUS	Dennis Dart 9.8SDL3035	Plaxton Pointer	B39F	1993	
L300BUS	Dennis Dart 9SDL3031	Marshall C35	B35F	1994	
L400BUS	Dennis Dart 9SDL3031	Marshall C35	B35F	1994	
L500BUS	Iveco Turbo City 480.10.21	Wadham Stringer Vanguard II	B47F	1994	Ex Iveco demonstrator, 1995
L600BUS	Optare MetroRider	Optare	B31F	1995	

Livery: Grey, blue and red

Previous Registrations:

D447FSP	D614FSL	L500BUS	M289OUR
JIL8238	A98WHE	LIL2288	B259AMG

Recent changes allowing vehicle index marks to be issued for any vehicle newer than and including the year letter chosen can be effective. Luckybus had reserved several of the L-BUS numbers and have used them for their new vehicles since 1993. One from that year is **L200BUS**, a Dennis Dart with Plaxton Pointer bodywork. Newly delivered are **L500BUS** and **L600BUS**. *Richard Godfrey*

THE LUTONIAN

Lutonian Buses Ltd, 6 High Town Road, Luton, Bedfordshire, LU2 0DD

C854AOW	Iveco 35-8	Robin Hood	M14	1986	Ex North Mymms, Potters Bar, 1989
D42PGJ	Iveco 35-8	Elme Orion	C16F	1987	Ex Stevens, West Bromwich, 1992
D210GLJ	Freight Rover Sherpa	Dormobile	B16F	1986	Ex London Country SW, 1990
D493YLN	Iveco 35-8	Elme Orion	C16F	1986	Ex Ruffle, Castle Hedingham, 1991
D494YLN	Iveco 35-8	Elme Orion	C16F	1986	Ex Dixon, Stevenage, 1990
D69YRF	Freight Rover Sherpa	Dormobile	B16F	1986	Ex Midland Red North, 1990
D352KVA	Freight Rover Sherpa	Dormobile	B16F	1986	Ex Sapwell-Autodouble, Woburn, 1993
D529NDA	Freight Rover Sherpa	Carlyle	B18F	1986	Ex Flavin, Corringham, 1993
D772PTU	Freight Rover Sherpa	Dormobile	B16F	1986	Ex Farmer, Ashford, 1993
D111TFT	Freight Rover Sherpa	Carlyle	B20F	1986	Ex RoadCar, 1994
D114TFT	Freight Rover Sherpa	Carlyle	B18F	1986	Ex RoadCar, 1994
D134TFT	Freight Rover Sherpa	Carlyle	B18F	1986	Ex RoadCar, 1994
D510NDA	Freight Rover Sherpa	Carlyle	B19F	1986	Ex
D155NON	Freight Rover Sherpa	Carlyle	B20F	1987	Ex RoadCar, 1995
E970SVP	Freight Rover Sherpa	Carlyle Citybus 2	B20F	1987	Ex Boulton, Peterborough, 1994
F358EKL	Talbot Express	Talbot	M12	1988	
G361FOP	Freight Rover Sherpa	Carlyle Citybus 2	B20F	1990	Ex Neal & Patterson, Chippenham, 1993
G276HDW	Freight Rover Sherpa	Carlyle Citybus 2	B20F	1990	Ex Robson, Thornaby, 1994
G277HDW	Freight Rover Sherpa	Carlyle Citybus 2	B20F	1990	Ex Robson, Thornaby, 1994
G146GOL	Iveco Daily 49.10	Carlyle Dailybus 2	B25F	1990	Ex Moffat & Williamson, Gauldry, 1995
J31UTG	Leyland DAF 400	Carlyle Citybus 2	B20F	1992	Ex Bebb, Llantwit Fardre, 1994
J32UTG	Leyland DAF 400	Carlyle Citybus 2	B20F	1992	Ex Bebb, Llantwit Fardre, 1994
N190DBH	Iveco TurboDaily 59-12	Marshall C31	B25F	1995	

Livery: White, blue and orange.

In 1994 The Lutonian added a pair of Leyland DAF 400 minibuses to the fleet which had run for Bebb of Llantwit Fardre when new. Seen in Luton is J31UTG showing the Carlyle Citybus 2 product which ceased to be available shortly after the batch was delivered. *Colin Lloyd*

MARSHALLS

F W Marshall, 16 North Street, Leighton Buzzard, Bedforshire LU7 9EN

Depots : Mark Road, Hemel Hempstead and North Street, Leighton Buzzard.

848FXN	Volvo B58-61	Plaxton Supreme IV	C53F	1979	Ex Windmill Coaches, Copford, 1987
JDB797V	Ford R1114	Plaxton Supreme IV	C49F	1980	Ex Transauto, Chesham, 1993
GSU384	Volvo B58-61	Jonckheere Bermuda	C53F	1981	Ex Transauto, Chesham, 1983
1404FM	Volvo B10M-61	Jonckheere Bermuda	C40FT	1981	Ex Trathens, 1983
FSU379	Aüwaerter Neoplan N122/3	Aüwaerter Skyliner	CH56/20CT	1982	Ex Ebdon, Sidcup, 1994
SM9562	Scania K112CRS	Jonckheere Bermuda P599	C51F	1984	
SJI8104	Scania K112CRS	Jonckheere Bermuda P599	C57F	1984	Ex Transauto, Chesham, 1983
MJI6253	Scania K112CRS	Jonckheere Bermuda P599	C53F	1985	
B891MAB	Bedford YNT	Duple Laser	C53F	1985	Ex Ronsway, Hemel Hempstead, 1994
SJI8101	Volvo B10M-61	Jonckheere Bermuda P50	C53F	1985	Ex Golden Boy, Hoddesdon, 1991
SJI8102	Volvo B10M-61	Jonckheere Bermuda P50	C53F	1985	Ex Collison, Stonehouse, 1992
SJI8103	Volvo B10M-61	Jonckheere Bermuda P50	C53F	1985	Ex Skill's, 1992
MJI3409	Volvo B10M-53	Jonckheere Bermuda P95	CH54/13DT	1985	Ex Happy Al's, Moreton, 1993
MJI6252	Volvo B10M-61	Jonckheere Bermuda P50	C51FT	1986	
SJI8107	Volvo B10M-61	Berkhof Esprite 350	C53FT	1987	
D508WNV	Bedford YNV Venturer	Caetano Algarve	C57F	1987	Ex Ronsway, Hemel Hempstead, 1994
SJI8105	Volvo B10M-61	Plaxton Paramount 3500 III	C53F	1988	Ex Transauto, Chesham, 1993
SJI8106	Volvo B10M-61	Plaxton Paramount 3500 III	C53F	1988	Ex Transauto, Chesham, 1993
SJI8100	Volvo B10M-60	Jonckheere Deauville P599	C34FT	1990	
H607SWG	Volvo B10M-60	Ikarus Blue Danube 336	C53F	1990	
H608SWG	Volvo B10M-60	Ikarus Blue Danube 336	C53F	1990	
L110RWB	Volvo B10M-60	Plaxton Excalibur	C53F	1994	
M250TAK	Scania K113CRB	Irizar Century	C49FT	1994	
M254TAK	Scania K93CRB	Berkhof Excellence 1000L	C55F	1995	
M255TAK	Scania K93CRB	Berkhof Excellence 1000L	C55F	1995	
M148KJF	MAN 11.190	Caetano Algarve II	C35F	1995	

Livery: Blue, red, orange and yellow; (Newbourne coaches) GSU384, SJI8104-7, D208VEV, E753/4YKU, M148KJF and M254TAK (Marshalls & Ronsway) remainder.

Previous Registrations:

1404FM	XNV150W	MJI6252	C414LRP	SJI8104	B68MLT, C951GWO
848FXN	BHX850T	MJI6253	B500GBD	SJI8105	E753YKU
B891MAB	LSV548	SJI8100	G166RBD	SJI8106	E754YKU
FSU379	GVL939Y	SJI8101	B39KAL	SJI8107	D208VEV
GSU384	XNV138W	SJI8102	B40KAL, UBM880, B794EGG	SM9562	A112SNH
MJI3409	B705EOF	SJI8103	B43KAL		

Photographed in Castle Meadow, Norwich is NRY333W, a Bedford YMT with Plaxton Supreme IV coachwork. A keen user of the marque, Neaves latest addition is another example that was added to the fleet in 1994.
Keith Grimes

MORLEY'S

J R Morley & Sons Ltd, West End Garage, Whittlesey, Cambridgeshire, PE7 1HH

Depots : Whitmore Street, Whittlesey; West End, Whittlesey and Low Cross, Whittlesey.

w	UEB782K	Bedford YRQ	Willowbrook 001	B47F	1972	
	UEB783K	Bedford YRQ	Willowbrook 001	B47F	1972	
	NER610M	Bedford YRT	Duple Dominant Express	C53F	1973	
	JFR397N	Leyland Atlantean AN68/1R	East Lancashire	H45/31F	1975	Ex Ribble, 1989
	ODU254P	Bedford YLQ	Duple Dominant	C45F	1976	Ex Wainfleet, Nuneaton, 1979
	NSJ19R	Seddon Pennine VII	Alexander AY	B53F	1976	Ex Western Scottish, 1987
	NSJ21R	Seddon Pennine VII	Alexander AY	B53F	1976	Ex Western Scottish, 1988
	NDP38R	Bristol VRT/LL3/6LXB	Northern Counties	H47/29D	1976	Ex Reading, 1990
w	OJD192R	Leyland Fleetline FE30AGR	MCW	H45/32F	1977	Ex London Transport, 1984
	OJD232R	Leyland Fleetline FE30AGR	MCW	H45/32F	1977	Ex Thamesdown, 1985
	RSD978R	Seddon Pennine VII	Alexander AY	B53F	1977	Ex Western Scottish, 1987
	SPA192R	Bedford YMT	Plaxton Supreme III Express	C53F	1977	Ex Jason, St Mary Cray, 1989
	WYV48T	Leyland Titan TNLXB2RRSp	Park Royal	H44/26D	1979	Ex London Buses, 1994
w	BTX39V	Ford R1114	Plaxton Supreme IV	C53F	1978	Ex Harrod, Wormegay, 1984
	UAV457X	Bedford YNT	Duple Dominant IV	C53F	1982	
	HBH411Y	Bedford YNT	Duple Laser	C53F	1983	Ex Hornsby, Ashby, 1990
	B220JPH	Mercedes-Benz L508D	Coachcraft	M15	1984	Ex Statham, Ibstock, 1989

Livery: Red and grey

NEAVES

H S Neave & Son Ltd, Fenside, The Street, Hickling Road,
Catfield, Norfolk, NR29 5AA

RYL728R	Bedford YMT	Duple Dominant II	C53F	1977	Ex Easton, Brandiston, 1989
VBH605S	Bedford YMT	Duple Dominant II	C53F	1978	Ex Smith, Blofield, 1989
AJD24T	Bedford YMT	Plaxton Supreme IV	C47F	1979	Ex Sales, Armes & Craske, Norwich, 1994
XHE754T	Ford R1114	Plaxton Supreme III	C53F	1978	Ex Chambers, Stevenage, 1983
ENM10T	Bedford YMT	Plaxton Supreme III	C53F	1979	Ex Court, Coventry, 1993
APH511T	Volvo B58-61	Plaxton Supreme IV	C53F	1979	Ex Embling, Guyhirn, 1984
JKV413V	Bedford YMT	Plaxton Supreme IV	C53F	1979	Ex Wood, Kirkby-le-Soken, 1984
KNK539V	Bedford YMT	Caetano Alpha	C53F	1979	Ex Tate, Markyate, 1985
GEG963W	Ford R1114	Plaxton Supreme IV Express	C53F	1980	Ex Embling, Guyhirn, 1987
UNK11W	Bedford YMT	Plaxton Supreme IV	C53F	1981	Ex Roffey, Flimwell, 1991
NRY333W	Bedford YMT	Plaxton Supreme IV	C53F	1982	Ex Parnaby, Tolworth, 1991
UHJ969Y	Bedford YNT	Plaxton Supreme V	C53F	1982	Ex Golden Boy, Roydon, 1991
A202LCL	Bedford YMP	Marshall Campaigner	B48F	1984	Ex Norfolk County Council, 1990

Livery: White, red and grey

Previous Registrations:
UHJ969Y   DNK582Y, YOI7374

NIBS

Nelson Independent Bus Services, W H Nelson Coaches (Wickford) Ltd, Bruce Grove, Wickford, Essex, SS11 8BZ

17	BIL9406	Leyland Leopard PSU3E/4R	Plaxton Supreme IV	C53F	1979	
29	BIL7894	Leyland Leopard PSU3E/4R	Plaxton Supreme IV	C53F	1980	Ex Pan Atlas, East Acton, 1983
30	BIL4539	Leyland Leopard PSU3E/4R	Plaxton Supreme III	C53F	1977	Ex Pan Atlas, East Acton, 1983
33	GHM803N	Daimler Fleetline CRL6	MCW	H44/27D	1974	Ex London Transport, 1984
35	SMU721N	Daimler Fleetline CRL6	MCW	H44/27D	1974	Ex London Transport, 1984
36	GHM797N	Daimler Fleetline CRL6	MCW	H44/27D	1974	Ex London Transport, 1984
38	TUO255J	Bristol RELL6G	Eastern Coach Works	B53F	1971	Ex Cullinan, London, 1986
40	TUO260J	Bristol RELL6G	Eastern Coach Works	B53F	1971	Ex Southern National, 1987
42	TUO261J	Bristol RELL6G	Eastern Coach Works	B53F	1971	Ex Southern National, 1987
43	TGX892M	Daimler Fleetline CRL6	Park Royal	H44/27D	1974	Ex Avro, Orsett, 1987
44	THM705M	Daimler Fleetline CRL6	MCW	H44/27D	1974	Ex Avro, Orsett, 1987
201	BIL4419	Renault-Dodge S56	East Lancashire	B21F	1986	Ex Ipswich, 1990
202	BIL6538	Renault-Dodge S56	East Lancashire	B21F	1986	Ex Ipswich, 1990
203	C566NHJ	Renault-Dodge S56	Northern Counties	B18F	1986	Ex GM Buses, 1991
	GUG132N	Leyland National 11351/1R		B52F	1975	Ex Jones, Shoeburyness, 1993
	MBZ7141	Leyland National 11351A/1R		B52F	1976	Ex Budget Busway, 1995
	MAU142P	Bristol VRT/SL3/6LXB	Eastern Coach Works	H39/31F	1976	Ex Europa, Pitsea, 1995
	NDL652R	Bristol VRT/SL3/6LXB	Eastern Coach Works	H43/31F	1976	Ex Pegg, Rotherham, 1991
	AUP714S	Bristol VRT/SL3/6LXB	Eastern Coach Works	H43/31F	1977	Ex Northumbria, 1994
	BIL4710	Bristol VRT/SL3/6LXB	Eastern Coach Works	H39/31F	1980	Ex Thamesway, 1991
	L890UVE	Mercedes-Benz 811D	Marshall C16	B33F	1994	
	L891UVE	Mercedes-Benz 811D	Marshall C16	B33F	1994	

Livery: Yellow (buses); White, maroon and grey (coaches)

Previous Registrations:

BIL4419	C201YDX	BIL6538	C202YDX	C566NHJ	C808CBU, BIL4710
BIL4539	VMJ960S	BIL7894	LVS431V	MBZ7141	RYG769R
BIL4710	STW25W	BIL9406	CTM404T		

Two Marshall-bodied Mercedes-Benz 811s were added to the NIBS fleet in 1994. Passing through Romford is L890UVE seen here on service 273. *BBP*

OSBORNE'S

G W Osborne & Sons, 62 New Road, Tollesbury, Essex, CM9 8QD

2	KUC228P	Daimler Fleetline CRL6	MCW	H45/32F	1975	Ex London Transport, 1983
4	GSL897N	Daimler Fleetline CRG6LXB	Alexander AL	H49/38F	1975	Ex Tayside, 1985
5	PHK620V	Volvo B58-56	Caetano Alpha	C53F	1980	
8	GVS984V	Leyland Tiger TRCTL11/2R	Plaxton Supreme VI Express	C53F	1983	
9	CPU125X	Leyland Tiger TRCTL11/2R	Plaxton Supreme VI Express	C53F	1982	
10	SJI4635	Leyland Tiger TRCTL11/3R	Berkhof Esprite 350	C53F	1983	
11	OSR191R	Bristol VRT/LL3/6LXB	Alexander AL	H49/34D	1977	Ex Tayside, 1980
14	MNK427V	Leyland Leopard PSU3E/4R	Duple Dominant II	C53F	1981	Ex Alder Valley, 1989
16	MNK429V	Leyland Leopard PSU3E/4R	Duple Dominant II	C53F	1981	Ex Alder Valley, 1989
17	XGS767X	Leyland Tiger TRCTL11/3R	Plaxton Supreme V	C57F	1981	Ex Ebdon, Sidcup, 1984
18	GSL901N	Daimler Fleetline CRG6LXB	Alexander AL	H49/34D	1975	Ex Tayside, 1984
19	MNK430V	Leyland Leopard PSU3E/4R	Duple Dominant II	C53F	1981	Ex Alder Valley, 1989
26	GSL900N	Daimler Fleetline CRG6LXB	Alexander AL	H49/34D	1975	Ex Tayside, 1984
30	TJI3130	Van Hool T815H	Van Hool Alizée	C49FT	1990	
31	TJI3131	Van Hool T815H	Van Hool Alizée	C49FT	1990	
32	SJI2954	Leyland Tiger TRCTL11/3R	LAG Galaxy	C53F	1985	
40	RWC40W	Leyland Leopard PSU3E/4R	Plaxton Supreme IV Express	C49F	1981	
41	RWC41W	Leyland Leopard PSU3E/4R	Plaxton Supreme IV Express	C49F	1981	
45	KBC2V	Volvo B58-61	Plaxton Supreme IV	C57F	1979	Ex Ementon, Cranfield, 1987
53	JIL5623	Leyland Tiger TRCTL11/3R	Plaxton Paramount 3200	C57F	1983	Ex Goldenport, London, 1985
54	LUA289V	Leyland Leopard PSU3F/4R	Plaxton Supreme IV	C53F	1980	Ex Wallace Arnold, 1986
60	EWW213T	Leyland Leopard PSU3E/4R	Plaxton Supreme IV	C53F	1979	Ex Wallace Arnold, 1984
70	TJI1670	Volvo B10M-60	Plaxton Paramount 3500 III	C49FT	1990	Ex Parks, 1992
75	L705CNR	DAF SB2305DHS585	Caetano Algarve II	C53F	1994	
76	L706CNR	DAF SB2305DHS585	Caetano Algarve II	C53F	1994	
77	M577JBC	Volvo B10M-62	Caetano Algarve II	C49FT	1995	
	CJH115V	Bristol VRT/SL3/6LXB	Eastern Coach Works	H43/31F	1979	Ex Stephensons, 1995
	CJH141V	Bristol VRT/SL3/6LXB	Eastern Coach Works	H43/31F	1979	Ex Stephensons, 1995
85	TJI1685	Volvo B10M-60	Plaxton Paramount 3500 III	C53F	1990	Ex Park's, 1992
88	TJI1688	Volvo B10M-60	Plaxton Paramount 3500 III	C53F	1990	Ex Park's, 1992 ###

Livery: Red, white and maroon (buses); white, blue and red (coaches)

Previous Registrations:

JIL5623	FNM860Y	SJI4635	JVW160Y	TJI1688	G88RGG		
JIL5628	C101AFX	TJI1670	G70RGG	TJI3130	G430VML		
SJI2954	B444BAR	TJI1685	G85RGG	TJI3131	G431VML		

The predecessor to the Volvo B10M, the B58 is shown here as a 12-metre version with Plaxton Supreme IV bodywork. The -61 in the chassis code represents the wheelbase of 6.1 metres, though not all Volvo models use this method to distinguish the types. Osborne's KBC2V was photographed in Trafalgar Square.
Colin Lloyd

PRESTWOOD TRAVEL

P & GL Baird, 152 Wrights Lane, Prestwood, Great Missenden,
Buckinghamshire, HP16 0LG

Depot: Binders Industrial Estate, Cryers Hill, High Wycombe.

WRO438S	AEC Reliance 6U3ZR	Plaxton Supreme III	C53F	1978	Ex Smith, Chesham, 1995
APM111T	AEC Reliance 6U2R	Plaxton Supreme IV Express	C53F	1979	Ex London Country, 1985
APM117T	AEC Reliance 6U2R	Plaxton Supreme IV Express	C49F	1979	Ex London Country, 1985
EPM140V	AEC Reliance 6U2R	Plaxton Supreme IV Express	C53F	1979	Ex Marchants, Cheltenham, 1990
EPM144V	AEC Reliance 6U2R	Plaxton Supreme IV Express	C53F	1979	Ex London Country, 1986
EPM146V	AEC Reliance 6U2R	Plaxton Supreme IV Express	C53F	1979	Ex London Country, 1986
RJI4670	Bova EL26/581	Bova Europa	C52F	1981	Ex Warren, Alton, 1992
PPJ162W	Leyland Leopard PSU5D/5R	Wadham Stringer Vanguard	B54F	1981	Ex MoD, 1995
CPE480Y	Leyland Leopard PSU5D/5R	Wadham Stringer Vanguard	B54F	1982	Ex MoD, 1995
RJI4668	Bova EL26/581	Bova Europa	C53F	1983	Ex Pan Atlas, East Acton, 1992
RJI4669	Bova EL26/581	Bova Europa	C53F	1983	Ex Pan Atlas, East Acton, 1992
8726FH	Bova EL26/581	Bova Europa	C53F	1983	Ex McAndrew, Leamington, 1990
E901LVE	Volkswagen LT55	Optare City Pacer	B25F	1987	Ex Cambus, 1993
E902LVE	Volkswagen LT55	Optare City Pacer	B25F	1987	Ex Cambus, 1993

Livery: White

Previous Registrations:

8726FH	CLX573Y	RJI4668	DOY133Y
CPE480Y	51AC05	RJI4669	DOY134Y
PPJ162W	50AC03	RJI4670	997GAT, VPG339X

Prestwood operate two Volkswagen LT55s with Optare City Pacer bodies. Photographed in High Wycombe, E901LVE was new to Cambus and shows this product which proved popular in the late 1980s when it was supplied to several major operators. Fleetnames of Prestwood Travel and Prestwood Holidays are used by this operator. *Keith Grimes*

RED ROSE

Red Rose Travel Ltd, 2 Brook End, Weston Turville,
Buckinghamshire HP22 5RF

Depot: Hartwell Sidings, Oxford Road, Aylesbury

Q956UOE	Bedford YRT	Willowbrook Warrior(1987)	B53F	1976	Ex Sussex Bus, Ford, 1992
WPH132Y	Leyland Tiger TRCTL11/2R	Eastern Coach Works B51	C53F	1982	Ex Darlington, 1995
B63APP	Ford Transit 190	Chassis Developments	M16	1985	Ex Cross Keys Coaches, Newingreen, 1994
D814BVT	Ford Transit 190	Ford	M8	1986	Ex private owner, 1991
D501MJA	Iveco Daily 49.10	Robin Hood City Nippy	B19F	1987	Ex GM Buses, 1992
D566NDA	Renault-Dodge S56	Reeve Burgess	B18F	1986	Ex Buckinghamshire RC, 1995
F725MNB	Ford Transit VE6	Mellor	M14	1989	Ex Darlington, 1995
F727EKR	Freight Rover Sherpa	Dormobile	B21F	1989	Ex Starline, Watford, 1995
H668ATN	Toyota Coaster HB31R	Caetano Optimo	C21F	1990	Ex Buffalo, Flitwick, 1993
H389SYG	Mercedes-Benz 811D	Optare StarRider E	B26F	1990	Ex Optare demonstrator, 1991
H733LOL	Mercedes-Benz 811D	Carlyle	DP33F	1990	Ex Lunt, Olney, 1995
K540OGA	Mercedes-Benz 811D	Dormobile Routemaker	B29F	1992	
M62MOG	Iveco TurboDaily 59.12	Mellor	B27F	1994	
M848MOL	Iveco TurboDaily 59.12	Mellor	B27F	1994	

Livery: Red, cream and black

Previous Registrations:
Q956UOE   NFP735P

Two Mellor-bodied Iveco TurboDaily 59.12s joined the Red Rose fleet in 1994. Photographed as it turns in Waterhouse Street, Hemel Hempstead on service 322 is M848MOL. *Richard Godfrey*

REG'S

Reg's Coaches Ltd, Spencer Street, Hertford, Hertfordshire, SG13 7AH

PHG186T	Leyland Leopard PSU5C/4R	Plaxton Supreme IV	C57F	1979	Ex Robinson's, Gt Harwood, 1985
YYL771T	Leyland Leopard PSU5C/4R	Duple Dominant II	C50F	1979	Ex Grey Green, 1985
CYH770V	Leyland Leopard PSU3E/4R	Duple Dominant II Express	C53F	1979	Ex Grey Green, 1986
NMJ269V	Bedford YMT	Duple Dominant II	C53F	1980	
LVS418V	Leyland Leopard PSU5C/4R	Duple Dominant II	C57F	1980	Ex Robinson's, Gt Harwood, 1986
HHG193W	Leyland Leopard PSU5C/4R	Duple Dominant II	C57F	1981	Ex Robinson's, Gt Harwood, 1988
LBZ2943	Leyland Tiger TRCTL11/3RZ	Plaxton Paramount 3200 III	C53F	1987	Ex Shearings, 1993
LBZ2944	Leyland Tiger TRCTL11/3RZ	Plaxton Paramount 3200 III	C53F	1987	Ex Shearings, 1993
LBZ2940	Hestair Duple SDA1512	Duple 425	C51FT	1988	Ex Pat's Coaches, New Broughton, 1994
LBZ2941	Dennis Javelin 12SDA1908	Plaxton Paramount 3200 III	C49FT	1988	Ex Go Whittle, Kidderminster, 1989
LBZ2942	Dennis Javelin 12SDA1908	Plaxton Paramount 3200 III	C57F	1988	Ex Go Whittle, Kidderminster, 1989
G541JBV	Dennis Dart 9SDL3002	Duple Dartline	B39F	1989	Ex Duple demonstrator, 1990
G350GCK	Dennis Dart 9SDL3002	Duple Dartline	B39F	1989	Ex Carlyle demonstrator, 1992
G624WPB	Dennis Dart 9SDL3002	Duple Dartline	B39F	1990	
J216XKY	Mercedes-Benz 709D	Alexander AM	B25F	1991	
J217XKY	Mercedes-Benz 709D	Alexander AM	B25F	1991	
N	Mercedes-Benz 709D	Marshall C19	B27F	1995	
N	Mercedes-Benz 709D	Marshall C19	B27F	1995	

Livery: White, green and black (buses); Green, black and red (coaches)

Previous Registrations:

LDZ2940	E612AEY	LDZ2942	E502JWP	LDZ2944	D594MVR
LDZ2941	E544JWP	LDZ2943	D593MVR		

Named vehicles: YYL771T *Reg's Caribbean Cruiser*; PHG186T *Reg's European Cruiser*; CYH770V *Reg's Sovereign Cruiser*; NMJ269V *Reg's Inter-Continental*; LVS418V *Reg's Panoramic Cruiser*; HHG193W *Reg's Pathfinder*; LBZ2940 *Reg's Enterprise*; LBZ2941 *Reg's Moonraker*; LBZ2942 *Reg's Starliner*; LBZ2943 *Reg's Highwayman*; LBZ2944 *Reg's Highlander*;

One of the original examples of the Dartline product, G350GCK was built by Duple. Production moved to Carlyle when the design was transferred after Duple pulled out of the market. Following a period on demonstration this vehicle joined Reg's in 1992 and is seen in Stevenage. *BBP*

RICHMOND'S COACHES

H V Richmond Ltd, The Garage, Barley, Hertfordshire SG8 8JA

Depots: Church Street, Barley and The Garage, Barley

648EAU	Ford R1114	Duple Dominant II Express	C53F	1980	
753LNU	Ford R1114	Plaxton Supreme IV	C53F	1980	
426YRA	Ford R1114	Duple Dominant II Express	C53F	1980	
XPP693X	Volvo B10M-61	Plaxton Supreme IV	C57F	1981	Ex Smith, Buntingford, 1994
275FUM	Volvo B10M-61	Plaxton Supreme VI	C57F	1982	
668PTM	Volvo B10M-61	Plaxton Supreme VI	C57F	1983	Ex Ralph's, Longford, 1985
239LYC	Volvo B10M-61	Plaxton P'mount 3200 III (1991)	C53F	1983	
559ABX	Volvo B10M-61	Plaxton Paramount 3200	C53F	1984	
HDT375	Volvo B10M-61	Plaxton Paramount 3500 II	C49FT	1984	Ex Smith, Buntingford, 1994
729KTO	Volvo B10M-61	Plaxton Paramount 3200 II	C57F	1985	
851FYD	Volvo B9M	Plaxton Paramount 3200 II	C39F	1986	
E408YLG	Mercedes-Benz 609D	PMT	DP24F	1987	Ex Cooper, Ashton, 1989
403NMM	Volvo B9M	Plaxton Paramount 3200 II	C39F	1987	
438XYA	Volvo B10M-61	Van Hool Alizée	C53F	1988	Ex Sworder, Walkern, 1990
E530VKH	Toyota Coaster HB31R	Caetano Optimo	C21F	1988	Ex Smith, Buntingford, 1994
F62MTM	Mercedes-Benz 609D	Reeve Burgess Beaver	DP19F	1989	
F810TMD	Volvo B10M-60	Van Hool Alizée	C57F	1989	Ex Tellings-Golden Miller, Byfleet, 1995
892LTV	Volvo B10M-60	Plaxton Paramount 3500 III	C48FT	1989	Ex Kenzie's, Shepreth, 1992
F37DAV	Volvo B10M-60	Van Hool Alizée	C53F	1989	Ex Kenzie's, Shepreth, 1995
593FGF	Volvo B10M-60	Van Hool Alizée	C55F	1990	
153WAR	Volvo B10M-60	Van Hool Alizée	C49FT	1993	
649ETF	Toyota Coaster HDB30R	Caetano Optimo II	C18F	1993	
M587BFL	Mercedes-Benz 709D	Marshall C19	B27F	1994	
M588BFL	Mercedes-Benz 709D	Marshall C19	B27F	1994	

Livery: Cream and brown

Previous Registrations:

153WAR	from new	559ABX	B618AMD	753LNU	KRO659V
239LYC	TMG671Y	593FGF	G85AUR	851FYD	C219FMF
275FUM	OMM675X	648EAU	KRO658V	892LTV	F404DUG
403NMM	D867YPH	649ETF	From new	A693NBM	STT608X
426YRA	PNM673W	668PTM	RMH868Y	HDT375	B617AMD
438XYA	F238HRO	729KTO	B29ABH		

Photographed in St Mary's Square, Hitchin, Richmond's 426YRA is a Ford R1114 with Duple Dominant II Express bodywork built in 1980 and qualifying for the then *bus grant*. The windscreen display shows the vehicle to be working a Hertfordshire County Council tendered service.
Richard Godfrey

ROVER BUS SERVICE

J R Dell, Delmar, Lycrome Road, Lye Green, Chesham,
Buckinghamshire, HP5 3LF

SFU718	Bedford YRT	Plaxton Supreme III	C53F	1976	Ex Morley's Grey, West Row, 1985
VUR118W	Ford R1114	Duple Dominant	B53F	1980	Ex Lee-Roy, Brentwood, 1984
VKX539	Leyland Tiger TRCTL11/3R	Plaxton Paramount 3500	C53F	1984	Ex Cavalier, Hounslow, 1985
PSU377	Leyland Tiger TRCTL11/3R	Plaxton Paramount 3500	C55F	1984	Ex Armchair, Brentford, 1987
IIB278	Leyland Tiger TRCTL11/3R	Plaxton Paramount 3500 II	C51F	1985	Ex Leyland demonstator, 1986
KIW3769	Leyland Tiger TRCTL11/3RZ	Plaxton Paramount 3200 II	C57F	1985	Ex Shearings, 1989
JIL9034	Mercedes-Benz L307D	Economy	M12	1986	Ex Coles, Eversley, 1995
HIL3470	Volvo B10M-61	Duple 320	C53F	1986	Ex Capital, West Drayton, 1991
JOI9820	Volvo B10M-61	Van Hool Alizée	C53F	1987	Ex Clarksons, South Elmsall, 1993
E240NSE	Mercedes-Benz 609D	Yeates	C19F	1988	Ex Mayne's, Buckie, 1989
OJR338	Volvo B10M-61	Plaxton Paramount 3500 III	C53F	1988	Ex Shearings, 1992
760BUS	Volvo B10M-60	Plaxton Paramount 3500 III	C53F	1989	Ex Horseshoe, Tottenham, 1991
F61RKX	Dennis Javelin 11SDL1905	Duple 320	C53F	1989	Ex Horsham Coaches, Warnham, 1993
G648ONH	Volvo B10M-60	Jonckheere Deauville P599	C51F	1990	Ex Redwood, Hernyock, 1994

Previous Registrations:

760BUS	F886SMU, 662JJO	KIW3769	B512UNB
D823UBH	D620PWA, 760BUS	OJR338	E659UNE
F61RKX	F491WPR, SRD733	PSU377	A151RMJ
HIL3470	C949TLF	SFU718	LHW508P
IIB278	B263AMG	VKX539	A148RMJ, SRD733
JIL9034	C532VPM	VUR118W	PNM663W, 662JJO
JOI9820	D560MVR, PJI5526, D710NYG		

Livery: Cream and blue

When Rover's G648ONH was photographed at South Mimms services the sign in the windscreen intimates that the bus was on hire to Wallace Arnold for a tour to Newquay. This Volvo B10M carries a Jonckheere Deauville P599 body which has since been renumbered to Deauville 45 during the latest facelift of this fashionable yet fashion-free style. *Colin Lloyd*

RULES

Rule's Coaches Ltd, Boxbank, Boxford, Suffolk, CO10 5HH

DAL771J	AEC Reliance 6U2R	Plaxton Elite Express	C53F	1970	Ex Overton, Stockton, 1981
YHA386J	Ford R192	Plaxton Derwent	B45F	1971	Ex Beeston's, Hadleigh, 1978
LIB1611	Leyland Leopard PSU5A/4R	Plaxton Supreme III	C53F	1976	Ex JD, Airdrie, 1990
GNK781T	AEC Reliance 6U2R	Duple Dominant II	C53F	1978	Ex Olde London Town, Luton, 1980
FBJ713T	AEC Reliance 6U3ZR	Plaxton Supreme IV Express	C53F	1979	
UWH314T	Ford Transit 130	Reeve Burgess	C17F	1979	Ex Davies, Bridgwater, 1990
EPM126V	AEC Reliance 6U2R	Duple Dominant II Express	C53F	1979	Ex Mulley's, Ixworth, 1995
WSF643Y	Volvo B10M-61	Van Hool Alizée	C49FT	1982	Ex Stuart, Carluke, 1995
KIB5227	Volvo B10M-61	Van Hool Alizée	C49FT	1983	Ex Caravelle, Felixstowe, 1990
D203NON	Freight Rover Sherpa	Carlyle	B20F	1986	Ex Bee Line Buzz, 1992

Livery: Red, maroon and white

Previous Registrations:

KIB5227	A51UMB	LIB1611	SFV202P	WSF643Y	KGG726Y, RRU345

New to London Country as RB126, EPM126V is now to be found operating with Rules of Boxford. The vehicle was photographed on Angel Hill, Bury St Edmunds in August 1995 having arrived from Mulley's Motorways earlier in the year. *Keith Grimes*

SANDERS COACHES

Sanders Coaches, Heath Drive, Hempstead Road, Holt, Norfolk, NR25 6JU

Depots: Cadogan Rd, Cromer; Heath Dr, Holt; Clay Pit Lane, Fakenham; Cornish Way, Lyngate Ind Estate, North Walsham.

1	WOA521P	Dennis Javelin 12SDA1908	Plaxton Paramount 3200 III	C49FT	1988	Ex Go Whittle, Kidderminster, 1992
2	SFC2T	Bedford YMT	Plaxton Supreme III	C53F	1978	Ex Blunsdon, Bladon, 1990
3	RDV903	DAF MB230LT615	Van Hool Alizée	C51FT	1988	Ex Robinson's, Great Harwood, 1995
4	RJI8604	Bedford YNV Venturer	Plaxton Paramount 3200 III	C57F	1987	Ex Mayne's, Buckie, 1988
5	FPP5T	Bedford YMT	Duple Dominant II	C53F	1978	Ex Premier, Watford, 1987
6	GFH6V	Bedford YMT	Plaxton Supreme IV	C53F	1979	Ex P & H, Ilford, 1991
7	J7FTG	Mercedes-Benz 811D	PMT Ami	DP33F	1992	Ex Flight's, Birmingham, 1995
8	J8FTG	Mercedes-Benz 811D	PMT Ami	DP33F	1992	Ex Flight's, Birmingham, 1995
9	YJE9T	Bedford YMT	Plaxton Supreme IV Express	C53F	1979	Ex Lloyd, Nuneaton, 1994
10	N597DWY	DAF SB220LC550	Ikarus CitiBus	B49F	1995	
12	ATL312X	Bedford YMT	Plaxton Supreme IV Express	C53F	1981	Ex The Delaine, Bourne, 1989
13	D129SHE	Bedford YNV Venturer	Caetano Algarve	C57F	1987	Ex McColl, Balloch, 1995
14	RJI8614	Bedford YNV Venturer	Duple 320	C55F	1986	Ex Maybury, Cranborne, 1989
15	SJI1615	Bedford YMT	Plaxton Supreme III	C53F	1977	Ex Martin, Sheffield, 1985
16	SJI1616	Bedford YMT	Plaxton Supreme IV	C53F	1979	Ex Torr, Gedling, 1991
17	SJI1617	Bedford YMT	Duple Dominant II	C53F	1980	Ex Matthews, Shouldham, 1987
18	SJI1618	Bedford YMT	Duple Dominant II	C53F	1981	Ex Felix, Stanley, 1988
19	SJI1619	Bedford YMT	Duple Dominant IV	C53F	1981	Ex Dereham Coachways, 1990
20	SJI1620	Bedford YMT	Plaxton Supreme IV	C53F	1979	Ex Tappins, Didcot, 1993
21	SJI1621	Bedford YMT	Plaxton Supreme IV	C53F	1979	Ex Tappins, Didcot, 1993
22	SJI1622	DAF MB200DKTL600	Plaxton Supreme IV	C57F	1979	Ex Crescent, North Walsham, 1993
23	SJI1623	DAF MB200DKTL600	Plaxton Supreme IV	C57F	1980	Ex Crescent, North Walsham, 1993
24	SJI1624	Bedford YMT	Plaxton Supreme IV	C53F	1979	Ex Boyden, Castle Donington, 1991
25	SJI1625	Bedford YMT	Plaxton Supreme IV	C53F	1979	Ex Tappins, Didcot, 1993
26	SJI1626	Bedford YNV Venturer	Plaxton Paramount 3200 III	C53F	1987	Ex Rainworth Travel, 1992
27	SJI1627	Bedford YNV Venturer	Plaxton Paramount 3200 II	C53F	1986	Ex Blue Line, Dallington, 1990
28	SJI1628	Bedford YNV Venturer	Plaxton Paramount 3200 II	C53F	1985	Ex Bammant, Fakenham, 1992
29	SJI1629	Bedford YNV Venturer	Plaxton Paramount 3200 II	C53F	1985	Ex Worth's, Enstone, 1993
30	SJI1630	Bedford YNV Venturer	Plaxton Paramount 3200 II	C55F	1986	
31	SJI1631	Bedford YNT	Plaxton Paramount 3200 III	C53F	1986	Ex Owen, Yateley, 1992
32	SJI1632	Bedford YNT	Plaxton Paramount 3200 E	C49F	1983	Ex Wide Horizon, Hinckley, 1992
34	C134USS	DAF SB2300DHS585	Plaxton Paramount 3200	C53F	1985	Ex Mayne's, Buckie, 1995
37	PVF377	DAF SB2300DHS585	Caetano Algarve	C53F	1987	Ex Miller, Foxton, 1993
38	J138OBU	Mercedes-Benz 609D	Made-to-Measure	C24F	1991	Ex Mason, Bo'ness, 1993
39	3990ME	Volvo B10M-60	Plaxton Paramount 3500 III	C53F	1989	Ex Wallace Arnold, 1992
40	MNM40V	DAF MB200DKTL600	Plaxton Supreme IV	C57F	1980	Ex Dhanoia, Orsett, 1995
41	D441CEW	Mercedes-Benz 609D	Reeve Burgess	C23F	1987	Ex Grey, Ely, 1990
42	APW942S	Bedford YMT	Duple Dominant II	C53F	1978	Ex Bebb, Llantwit Fardre, 1983
44	GJI4481	Mercedes-Benz L608D	Whittaker	C19F	1984	Ex Ward, Mundesley, 1994
47	OGR647	DAF MB200DKTL600	Plaxton Paramount 3500	C55F	19..	Ex ?, 1994
48	PJI7348	Bedford YNV Venturer	Plaxton Paramount 3200 II	C57F	1985	Ex Larratt Pepper, Thurnscoe, 1992
49	BIL8949	DAF MB200DKTL600	Plaxton Supreme IV	C53F	1982	Ex Irvine, Law, 1994
50	JDN506L	Bedford YRT	Plaxton Elite III	C53F	1973	Ex York Pullman, 1981
51	JNK551N	Bedford YRT	Plaxton Elite III	C53F	1975	Ex JR Deluxe, Foulden, 1982
52	SJI5629	DAF MB200DKTL600	Plaxton Supreme IV	C53F	1981	Ex Brijon Tours, Swanmore, 1995
53	WXI9253	DAF MB200DKTL600	Plaxton Supreme IV	C57F	1980	Ex Embling, Guyhirn, 1995
54	354TRT	DAF MB200DKTL600	Plaxton Supreme IV	C57F	1980	Ex Kingsman, Holbrook, 1995
55	FTO551V	Bedford YMT	Plaxton Supreme IV Express	DP53F	1979	Ex Baker, Weston-super-Mare, 1994
56	PJI5637	DAF MB200DKL600	Plaxton Supreme IV	C53F	1979	Ex Haynes, Ringstead, 1994
57	FTO557V	Bedford YMT	Plaxton Supreme IV Express	DP53F	1979	Ex Baker, Weston-super-Mare, 1994
59	259VYC	Bova FLD12.250	Bova Futura	C57F	1986	Ex Marchwood Motorways, Totton, 1993
61	MIW3561	DAF MB200DKVL600	Duple Caribbean	C51FT	1986	Ex Ward, Mundeley, 1994
62	D624KJT	Mercedes-Benz 609D	Yeates	C19F	1987	Ex Excelsior, 1990
64	GOE264V	DAF MB200DKVL600	Plaxton Supreme IV	C53F	1979	Ex Mike de Courcey Travel, 1994
65	SGF965	Volvo B10M-60	Plaxton Paramount 3500 III	C49FT	19..	Ex ?, 1995
67	YVJ677	DAF MB200DKTL600	Van Hool Alizée	C51FT	1983	Ex Crescent, North Walsham, 1993
69	F269GUD	Mercedes-Benz 609D	Reeve Burgess Beaver	C19F	1989	Ex Pearce, Berinsfield, 1992
70	B670EHL	Mercedes-Benz L307	Reeve Burgess	M12	1985	Ex Ward, Mundesley, 1994
71	M971CVG	Mercedes-Benz 711D	Plaxton Beaver	C25F	1995	
72	A22UBD	Mercedes-Benz L307D	Reeve Burgess	M12	1983	Ex Bammant, Fakenham, 1992
73	H113DVM	Mercedes-Benz 609D	Reeve Burgess Beaver	C19F	1991	Ex Shearings, 1995
74	KAU574V	Bedford YMT	Plaxton Supreme IV Express	DP53F	1980	Ex Baker, Weston-super-Mare, 1994
75	KAU575V	Bedford YMT	Plaxton Supreme IV Express	DP53F	1980	Ex Baker, Weston-super-Mare, 1994

Sanders PJI8327 was operating a National Express service when photographed in Elizabeth Street, London. This Bova Futura is one of a pair that joined the fleet from Crescent of North Walsham in 1993. *BBP*

One of the few Bedford chassis types to be given a name was the YNV. Marketed as the Venturer it was also one of the last to be produced before Bedford withdrew from the UK coaching market. RJI8607 is seen in Stevenage in August 1995. *Colin Lloyd*

78	EAC878T	Bedford YMT	Plaxton Supreme IV Express	DP53F	1979	Ex Lloyd, Nuneaton, 1994
79	JJF879V	Bedford YMT	Plaxton Supreme IV	C53F	1980	Ex Skinner, Saltby, 1990
80	KPT800T	Bedford YMT	Plaxton Supreme IV	C53F	1979	Ex Bammant, Fakenham, 1992
81	LNU581W	Bedford YMT	Plaxton Supreme IV Express	DP53F	1980	Ex Baker, Weston-super-Mare, 1994
82	VKC832V	Bedford YMT	Plaxton Supreme IV	C53F	1980	Ex Amberline, Liverpool, 1983
83	VKC833V	Bedford YMT	Plaxton Supreme IV	C53F	1980	Ex Amberline, Liverpool, 1983
84	BIL8430	Bedford YMT	Plaxton Supreme IV	C53F	1980	Ex Coleman, Leverington, 1986
86	XVG686X	Bedford YNT	Duple Dominant III	C53F	1982	Ex Crescent, North Walsham, 1993
87	PJI8327	Bova FHD12.280	Bova Futura	C49FT	1984	Ex Crescent, North Walsham, 1993
88	PJI8328	Bova FHD12.280	Bova Futura	C49FT	1984	Ex Crescent, North Walsham, 1993
89	G389LDT	Mercedes-Benz 609D	Whittaker	C24F	1990	Ex Crescent, North Walsham, 1993
90	MIB9067	Bedford YNT	Plaxton Supreme IV	C53F	1981	Ex Dore, Leafield, 1992
93	FIL8693	DAF MB200DKTL600	Plaxton Supreme V	C53F	1982	Ex Crescent, North Walsham, 1993
94	DJI1594	Bova FHD12.280	Bova Futura	C49FT	1984	Ex Garnett, Tindale Crescent, 1994
95	DHE695V	Bedford YMT	Plaxton Supreme IV	C53F	1979	Ex Boyden, Castle Donington, 1991
96	D694MAG	Mercedes-Benz 709D	Coachcraft	C26F	1987	Ex Upham, Wickford, 1990
97	HGG997T	Bedford YMT	Plaxton Supreme IV	C53F	1979	Ex Constable, Felixstowe, 1984
99	BWK9T	Bedford YMT	Plaxton Supreme IV Express	C53F	1979	Ex Lloyd, Nuneaton, 1994
100	RRT100W	Bedford YMT	Plaxton Supreme IV Express	C53F	1981	Ex Bammant, Fakenham, 1992
101	LAH817A	AEC Reliance 2U3RA	Plaxton Elite	C49F	1962	Ex preservation, 1994
102	C220VCT	Mercedes-Benz L608D	Reeve Burgess	C19F	1985	Ex Dunthorne, Wells, 1994
103	WSV503	Bedford YNV Venturer	Duple 320	C53F	1987	Ex Enterprise, Chatteris, 1990
105	HUX15V	Bedford YMT	Duple Dominant II Express	C53F	1980	Ex Rover, Bromsgrove, 1990
106	XFE649S	Bedford YMT	Plaxton Supreme III Express	C53F	1977	Ex Harrod, Wormegay, 1988
107	RJI8607	Bedford YNV Venturer	Plaxton Paramount 3200 III	C57F	1987	Ex Owen, Oswestry, 1989
108	CVA108V	Bedford YMT	Plaxton Supreme IV	C53F	1980	Ex Crescent, North Walsham, 1993
109	MMJ547V	Bedford YMT	Duple Dominant II	C53F	1980	Ex Hoerty, Birkenhead, 1987
110	WVF635S	Bedford YMT	Duple Dominant	C53F	1977	Ex Keymer, Aylsham, 1990
111	JTL805V	Bedford YMT	Duple Dominant II Express	C53F	1979	Ex The Delaine, Bourne, 1989
112	GVF755T	Bedford YLQ	Duple Dominant II	C45F	1979	Ex Pullman, Norwich, 1982
113	HUX82V	Bedford YMT	Duple Dominant II Express	C53F	1980	Ex Bammant, Fakenham, 1992
114	JGU938V	Bedford YMT	Duple Dominant II	C53F	1979	Ex Goodwin, Stockport, 1988
115	CYD133S	Bedford YMT	Duple Dominant II	C53F	1977	Ex Spratt, Wreningham, 1990
116	D447PGH	Bedford YNV Venturer	Duple 320	C55F	1987	Ex McColl, Balloch, 1995
117	E787DNG	Freight Rover Sherpa	Crystals	M16	1989	
	SNT925H	Bedford VAL70	Plaxton Elite	C53F	1970	Ex Woolley, Llanedwen, 1994

Livery: White, light blue and orange

Previous Registrations:

259VYC	C954VAY	RJI8614	C444KGP
354TRT	MNM44V	SGF965	J503LGA
3990ME	F440DUG	SJI1615	DVY755S
APW942S	TPJ285S, BIL8949	SJI1616	FRR686V
BIL8430	KUM983V	SJI1617	NPV307W, PVF377
BIL8949	TND421X, RDV903	SJI1618	ORA688W
BWK9T	EAC877T	SJI1619	RJU259W
C134USS	C301UFP, CXI7390, C57USS	SJI1620	YAN814T, 3990ME
CYD133S	NHF333S, CJS447, APW668S, 259VYC	SJI1621	YAN822T, WDA521
DJI1594	A771HPY	SJI1622	SWP666V
FIL8693	TND408X, XRL923	SJI1623	JJU68V, 3367PP, FIL8693, NPW444W
GJI4481	A826LVF	SJI1624	HDB353V
GOE264V	LBM146V, MJI2367	SJI1625	YAN821T, SGF965
GVF755T	YJE9T	SJI1626	D342SWB
J7FTG	J457UFS	SJI1627	C115AFX
LAH817A	521FN	SJI1628	B283AMG
MIB9067	KHB14W	SJI1629	B918SPR
MIW3561	C789MVH	SJI1630	C294BVF
OGR647	E180TVG	SJI1631	D125VRM, 748COF, D410BDP
PJI5637	FTW131T	SJI1632	LCJ633Y
PJI7348	C514MWJ	SJI5629	RAY7W, UVY412
PJI8327	A604VAV	WSV503	E863LFL, RJI8613
PJI8328	A258SBM	WOA521	E511JWP
PVF377	D522WNV	WXI4253	PNM666W
RDV903	E221KFV	YJE9T	FDU807T
RJI8604	E440MSE	YVJ677	ORP204Y
RJI8607	E917EAY		

SEAMARKS

Seamarks Coach & Travel Ltd, Seamarks House, 387-397 Dunstable Road, Luton, Bedfordshire, LU4 8BY

182	EPP819Y	Bova EL26/581	Bova Europa	C53F	1982	
183	2267MK	Kässbohrer Setra S215HD	Kässbohrer Tornado	C49FT	1982	
192	HRO982V	Bedford YMT	Duple Dominant II	C53F	1979	Ex Kirby, High Wycombe, 1983
197	2917MK	Kässbohrer Setra S215HR	Kässbohrer Rational	C53F	1984	
198	Q684LPP	Kässbohrer Setra S215HU	Kässbohrer	C49FT	1984	
199	9569KM	Kässbohrer Setra S215HR	Kässbohrer Rational	C53F	1984	
200	MJI7855	Kässbohrer Setra S215H	Kässbohrer	C53F	1984	
201	MJI7856	Kässbohrer Setra S215H	Kässbohrer	C53F	1984	
202	MJI7857	Kässbohrer Setra S215H	Kässbohrer	C53F	1984	
205	B817BPP	Volvo B10M-61	Plaxton Paramount 3500 II	C57F	1985	
206	MJI8660	Volvo B10M-61	Plaxton Paramount 3500 II	C57F	1985	
207	MJI8661	Volvo B10M-61	Plaxton Paramount 3500 II	C57F	1985	
208	MJI8662	Volvo B10M-61	Plaxton Paramount 3500	C53F	1985	
209	MJI8663	Volvo B10M-61	Plaxton Paramount 3500	C53F	1985	
210	25CTM	Volvo C10M-70	Ramseier & Jenser	C49FT	1985	
211	MJI7854	Volvo B10M-61	Caetano Algarve	C53F	1985	
214	F791DWT	DAF SB220LC550	Optare Delta	B47F	1989	
215	F370BUA	DAF SB220LC550	Optare Delta	B51F	1988	Ex Optare demonstrator, 1989
219	G971TTM	DAF SB220LC550	Optare Delta	B47F	1989	

Kässbohrer Setra products are renowned for quality, the S215H being the most common model supplied to the UK. A later product in the 300 series is now built in left-hand drive format but right-hand drive models are not yet envisaged. However, an additional model, the S250 has recently been introduced to the UK market. Photographed on a school excursion is Seamark's MJI7856 an earlier S215. *BBP*

Seamarks operate four Optare Deltas on their Hertfordshire services. Seen heading for St Albans as it passes through Borehamwood is G278WKX. *Colin Lloyd*

220	G278WKX	DAF SB220LC550	Optare Delta	B47F	1989	
223	6101MV	Volvo C10M-70	Ramseier & Jenser	C49F	1986	Ex Park's, 1991
224	9683ML	Volvo C10M-70	Ramseier & Jenser	C49F	1986	Ex Park's, 1991
225	J208RVS	Optare MetroRider	Optare	B31F	1992	
226	H846UUA	MAN 11.190 HOCL	Optare Vecta	B41F	1991	Ex Optare demonstrator, 1992
227	D207MKK	Scania K92CRB	East Lancashire	B55F	1987	Ex Boro'line, 1992
228	D81NWW	Volkswagen LT55	Optare City Pacer	B25F	1987	Ex Lancaster, 1992
229	J367BNW	MAN 11.190 HOCL	Optare Vecta	B41F	1992	Ex Optare demonstrator, 1993
230	L834MWT	MAN 11.190 HOCL	Optare Vecta	B40F	1993	Ex Optare demonstrator, 1994
231	M702RVS	MAN 11.190 HOCL	Optare Vecta	B40F	1994	
232	M231SGS	Mercedes-Benz 709D	Marshall C19	B25F	1995	

Livery: White and green

Previous Registrations:

25CTM	from new	B817BPP	B541BMH, 9683ML	MJI8660	B542BMH
2267MK	from new	HRO982V	GTM141T	MJI8661	B543BMH
2917MK	A608RNM	MJI7854	B455AUR	MJI8662	B544BMH
6101MV	C651KDS	MJI7855	B265XNK	MJI8663	B545BMH
9569KM	A531STM	MJI7856	B266XNK	Q684LPP	?
9683ML	C345GSD	MJI7857	B267XNK		

In 1992 Seamarks added a Scania K92 bus to their fleet. East Lancashire-bodied D207MKK was previously with Boro'line of Maidstone and can now be seen on Hertfordshire services. It was photographed while parked in Hemel Hempstead bus station. *Ivor Norman*

Newly delivered into the Seamarks fleet for their 355 service is Mercedes-Benz 709D M231SGS, showing the latest version of Marshall's bodywork in this picture taken in St Albans. *BBP*

SEMMENCE

H Semmence & Co Ltd, 34 Norwich Road, Wymondham, Norfolk, NR18 0NS

NKE307P	Bedford YRT	Duple Dominant	B53F	1976	Ex Maidstone, 1982
RYL706R	Bedford YMT	Duple Dominant II	C49F	1977	Ex Grey-Green, 1982
VYU753S	Bedford YMT	Duple Dominant II	C53F	1978	Ex Grey-Green, 1982
VYU759S	Bedford YMT	Duple Dominant II	C53F	1978	Ex Dix, Dagenham, 1985
YYL791T	Bedford YMT	Duple Dominant II	C53F	1979	Ex Dix, Dagenham, 1984
JKV420V	Bedford YMT	Plaxton Supreme IV	C53F	1979	Ex Wood, Wickford, 1989
JKV422V	Bedford YMT	Plaxton Supreme IV	C53F	1979	Ex Clarke and Goodman, Pailton, 1986
EPH27V	Bedford YLQ	Duple Dominant	B52F	1979	Ex Tillingbourne, Cranleigh, 1985
JGV336V	Bedford YMT	Plaxton Supreme IV	C53F	1979	Ex Morley's Grey, West Row, 1985
ECT999V	Bedford YMT	Duple Dominant II	C53F	1980	Ex Wing, Sleaford, 1985
KNR310V	Bedford YMT	Duple Dominant II	C53F	1980	Ex Shelton-Orsborn, Wollaston, 1985
GWO111W	Bedford YMT	Plaxton Supreme IV	C53F	1980	Ex Hunt, Alford, 1986
NUF990W	Bedford YMT	Plaxton Supreme IV	C53F	1981	Ex Watts, Gillingham, 1986
TKV18W	Bedford YNT	Plaxton Supreme IV	C53F	1981	Ex Lambert, Beccles, 1987
OTO677W	Bedford YNT	Duple Dominant III	C57F	1981	Ex Bailey, Kirby-in-Ashfield, 1988
CBE882X	Bedford YNT	Plaxton Supreme IV Express	C53F	1981	Ex Enterprise & Silver Dawn, 1987
PTV597X	Bedford YNT	Plaxton Supreme IV Express	C53F	1981	Ex Gagg, Bunny, 1988
WAY456X	Bedford YNT	Duple Dominant III	C57F	1982	Ex Bexleyheath Transport, 1987
CKM140Y	Bedford YMT	Wright TT	B61F	1982	Ex Boro'line, 1992
CKM141Y	Bedford YMT	Wright TT	B61F	1982	Ex Boro'line, 1992
EUB552Y	Bedford YNT	Plaxton Paramount 3200	C53F	1982	Ex Dereham Coachways, 1990
OSU314	Bedford YNT	Plaxton Paramount 3200	C53F	1982	Ex Jamieson, Cullivoe, 1989
XBJ876	Bedford YNT	Plaxton Paramount 3200	C53F	1982	Ex Palmer, Dunstable, 1989
XNR997Y	Bedford YNT	Duple Dominant III	C57F	1983	Ex Torquay Travel, 1988
PVV312	Bova EL26/581	Bova Europa	C52F	1983	Ex Tourmaster, Loughborough, 1990
PVV313	Bova EL26/581	Bova Europa	C52F	1983	Ex County, Leicester, 1989
A266BTY	Bedford YNT	Plaxton Paramount 3200	C53F	1984	Ex Rochester & Marshall, 1992
A33UGA	Bova EL28/581	Duple Calypso	C57F	1984	Ex Henry Crawford, Neilston, 1990
149GJF	DAF SB2300DHS585	Plaxton Paramount 3200	C53F	1984	Ex Fleet Coaches, Fleet, 1992
A583MEH	Bova FLD12.250	Bova Futura	C53F	1984	Ex Stoddards, Cheadle, 1993
A301KFP	Bova FLD12.250	Bova Futura	C53F	1984	Ex Sykes, Appleton Roebuck, 1993
B512JJR	Bedford YNT	Plaxton Paramount 3200 II	C57F	1985	Ex Kerr, Wallsend, 1991
B513JJR	Bedford YNT	Plaxton Paramount 3200 II	C57F	1985	Ex Kerr, Wallsend, 1991
BXI3079	DAF SB2300DHS585	Plaxton Paramount 3500 II	C53F	1985	Ex Burgin, Sheffield, 1994
C72HDT	Bedford YNV Venturer	Plaxton Paramount 3200 II	C53F	1985	Ex Fourways, Leeds, 1992
D616YCX	DAF SB2300DHS585	Duple 340	C57F	1987	Ex Wilson, Carnwath, 1992
E218ARM	Mercedes-Benz 609D	Reeve Burgess Beaver	C20F	1988	Ex Stonebridge, Biggleswade, 1994
E677UND	Mercedes-Benz 609D	Made-to-Measure	C20F	1988	Ex Cunningham Carriage Co, 1994
RJI5723	Dennis Javelin 12SDA1907	Plaxton Paramount 3200 III	C53F	1988	Ex Baker, Weston-super-Mare, 1994
RJI5721	Dennis Javelin 12SDA1907	Plaxton Paramount 3200 III	C57F	1988	Ex Baker, Weston-super-Mare, 1994
G407DPD	Iveco Daily 49.10	Carlyle Dailybus 2	C21F	1989	Ex Metrobus, Orpington, 1994

Livery: Cream, orange and brown

Previous Registrations:

149GJF	A272KEL	OSU314	RPS380Y	RJI5721	F421PSE
A301KFP	WDL124, 124YTW	PVV312	JRO613Y	RJI5723	E761HJF
A583MEH	A866XOP, A10MPS	PVV313	JRO614Y	XBJ876	HBH422Y
BXI3079	B643OFP				

Shown here are a pair of coaches from the Semmence fleet. Above is one of the many Bedford products which still dominate the fleet typified by XNR997Y, a YNT with the distinctive sloping windows profile of the Duple Dominant III body design. In contrast is a similarly aged coach from Bova, PVV312, showing the Europa design of body. *David Donati*

THE SHIRES

LDT Ltd, Castle Street, Luton, Bedfordshire, LU1 3AJ

Depots and outstations: Amersham Old Town; Rabans Lane Industrial Estate, Smeaton Close, Aylesbury; Tavistock Street, Dunstable; Whiteleaf Road, Hemel Hempstead; Lincoln Road, Cressex Industrial Estate, High Wycombe; Fishponds Road, Hitchin; Plantation Road, Leighton Buzzard; Castle Street, Luton; Norton Green Road, Stevenage and St Albans Road, Garston, Watford.

A subsidiary of British Bus plc.

Coaches;

TP13	A113EPA	Leyland Tiger TRCTL11/2R	Plaxton Paramount 3200 E	C53F	1983	Ex London Country NW, 1991
TP15	A115EPA	Leyland Tiger TRCTL11/2R	Plaxton Paramount 3200 E	C53F	1983	Ex London Country NW, 1991
TP36	A136EPA	Leyland Tiger TRCTL11/2R	Plaxton Paramount 3200 E	C53F	1984	Ex London Country NW, 1991
BTL47	C147SPB	Leyland Tiger TRCTL11/3R	Berkhof Everest 370	C53F	1986	Ex London Country NW, 1991
BTL48	C148SPB	Leyland Tiger TRCTL11/3R	Berkhof Everest 370	C53F	1986	Ex London Country NW, 1991
BTL49	C149SPB	Leyland Tiger TRCTL11/3R	Berkhof Everest 370	C53F	1986	Ex London Country NW, 1991
TPL50	A150EPA	Leyland Tiger TRCTL11/3R	Plaxton Paramount 3200 E	C51F	1984	Ex London Country SW, 1989

TPL51-57		Leyland Tiger TRCTL11/3R	Plaxton Paramount 3200 E	C57F	1984	Ex London Country NW, 1991

51	A151EPA	**52**	A152EPA	**53**	A153EPA	**55**	A155EPA	**57**	A157EPA

TPL84	B284KPF	Leyland Tiger TRCTL11/3R	Plaxton Paramount 3200 IIE	C51F	1985	Ex London Country NW, 1991
TPL92	B292KPF	Leyland Tiger TRCTL11/3R	Plaxton Paramount 3200 IIE	C51F	1985	Ex London Country NW, 1991
TPL93	B293KPF	Leyland Tiger TRCTL11/3R	Plaxton Paramount 3200 IIE	C51F	1985	Ex London Country NW, 1991
TPL98	E323OMG	Leyland Tiger TRCTL11/3R	Plaxton Paramount 3200 III	C53F	1988	Ex London Country NW, 1991

The fleet numbering system used by The Shires is still influenced by the two previous systems inherited from Luton & District and London Country North West. We have arranged the vehicles here by type to try and separate some of the number duplication. Many coaches operate Green Line services. Seen in dedicated livery for the 797 Stevenage to London service is 135, IIL4579.
Colin Lloyd

Dedicated livery for the 757 service between Luton Airport, where this picture was taken, and London is worn by 193, GIL6949, a Volvo B10M with Plaxton Paramount 3200 body. *BBP*

109-113

109-113		Leyland Tiger TRCTL11/3RZ	Plaxton Paramount 3200 III	C53F	1988			
109	E881YKY	110	E882YKY	111	E661AWJ	112	E662AWJ	113	E663AWJ

119	C249SPC	Leyland Tiger TRCTL11/3RH	Duple 320	C53F	1986	Ex Sovereign, 1990
121	A121EPA	Leyland Tiger TRCTL11/2R	Plaxton Paramount 3200 E	C53F	1983	Ex London Country NW, 1991
TP128	A101EPA	Leyland Tiger TRCTL11/2R	Plaxton Paramount 3200 E	C53F	1983	Ex London Country NW, 1991
134	HIL7596	Dennis Javelin 11SDL1905	Duple 320	C49F	1988	Ex Rochester & Marshall, 1994
135	IIL4579	Dennis Javelin 11SDL1905	Duple 320	C53F	1988	Ex Rochester & Marshall, 1994
136	IIL4580	Dennis Javelin 11SDL1905	Duple 320	C53F	1988	Ex Rochester & Marshall, 1994
137	GIL8487	Dennis Javelin 11SDL1905	Duple 320	C53F	1988	Ex Rochester & Marshall, 1994
138	GIL8488	Dennis Javelin 11SDL1905	Duple 320	C53F	1988	Ex Rochester & Marshall, 1994
DJ139	429UFM	Dennis Javelin 11SDL1905	Duple 320	C53F	1988	Ex Crosville Wales, 1995
DJ140	430UFM	Dennis Javelin 11SDL1905	Duple 320	C53F	1988	Ex Crosville Wales, 1995
143	A143EPA	Leyland Tiger TRCTL11/3R	Plaxton Paramount 3200 E	C51F	1984	Ex London Country NW, 1991
191	SMY630X	Leyland Tiger TRCTL11/3R	Plaxton Supreme V	C53F	1982	Ex London Country NW, 1991
192	GIL6253	Volvo B10M-61	Plaxton Paramount 3200 III	C50F	1987	Ex Moor Dale, 1994
193	GIL6949	Volvo B10M-61	Plaxton Paramount 3200 III	C50F	1987	Ex Moor Dale, 1994
194	HIL7594	Volvo B10M-61	Plaxton Paramount 3500 III	C53F	1988	Ex Moor Dale, 1994
195	HIL7595	Volvo B10M-61	Plaxton Paramount 3500 III	C53F	1988	Ex Moor Dale, 1994
196	HIL7597	Volvo B10M-61	Plaxton Paramount 3500 III	C53F	1988	Ex Moor Dale, 1994
STL201	SIB8529	Leyland Tiger TRCL10/3ARZA	Plaxton Paramount 3200 III	C51F	1988	Ex London Country NW, 1991
STL202	SIB7480	Leyland Tiger TRCL10/3ARZA	Plaxton Paramount 3200 III	C51F	1988	Ex London Country NW, 1991
STL203	SIB7481	Leyland Tiger TRCL10/3ARZA	Plaxton Paramount 3500 III	C51FT	1988	Ex London Country NW, 1991
204	SIB4846	Leyland Tiger TRCL10/3ARZA	Plaxton Paramount 3200 III	C53F	1988	Ex London Country NW, 1991

Double-deck buses:

LRL29	G129YEV	Leyland Olympian ONCL10/2RZ	Northern Counties	H49/33F	1989	Ex London Country NW, 1991
LRL30	G130YEV	Leyland Olympian ONCL10/2RZ	Northern Counties	H49/33F	1989	Ex London Country NW, 1991
LRL31	G131YWC	Leyland Olympian ONCL10/2RZ	Northern Counties	H49/33F	1989	Ex Ensign, Purfleet, 1991
LRL32	G132YWC	Leyland Olympian ONCL10/2RZ	Northern Counties	H49/33F	1989	Ex London Country NW, 1991
LR33	A698EAU	Leyland Olympian ONTL11/1R	Northern Counties	H47/33D	1984	Ex Buffalo, Flitwick, 1995
LR34	A699EAU	Leyland Olympian ONTL11/1R	Northern Counties	H47/33D	1984	Ex Buffalo, Flitwick, 1995
LR35	F506OYW	Leyland Olympian ONTL11/1R	Northern Counties	H47/30F	1988	Ex Yellow Bus, Stoke Mandeville, 1995

Double deck buses with The Shires include Olympians, Atlanteans and Bristol VRs from the fleets of predecessors and several vehicles recently acquired from independents. The cover picture shows The Shires' livery on an Alexander-bodied Leyland Olympian acquired from A1 in 1995. Above is the former green livery seen on Atlantean 244, TRN470V seen in High Wycombe while below is a Roe-bodied Olympian LR49, A149FPG, in overall advert livery. *Richard Godfrey, Cover: Malc McDonald*

LR49-55

Leyland Olympian ONTL11/1R Roe H43/29F 1984 Ex London Country NW, 1991

49	A149FPG	52	A152FPG	53	A153FPG	54	A154FPG	55	A155FPG
51	A151FPG								

LR70	B270LPH	Leyland Olympian ONTL11/1R	Eastern Coach Works	H43/29F	1985	Ex London Country NW, 1991
LR71	B271LPH	Leyland Olympian ONTL11/1R	Eastern Coach Works	H43/29F	1985	Ex London Country NW, 1991
LR72	B272LPH	Leyland Olympian ONTL11/1R	Eastern Coach Works	H43/29F	1985	Ex London Country NW, 1991
LR73	B273LPH	Leyland Olympian ONTL11/1R	Eastern Coach Works	H43/29F	1985	Ex London Country NW, 1991

LR81-95

Leyland Olympian ONCL10/1RZ Leyland H47/31F 1989-90 Ex London Country NW, 1991

81	G281UMJ	84	G284UMJ	87	G287UMJ	90	G290UMJ	93	G293UMJ
82	G282UMJ	85	G285UMJ	88	G288UMJ	91	G291UMJ	94	G294UMJ
83	G283UMJ	86	G286UMJ	89	G289UMJ	92	G292UMJ	95	G295UMJ

LR96-102

Leyland Olympian ON2R50C13Z4 Leyland H47/29F 1991 Ex London Country NW, 1991

96	H196GRO	98	H198GRO	100	H201GRO	101	H202GRO	102	H203GRO
97	H197GRO	99	H199GRO						

LR103	F747XCS	Leyland Olympian ONCL10/1RZ	Alexander RL	H47/32F	1989	Ex A1 Service (McMenemy), 1995
AN195	XPG195T	Leyland Atlantean AN68A/1R	Roe	H43/30F	1979	Ex London Country NW, 1991

AN233-243

Leyland Atlantean AN68B/1R Roe H43/30F 1980 Ex London Country NW, 1991

233	JPE233V	236	JPE236V	239	KPJ239W	242	KPJ242W	243	KPJ243W
234	JPE234V	237	JPE237V	241	KPJ241W				

AN244	TRN470V	Leyland Atlantean AN68A/1R	Eastern Coach Works	H43/31F	1979	Ex Ribble, 1994
AN245	TRN477V	Leyland Atlantean AN68A/1R	Eastern Coach Works	H43/31F	1980	Ex Ribble, 1994
600	MUH284X	Leyland Olympian ONLXB/1R	Eastern Coach Works	H45/32F	1982	Ex Rhondda, 1995
601	MUH287X	Leyland Olympian ONLXB/1R	Eastern Coach Works	H45/32F	1982	Ex Rhondda, 1995

612-620

Leyland Olympian ONLXB/1R Eastern Coach Works H45/32F 1981-82 Ex United Counties, 1986

612	ARP612X	614	ARP614X	616	ARP616X	618	ARP618X	620	ARP620X
613	ARP613X	615	ARP615X	617	ARP617X	619	ARP619X		

633-644

Leyland Olympian ONCL10/1RZ Alexander RL H47/32F* 1988 *641 is DPH47/29F

633	F633LMJ	LR636	F636LMJ	639	F639LMJ	641	F641LMJ	643	F643LMJ
634	F634LMJ	637	F637LMJ	640	F640LMJ	642	F642LMJ	644	F644LMJ
635	F635LMJ	638	F638LMJ						

645-657

Leyland Olympian ON2R50C13Z4 Alexander RL H47/32F* 1989-90 *654 is DPH47/29F
649-53 are H47/34F

645	G645UPP	648	G648UPP	651	G651UPP	654	G654UPP	656	G656UPP
646	G646UPP	649	G649UPP	652	G652UPP	655	G655UPP	657	G657UPP
647	G647UPP	650	G650UPP	653	G653UPP				

661	A141DPE	Leyland Olympian ONTL11/1R	Roe	H43/29F	1983	Ex Sovereign, 1990
LR662	A142DPE	Leyland Olympian ONTL11/1R	Roe	H43/29F	1983	Ex Sovereign, 1990
663	A143DPE	Leyland Olympian ONTL11/1R	Roe	H43/29F	1983	Ex Sovereign, 1990
664	B262LPH	Leyland Olympian ONTL11/1R	Eastern Coach Works	H43/29F	1985	Ex Sovereign, 1990
665	BPF135Y	Leyland Olympian ONTL11/1R	Roe	H43/29F	1983	Ex Sovereign, 1990
666	BPF136Y	Leyland Olympian ONTL11/1R	Roe	H43/29F	1983	Ex Sovereign, 1990

779-800

Bristol VRT/SL2/6LX Eastern Coach Works H39/31F 1972-73 779-797 ex United Counties, 1986
798-800 ex Milton Keynes City Bus, 1987

779	CBD779K	797	JRP797L	798	JRP798L	799	JRP799L	800	JRP800L
796	JRP796L								

802-833

Bristol VRT/SL2/6LX Eastern Coach Works H43/31F 1974-75 Ex United Counties, 1986

802	PRP802M	804	PRP804M	812	RRP812M	823	GNV332N	833	HRP673N
803	PRP803M	805	PRP805M	815	RRP815M	825	GNV334N		

837	LBD837P	Bristol VRT/SL3/6LX	Eastern Coach Works	H43/31F	1975	Ex United Counties, 1986
841	KKY841P	Bristol VRT/SL3/501	Eastern Coach Works	H43/34F	1976	Ex RoadCar, 1986

Displaying number 971 in The Shires fleet is THX481S, a former London Buses Leyland Fleetline latterly operating for Stuart Palmer Travel whose local services were acquired late in 1994. *Richard Godfrey*

MCW30, E731DNM is an MCW MetroRider now painted in the latest blue and yellow livery for the *network Watford* operation. Photographed at Watford Junction rail station, it is seen departing on service W21 for South Oxhey. *Richard Godfrey*

851-904 — Bristol VRT/SL3/6LXB — Eastern Coach Works — H43/31F — 1976-78 Ex United Counties, 1986

851	OVV851R	864	TNH864R	874	WBD874S	894	YVV894S	899	CBD899T
852	OVV852R	865	TNH865R	877	WBD877S	895	YVV895S	900	CBD900T
853	OVV853R	866	TNH866R	892	YVV892S	897	CBD897T	904	CBD904T
855	OVV855R	867	TNH867R	893	YVV893S	898	CBD898T		

913	HBD913T	Bristol VRT/SL3/6LXB	Eastern Coach Works	H43/31F	1979	Ex Milton Keynes City Bus, 1987
VR916	OCY916R	Bristol VRT/SL3/501	Eastern Coach Works	H43/31F	1977	Ex South Wales, 1987
VR917	RTH917S	Bristol VRT/SL3/501	Eastern Coach Works	H43/31F	1977	Ex South Wales, 1987
918	HBD918T	Bristol VRT/SL3/6LXB	Eastern Coach Works	DPH40/28F	1979	Ex United Counties, 1986

925-960 — Bristol VRT/SL3/6LXB — Eastern Coach Works — H43/31F* — 1980-81 Ex United Counties, 1986
*955 is DPH40/28F

925	ONH925V	932	SNV932W	938	SNV938W	951	VVV951W	957	VVV957W
928	ONH928V	933	SNV933W	946	URP946W	955	VVV955W	960	VVV960W
929	ONH929V	934	SNV934W	947	URP947W	956	VVV956W		

961	OUD483T	Bristol VRT/SL3/6LXB	Eastern Coach Works	H43/27D	1978	Ex Stuart Palmer, 1995
962	OUD484T	Bristol VRT/SL3/6LXB	Eastern Coach Works	H43/27D	1978	Ex Stuart Palmer, 1995
963	OUD485T	Bristol VRT/SL3/6LXB	Eastern Coach Works	H43/27D	1978	Ex Stuart Palmer, 1995
964	OJD363R	Leyland Fleetline FE30ALRSp	Park Royal	H44/24D	1977	Ex Stuart Palmer, 1995
965	OJD425R	Leyland Fleetline FE30ALRSp	Park Royal	H44/24D	1977	Ex Stuart Palmer, 1995
966	THX312S	Leyland Fleetline FE30ALRSp	MCW	H44/24D	1978	Ex Stuart Palmer, 1995
967	THX332S	Leyland Fleetline FE30ALRSp	MCW	H44/24D	1978	Ex Stuart Palmer, 1995
969	THX345S	Leyland Fleetline FE30ALRSp	MCW	H44/24D	1978	Ex Stuart Palmer, 1995
970	THX480S	Leyland Fleetline FE30ALRSp	Park Royal	H44/24D	1977	Ex Stuart Palmer, 1995
971	THX481S	Leyland Fleetline FE30ALRSp	Park Royal	H44/24D	1977	Ex Stuart Palmer, 1995
973	THX525S	Leyland Fleetline FE30ALRSp	Park Royal	H44/24D	1978	Ex Stuart Palmer, 1995
974	THX560S	Leyland Fleetline FE30ALRSp	Park Royal	H44/27D	1978	Ex Stuart Palmer, 1995
975	OJD368R	Leyland Fleetline FE30ALRSp	Park Royal	H44/24D	1977	Ex Stuart Palmer, 1995
976	OJD261R	Leyland Fleetline FE30ALRSp	MCW	H44/24D	1977	Ex Stuart Palmer, 1995

Minibuses

MCW1-32 — MCW MetroRider MF150/81* — MCW — B23F — 1988 Ex London Country NW, 1991
*MCW19-30 are MF150/83; MCW31/2 are MF150/72

1	E971DNK	7	E977DNK	15	E985DNK	21	E991DNK	27	E997DNK
2	E972DNK	8	E978DNK	16	E986DNK	22	E992DNK	28	E998DNK
3	E973DNK	9	E979DNK	17	E987DNK	23	E993DNK	29	E999DNK
4	E974DNK	10	E980DNK	18	E988DNK	24	E994DNK	30	E731DNM
5	E975DNK	11	E981DNK	19	E989DNK	25	E995DNK	31	E478CNM
6	E976DNK	14	E984DNK	20	E990DNK	26	E996DNK	32	E479CNM

MCW33	E486CNM	MCW MetroRider MF150/74	MCW	B23F	1987	Ex Sovereign, 1990
MCW34	E484CNM	MCW MetroRider MF150/72	MCW	B23F	1987	Ex Sovereign, 1990

MBI52-63 — Iveco Daily 49.10 — Robin Hood City Nippy — B21F — 1987 Ex London Country NW, 1991

52	D495RNM	55	D498RNM	61	D26RPP	62	D25RPP	63	D23RPP
54	D497RNM	60	D472RVS						

1	K8BUS	Mercedes-Benz 811D	Wright	B33F	1993	Ex Patterson, Birmingham, 1995
2	K580YOJ	Mercedes-Benz 811D	Wright	B33F	1993	Ex Patterson, Birmingham, 1995
3	H35DGD	Mercedes-Benz 811D	Dormobile Routemaker	B33F	1991	Ex Pathfinder, Newark, 1995
4	G896TGG	Mercedes-Benz 811D	Reeve Burgess Beaver	B33F	1990	Ex Stevensons, 1995

6-14 — Mercedes-Benz 709D — Reeve Burgess Beaver — B25F — 1988-91 6-11 ex Kentish Bus, 1991
12-14 ex Argyll Bus & Coach, 1992

6	F121TRU	8	F123TRU	10	F125TRU	12	J917HGD	14	F598CET
7	F122TRU	9	F124TRU	11	F128TRU	13	H848AUS		

15-21 — Mercedes-Benz 709D — Made-to-Measure — B24F — 1992 Ex Birmingham Omnibus, Tividale, 1995

15	K25WND	17	K27WND	19	K29WND	20	K31WND	21	K32WND
16	K26WND	18	K28WND						

No.	Reg	Type	Body	Seat	Year	Notes
ML18	L326AUT	Mercedes-Benz 709D	Leicester Carriage Builders	B25F	1994	Ex Midland Fox, 1994
ML19	L327AUT	Mercedes-Benz 709D	Leicester Carriage Builders	B25F	1994	Ex Midland Fox, 1994
ML20	L328AUT	Mercedes-Benz 709D	Leicester Carriage Builders	B25F	1994	Ex Midland Fox, 1994
23	H408BVR	Mercedes-Benz 709D	Reeve Burgess Beaver	B25F	1990	Ex Starline, Knutsford, 1995
24	H409BVR	Mercedes-Benz 709D	Reeve Burgess Beaver	B25F	1990	Ex Starline, Knutsford, 1995
25	K579YOJ	Mercedes-Benz 709D	Dormobile Routemaker	B29F	1993	Ex Patterson, Birmingham, 1995
26	K543OGA	Mercedes-Benz 811D	Dormobile Routemaker	B29F	1992	Ex ??, 1995
27	H641UWE	Mercedes-Benz 814D	Europa Enterprise	B31F	1991	Ex Buffalo, Flitwick, 1995
28	H614CGG	Mercedes-Benz 709D	Dormobile Routemaker	B33F	1991	Ex Pathfinder, Newark, 1995
29	K578YOJ	Mercedes-Benz 709D	Dormobile Routemaker	B29F	1993	Ex Patterson, Birmingham, 1995
30	K202FEH	Mercedes-Benz 709D	Dormobile Routemaker	B27F	1993	Ex Stevensons, 1995
31	K203FEH	Mercedes-Benz 709D	Dormobile Routemaker	B27F	1993	Ex Stevensons, 1995
32	H642UWE	Mercedes-Benz 811D	Europa Enterprise	B31F	1991	Ex Buffalo, Flitwick, 1995
33	G58BEL	Mercedes-Benz 811D	Wadham Stringer Wessex	DP31F	1989	Ex Buffalo, Flitwick, 1995
34	H231KBH	Mercedes-Benz 709D	Carlyle	B27F	1992	Ex Buffalo, Flitwick, 1995
36	H523SWE	Mercedes-Benz 709D	Whittaker Europa	B29F	1990	Ex Rhondda, 1995

38-42   Iveco Daily 49.10   Robin Hood City Nippy   B19F   1986

38	D755MUR	**39**	D756MUR	**40**	D757MUR	**41**	D758MUR	**42**	D759MUR

43	E454TYG	Iveco Daily 49.10	Robin Hood City Nippy	B23F	1988	Ex Harrogate & District, 1992

44-53   Iveco Daily 49.10   Robin Hood City Nippy   B19F   1986

44	D761MUR	**46**	D763MUR	**48**	D765MUR	**51**	D768MUR	**53w**	D770MUR
45	D762MUR	**47**	D764MUR	**50**	D767MUR	**52w**	D769MUR		

56	D499RNW	Iveco Daily 49.10	Robin Hood City Nippy	B21F	1987	Ex United Counties, 1994
57	E48MRP	Iveco Daily 49.10	Robin Hood City Nippy	B23F	1988	Ex United Counties, 1994
58	D21RPP	Iveco Daily 49.10	Robin Hood City Nippy	B21F	1987	Ex United Counties, 1994
59	D934EBP	Iveco Daily 49.10	Robin Hood City Nippy	B19F	1986	Ex United Counties, 1994

60-78   Iveco Daily 49.10   Dormobile   B25F*   1988   *77/8 are DP25F

60	E338DRO	**65**	E336DRO	**69**	E335DRO	**73**	E344DRO	**76**	E347DRO
62	E340DRO	**66**	E331DRO	**70**	E341DRO	**74**	E345DRO	**77**	E348DRO
63	E334DRO	**67**	E332DRO	**71**	E342DRO	**75**	E346DRO	**78**	E349DRO
64	E337DRO	**68**	E333DRO	**72**	E343DRO				

99-104   Iveco Daily 49.10   Robin Hood City Nippy   B21F   1986   Ex London Buses, 1993

99	C509DYM	**101**	D519FYL	**102**	C502DYM	**103**	C503DYM	**104**	TC504DYM
100	C506DYM								

106	E64BVS	Iveco Daily 49.10	Robin Hood City Nippy	B25F	1988	Ex East Midland, 1994
107	E66BVS	Iveco Daily 49.10	Robin Hood City Nippy	B25F	1988	Ex United Counties, 1994

IV150-160   Iveco TurboDaily 59-12   Marshall C31   B27F   1994   *IV150/1 are B29F

IV150	M150RBH	**152**	M152RBH	**154**	M154RBH	**157**	M157RBH	**159**	M159RBH
IV151	M151RBH	**153**	M153RBH	**156**	M156RBH	**158**	M158RBH	**160**	M160RBH

161	F269CEY	Iveco Daily 49.10	Robin Hood City Nippy	B21F	1988	Ex Crosville Wales, 1994
162	F251ACC	Iveco Daily 49.10	Robin Hood City Nippy	B21F	1988	Ex Crosville Wales, 1994
163	F268CEY	Iveco Daily 49.10	Robin Hood City Nippy	B21F	1988	Ex Crosville Wales, 1994
164	F634UEF	Iveco Daily 49.10	Carlyle Dailybus 2	B23F	1989	Ex OK Travel, 1994
165	F657KNL	Iveco Daily 49.10	Carlyle Dailybus 2	B23F	1989	Ex OK Travel, 1994
166	F660KNL	Iveco Daily 49.10	Carlyle Dailybus 2	B23F	1989	Ex OK Travel, 1994
167	F554TLW	Iveco Daily 49.10	Robin Hood City Nippy	B25F	1989	Ex R&I, Park Royal, 1994
169	L863BEA	Iveco Daily 49.10	Marshall	B23F	1993	Ex Buffalo, Flitwick, 1994
170	L864BEA	Iveco Daily 49.10	Marshall	B23F	1993	Ex Buffalo, Flitwick, 1994
173	F969GKJ	Iveco Daily 49.10	Robin Hood City Nippy	B21F	1989	Ex Buffalo, Flitwick, 1994
174	F287FGL	Iveco Daily 49.10	Carlyle Dailybus 2	B23F	1988	Ex Buffalo, Flitwick, 1994

Opposite: **The Shires fleet is gradually gaining the new blue and yellow livery with priority being given to recently acquired vehicles and new deliveries. Examples to show the scheme are 25, K579YOJ a Mercedes-Benz with *Luton & Dunstable* names and DC3, H925LOX a Dennis Dart with *network Watford* names and showing the continued use of class lettering at Watford, Hemel and High Wycombe depots.** *Colin Lloyd/Richard Godfrey*

Two Plaxton-bodied Darts joined the fleet in 1992 and given DC classification. DC14, K447XPA though allocated to Watford is seen at St Albans bound for Dunstable during the hot 1995 summer.

175	K184GDU	Mercedes-Benz 811D	Wright	B31F	1993	Ex Yellow Bus, Stoke Mandeville, 1995
176	J171GGG	Mercedes-Benz 709D	Dormobile Routemaker	B29F	1991	Ex Yellow Bus, Stoke Mandeville, 1995
177	G360FOP	Mercedes-Benz 709D	Carlyle	B25F	1989	Ex Yellow Bus, Stoke Mandeville, 1995

178-200

		Mercedes-Benz 709D		Plaxton Beaver		B25F		1995	

178	M38WUR	180	M41WUR	182	M43WUR	184	M46WUR	185	M47WUR
179	M39WUR	181	M42WUR	183	M45WUR				

Midi-buses

DC1-8

		Dennis Dart 9.8SDL3004		Carlyle Dartline		B40F		1990	Ex London Country NW, 1991

1	H922LOX	3	H925LOX	5	H242MUK	7	H244MUK	8	H245MUK
2	H923LOX	4	H926LOX	6	H243MUK				

DW9-13

		Dennis Dart 9.8SDL3054		Wright Handy-bus		B40F		1994	

9	M247SPP	10	M248SPP	11	M249SPP	12	M250SPP	13	M251SPP

DC14	K447XPA	Dennis Dart 9.8SDL3017	Plaxton Pointer	B40F	1992	Ex Buffalo, Flitwick, 1995
DC15	K448XPA	Dennis Dart 9.8SDL3017	Plaxton Pointer	B40F	1992	Ex Buffalo, Flitwick, 1995

305-336

		Volvo B6-9.9M		Northern Counties Paladin		B40F		1994	

305	L305HPP	VN312	L312HPP	VN319	M719OMJ	VN325	M725OMJ	331	M711OMJ
306	L306HPP	VN313	L313HPP	VN320	M720OMJ	VN326	M726OMJ	332	M712OMJ
307	L307HPP	VN314	L314HPP	VN321	M721OMJ	VN327	M727OMJ	333	M713OMJ
308	L308HPP	VN315	L315HPP	VN322	M722OMJ	328	M728OMJ	334	M714OMJ
309	L309HPP	VN316	L316HPP	VN323	M723OMJ	329	M729OMJ	335	M715OMJ
VN310	L310HPP	VN317	M717OMJ	VN324	M724OMJ	330	M710OMJ	336	M716OMJ
VN311	L311HPP	VN318	M718OMJ						

337	L43MEH	Volvo B6-9.9M	Plaxton Pointer	B40F	1994	Ex Stevensons, 1994
VN338	L922LJO	Volvo B6-9.9M	Northern Counties Paladin	B40F	1994	Ex Yellow Bus, Stoke Mandeville, 1995
VN339	L923LJO	Volvo B6-9.9M	Northern Counties Paladin	B40F	1994	Ex Yellow Bus, Stoke Mandeville, 1995

Photographed in Dunstable is Leyland Lynx 410, H410ERO. The fleet contains thirteen Lynx of which nine are based at Stevenage, one at Aylesbury and three, including 410, at Luton. *Colin Lloyd*

Single-deck buses

LN69	NPD169L	Leyland National 1151/1R/0402		DP21DL	1973	Ex London Country NW, 1991
300	F300MNK	Leyland Swift LBM6T/2RA	Wadham Stringer Vanguard II B35F		1989	
301	F301MNK	Leyland Swift LBM6T/2RA	Wadham Stringer Vanguard II B35F		1989	
302	F302MNK	Leyland Swift LBM6T/2RA	Wadham Stringer Vanguard II B35F		1989	
303	F303MNK	Leyland Swift LBM6T/2RA	Wadham Stringer Vanguard II B35F		1989	
304	G97VMM	Leyland Swift LBM6T/2RS	Wadham Stringer Vanguard II B39F		1989	Ex London Country NW, 1990
350	L133HVS	Volvo B10B-58	Alexander Strider	B51F	1993	Ex Buffalo, Flitwick, 1995
351	F314RMH	Volvo B10M-56	Plaxton Derwent II	B54F	1988	Ex Buffalo, Flitwick, 1995
352	F151KGS	Volvo B10M-56	Plaxton Derwent II	B54F	1988	Ex Buffalo, Flitwick, 1995
353	F152KGS	Volvo B10M-56	Plaxton Derwent II	B54F	1988	Ex Buffalo, Flitwick, 1995
354	F153KGS	Volvo B10M-56	Plaxton Derwent II	B54F	1988	Ex Buffalo, Flitwick, 1995
355	NIB8459	Volvo B10M-61	East Lancs EL2000(1992)	B55F	1988	Ex Buffalo, Flitwick, 1995
356	URY598	Volvo B10M-61	East Lancs EL2000(1992)	B55F	1985	Ex Buffalo, Flitwick, 1995
357	HIL7467	Volvo B10M-61	East Lancs EL2000(1991)	B55F	1983	Ex Buffalo, Flitwick, 1995
358	RDS83W	Volvo B58-56	Duple Dominant	B53F	1980	Ex Buffalo, Flitwick, 1995
359	RDS84W	Volvo B58-56	Duple Dominant	B53F	1980	Ex Buffalo, Flitwick, 1995
360	GHB574V	Volvo B58-61	East Lancs EL2000(1994)	B53F	1980	Ex Parfitt's, 1995

400-404 Leyland Lynx LX112L10ZR1R   Leyland Lynx   B51F   1989

400	F400PUR	**401**	F401PUR	**402**	F402PUR	**403**	F403PUR	**404** F404PUR

405	D603ACW	Leyland Lynx LX112L10ZR1R	Leyland Lynx	B51F	1987	Ex Sovereign, 1990
406	E970NMK	Leyland Lynx LX112TL11ZR1S	Leyland Lynx	B49F	1987	Ex Sovereign, 1990
407	H407ERO	Leyland Lynx LX2R11C15Z4S	Leyland Lynx	DP29F	1990	
408	H408ERO	Leyland Lynx LX2R11C15Z4S	Leyland Lynx	DP29F	1990	
409	H409ERO	Leyland Lynx LX2R11C15Z4S	Leyland Lynx	DP29F	1990	
410	H410ERO	Leyland Lynx LX2R11C15Z4S	Leyland Lynx	DP45F	1990	
416	UPB316S	Leyland National 10351A/1R		B41F	1977	Ex Sovereign, 1990

Smartly turned out with an example of *the Stevenage line* names is 420, F155KGS, a Leyland Swift with Wadham Stringer's Vanguard body. Previously with Buffalo it was allocated to Hitchin on the acquisition of the bus services of that operator. *BBP*

417	E969PME	Leyland Lynx LX112L10ZR1R	Leyland Lynx	B49F	1988	Ex Atlas Bus, Harlesden, 1994
418	E970PME	Leyland Lynx LX112L10ZR1R	Leyland Lynx	B49F	1988	Ex Atlas Bus, Harlesden, 1994
419	F154KGS	Leyland Swift LBM6T/2RA	Wadham Stringer Vanguard II B39F		1988	Ex Buffalo, Flitwick, 1995
420	F155KGS	Leyland Swift LBM6T/2RA	Wadham Stringer Vanguard II B39F		1988	Ex Buffalo, Flitwick, 1995
422	E966PME	Leyland Lynx LX112L10ZR1R	Leyland Lynx	B49F	1988	Ex Yellow Bus, Stoke Mandeville, 1995
423	E965PME	Leyland Lynx LX112L10ZR1R	Leyland Lynx	B49F	1988	Ex Yellow Bus, Stoke Mandeville, 1995
SN328	UPB328S	Leyland National 10351A/1R		B41F	1977	Ex London Country NW, 1991
SN343	UPB343S	Leyland National 10351A/1R		B41F	1977	Ex London Country NW, 1991
SN368	YPF768T	Leyland National 10351A/1R		B41F	1978	Ex London Country NW, 1991
SN370	YPF770T	Leyland National 10351A/1R		B41F	1978	Ex London Country NW, 1991

SN396-458

SN396-458		Leyland National 10351B/1R				B41F		1978-79	Ex London Country NW, 1991
396	YPL396T	410	YPL410T	424	YPL424T	441	YPL441T	454	YPL454T
398	YPL398T	415	YPL415T	426	YPL426T	446	YPL446T	456	YPL456T
404	YPL404T	417	YPL417T	434	YPL434T	449	YPL449T	457	YPL457T
405	YPL405T	418	YPL418T	436	YPL436T	451	YPL451T	458	YPL458T
409	YPL409T	421	YPL421T	438	YPL438T				

437	UPB337S	Leyland National 10351A/1R	B41F	1978	Ex Sovereign, 1990
441	UPB341S	Leyland National 10351A/1R	B41F	1977	Ex Sovereign, 1990
466	RYG766R	Leyland National 11351A/1R	B52F	1977	Ex Sovereign, 1990
LN468	ORP468M	Leyland National 1151/1R/0401	B49F	1974	Ex Milton Keynes City Bus, 1986
469	YPF769T	Leyland National 10351A/1R	B41F	1978	Ex Sovereign, 1990

SN460-473

SN460-473		Leyland National 10351B/1R				B41F		1979	Ex London Country NW, 1991
460	BPL460T	464	BPL464T	467	BPL467T	469	BPL469T	471	BPL471T
462	BPL462T	465	BPL465T	468	BPL468T	470	BPL470T	473	BPL473T
463	BPL463T	466	BPL466T						

485-513 — Leyland National 11351/1R — B49F — 1974-76

485	RNV485M	488	GNV655N	491	GNV658N	LN498	GVV889N	513	KNV513P
486	GNV653N	489	GNV656N	LN493	GNV660N	509	KNV509P		

SN501-523 — Leyland National 10351B/1R — B41F* — 1979 — Ex London Country NW, 1991 *514/5 are DP41F

501	DPH501T	512	EPD512V	515	EPD515V	521	EPD521V	523	EPD523V
505	EPD505V	514	EPD514V	517	EPD517V				

518-579 — Leyland National 11351A/1R — B49F* — 1976-79 *548 is DP47FL
Ex United Counties, 1986; 531/72/3 ex Milton Keynes City Bus, 1987
532 rebuilt to East Lancs Greenway, 1994

518	OVV518R	533	VRP533S	545	BVV545T	563	KRP563V	573	MNH573V
519	OVV519R	537	XVV537S	547	BVV547T	565	KRP565V	574	MNH574V
523	SBD523R	538	XVV538S	548	BVV548T	566	KRP566V	577	MNH577V
524	SBD524R	539	XVV539S	550	ERP550T	569	MNH569V	578	MNH578V
531	VRP531S	542	BVV542T	560	KRP560V	572	MNH572V	579	MNH579V
532	VRP532S								

SN524	IIL4821	Leyland National 10351/1R/SC(6HLX)# East Lancs Greenway (1993)	B41F	1974	Ex Crosville Wales, 1995
SN525	IIL4822	Leyland National 10351/1R/SC(6HLX)# East Lancs Greenway (1993)	B41F	1976	Ex Crosville Wales, 1995
SN526	IIL4823	Leyland National 10351B/1R(6HLX)# East Lancs Greenway (1993)	B41F	1978	Ex Crosville Wales, 1995
SN527	IIL4824	Leyland National 10351/1R(6HLX)# East Lancs Greenway (1993)	B41F	1975	Ex Crosville Wales, 1995
SN528	BAZ6869	Leyland National 10351B/1R(6HLX)# East Lancs Greenway (1994)	B41F	1979	Ex Crosville Wales, 1995
SN529	RJI6861	Leyland National 10351B/1R(6HLX)# East Lancs Greenway (1994)	B41F	1979	Ex Crosville Wales, 1995
SN534	TIB4886	Leyland National 10351/1R(6HLX)# East Lancs Greenway (1993)	B41F	1975	Ex Crosville Wales, 1995
SN535	RJI6862	Leyland National 10351B/1R(6HLX)# East Lancs Greenway (1994)	B41F	1979	Ex Crosville Wales, 1995
SN536	TIB4873	Leyland National 10351B/1R(6HLX)# East Lancs Greenway (1993)	B41F	1979	Ex Crosville Wales, 1995
SN540	BTX152T	Leyland National 10351A/2R(6HLX)# East Lancs Greenway (1994)	B44F	1979	Ex Parfitts, 1995
581	NRP581V	Leyland National 2 NL116L11/1R	B49F	1980	
588	SVV588W	Leyland National 2 NL116L11/1R	B49F	1980	

Livery: Blue and yellow
Green Line: BTL48/9, TDL57, TP13/5,21,36, TPL50-98
Jetlink: BTL47; School bus: 795-812

Previous Registrations:
To follow!

On order: 2 MB 811D/Plaxton; 27 MB 709D/Plaxton; 23 Scania L113/East Lancashire; 25 Dennis Lance SLF

Another vehicle from the Buffalo fleet is 355, NIB8459, a Volvo B10M which was re-bodied by East Lancashire in 1992. The EL2000 style body is shown carrying *Luton & Dunstable* names and the vehicle is based at Dunstable. It was photographed in Midsummer Boulevard, Milton Keynes in August 1995. *Colin Lloyd*

Two vehicles from the Simmonds fleet are seen here. Above is A818XMK, with a MAN chassis and a Reeve Burgess Riviera coach body. The vehicle has been withdrawn since this picture was taken at Epsom on Derby Day. Below is F305RMH, one of four Volvo B10Ms operating with Simmonds, all of which carry Plaxton Paramount bodywork. It is seen in Parliament Square, London. *BBP*

SHOREY

E C J Shorey, 28 Ampthill Road, Flitwick, Bedfordshire MK45 1BT

Depot: Clophill Road, Maulden,

GHV999N	Daimler Fleetline CRL6	Park Royal	H44/27D	1974	Ex Ensign, Purfleet, 1986
DDA66	Daimler Fleetline CRL6	MCW	H45/32F	1975	Ex London Transport, 1984
GHV51N	Daimler Fleetline CRL6	Park Royal	H44/32F	1975	Ex Pathfinder, Chadwell Heath, 1987
OJD357R	Leyland Fleetline FE30ALR	Park Royal	H44/24D	1977	Ex London Buses, 1991
THX580S	Leyland Fleetline FE30ALR	Park Royal	H44/27D	1978	Ex London Buses, 1992
BNO670T	Leyland National 11351A/1R		B49F	1978	Ex Thamesway, 1995
17EJU	Volvo B10M-61	Van Hool Astral	CH47/10DT	1984	
PIA892	Volvo B10M-53	Berkhof Emperor 395	CH47/11FT	1984	Ex The Kings Ferry, Gillingham, 1993
SIB6441	LAG G355Z	LAG Panoramic	C49FT	1988	

Livery: White

Named Vehicles: 17 EJU *Lady Donna*

Previous Registrations:

17EJL	From new	PIA892	B570YJN	
DDA66	GHM893N	SIB6441	E672NNV	

SIMMONDS

Simmonds Coaches Ltd, 9 Broadwater Avenue, Letchworth, Hertfordshire, SG6 3HE

Depot: Norton Way North, Letchworth.

KUC948P	Daimler Fleetline CRL6	MCW	H44/24D	1975	Ex London Transport, 1984
KJD89P	Leyland Fleetline FE30ALR	Park Royal	H44/24D	1976	Ex London Transport, 1983
RHD660X	Volvo B58-56	Duple Dominant	C51F	1982	Ex Blue Link, Dallington, 1985
XGS763X	Leyland Leopard PSU5D/4R	Plaxton Supreme IV	C51F	1982	Ex Ebdon, Sidcup, 1983
A819XMK	Volvo B10M-61	Plaxton Paramount 3500	C53F	1984	
C326DND	Volvo B10M-61	Van Hool Alizée	C53F	1986	Ex Shearings, 1992
C117EMG	Volvo B10M-61	Plaxton Paramount 3200 II	C57F	1986	
E339MMM	Van Hool T809H	Van Hool Alicron	C32F	1988	Ex North Mymms, Potters Bar, 1992
F305RMH	Volvo B10M-61	Plaxton Paramount 3200 III	C57F	1988	
F183UEE	Mercedes-Benz 408D	Coachcraft	M15	1989	
G104SVM	Mazda E2200	Made-to-Measure	M14	1990	
J61NTM	Volvo B10M-60	Plaxton Paramount 3500 III	C53F	1991	
L355HFU	Mercedes-Benz 814D	Auto Classique 2	C33F	1993	
L980CRY	Toyota Coaster HZB50R	Caetano Optimo III	C21F	1994	
M136SKY	Volvo B10M-62	Van Hool Alizée	C53F	1995	

Livery: White, blue and red

Two vehicles from the Simonds of Botesdale fleet are seen here earning their keep. Above is 256JPA, a Plaxton Paramount 3500 based on a Volvo B10M while below is a similar mid-engined chassis this time with a Van Hool Alizée body. The Van Hool factory is located in Lier, Belgium and produced many buses for the home market as well as coaches. *Colin Lloyd*

SIMONDS

Simonds of Botesdale Ltd, The Garage, Botesdale, Diss, Norfolk, IP22 1BX

Depots: The Garage, Botesdale; Victoria Road, Diss and Harleston.

RBJ46R	Bedford YMT	Plaxton Derwent	B66F	1976	
TPV41R	Ford R1114	Plaxton Supreme III Express	C53F	1977	Ex Bickers, Coddenham, 1983
PFL435R	Ford R1114	Plaxton Supreme III	C53F	1977	Ex Duncan, Sawtry, 1983
UUX360S	Ford R1114	Plaxton Supreme III	C49F	1977	Ex Salopia, Whitchurch, 1983
CPV2T	Ford R1114	Plaxton Supreme III	C53F	1978	Ex Bickers, Coddenham, 1983
MBT551T	Ford R1114	Plaxton Supreme III	C53F	1978	Ex Rydal, Richmond, 1984
XVA545T	Ford R1114	Plaxton Supreme IV	C53F	1979	Ex Safford, Little Gransden, 1984
FDX270T	Bedford YMT	Duple Dominant II	B63F	1979	
HIB664	Bedford YMT	Plaxton Supreme IV	C53F	1979	Ex private owner, 1992
XCG264V	Ford T152	Plaxton Supreme IV	C33F	1979	Ex Summerbee, Southampton, 1983
RLJ93X	Bedford YNT	Plaxton Supreme IV	C53F	1981	Ex Amport & District, Thruxton, 1986
460UEV	Bedford YNT	Plaxton Supreme V	C53F	1981	Ex Kiddle, St Ives, 1990
LTG276X	Ford R1114	Plaxton Supreme	C53F	1981	Ex Capitol, Cwmbran, 1984
WDX663X	Ford R1114	Plaxton Supreme VI Express	C53F	1982	
XJO46	Bedford YNT	Plaxton Supreme VI Express	C53F	1982	Ex Cornishman, Wadebridge, 1985
JGV929	Bedford YMT	Plaxton Supreme IV	C53F	1982	Ex Sovereign, Eye, 1992
166UMB	Bedford YNT	Plaxton Supreme V Express	C53F	1982	Ex Chapel End, Nuneaton, 1986
TCF496	Bedford YNT	Plaxton Supreme V	C53F	1982	Ex Freeman, Uffington, 1988
TVG397	Bedford YNT	Plaxton Paramount 3200 E	C53F	1983	Ex Davies Bros, Pencader, 1986
SIA488	Volvo B10M-61	Plaxton Paramount 3500	C53F	1983	Ex Berkeley, Paulton, 1993
YVF158	Bedford YNT	Plaxton Paramount 3200	C53F	1983	Ex Glennie, Newmachar, 1989
538ELX	Bedford YNV Venturer	Plaxton Paramount 3200 II	DP69F	1985	
4512UR	Bedford YNT	Plaxton Paramount 3200 II	C53F	1985	Ex Capitol, Cwmbran, 1987
8333UR	Bedford YNT	Plaxton Paramount 3200 II	C53F	1985	Ex Capitol, Cwmbran, 1988
7236PW	Volvo B10M-61	Plaxton Paramount 3500 II	C49FT	1985	Ex Worthing Coaches, 1988
98TNO	Volvo B10M-61	Plaxton Paramount 3500 II	C49FT	1986	Ex Moon, Warnham, 1989
VRY841	Volvo B10M-61	Plaxton Paramount 3500 III	C49FT	1987	Ex Berkeley, Paulton, 1992
256JPA	Volvo B10M-61	Plaxton Paramount 3500 III	C49FT	1987	Ex Dodsworth, Boroughbridge, 1992
SIJ82	Volvo B10M-61	Plaxton Paramount 3200 III	C53F	1987	Ex Excelsior, 1989
4940VF	Volvo B10M-61	Plaxton Paramount 3500 III	C53F	1987	Ex Berkeley, Paulton, 1992
KIA891	Volvo B10M-61	Plaxton Paramount 3500 III	C49FT	1988	Ex National Plant, Bilsthorpe, 1993
SLK886	Mercedes-Benz 609D	Reeve Burgess Beaver	DP19F	1988	
9983PW	Volvo B10M-61	Van Hool Alizée	C49FT	1988	Ex Excelsior, 1991
DSK648	Volvo B10M-61	Van Hool Alizée	C53F	1989	Ex Kenzie's, Shepreth, 1994
LIB226	Volvo B10M-61	Van Hool Alizée	C51F	1989	Ex Wilson, Carnwath, 1994
9383MX	Volvo B10M-60	Van Hool Alizée	C53F	1990	Ex Kenzies, Shepreth, 1995
M2SOB	Toyota Coaster HZB50R	Caetano Optimo III	C21F	1995	
M3SOB	Volvo B10M-62	Plaxton Excalibur	C49FT	1995	

Livery: Red, white and black

Previous Registrations:

166UMB	XVC9X, AAC866X	HIB664	APH510T
256JPA	D709MWX	JGV929	AVS632X
4512UR	B610DDW	KIA891	E582UHS, A1NPT
460UEV	TRY6X	LIB226	F711SFS
4940VF	D807SGB	SIA488	OOU855Y
538ELX	From new	SIJ82	D252HFX
7236PW	C196WJT	SLK886	E346HBJ
8333UR	B631DDW	TCF496	YRU296Y
9383MX	G41SAV	TVG397	OBX454Y, 9983PW
98TNO	C547RWV	VRY841	D402HEU
9983PW	E306OPR, XEL941, E407SEL	XJO46	NGL276X
DSK648	F38DAV	YVF158	A807ASE

SOUTHEND TRANSPORT

Southend Transport Ltd, 87 London Road, Southend-on-Sea, Essex, SS1 1PP

A subsidiary of British Bus plc

208	JTD388P	Daimler Fleetline CRL6-33	Northern Counties	H49/31D	1975
211	JTD391P	Daimler Fleetline CRL6-33	Northern Counties	H49/31D	1975
212	JTD392P	Daimler Fleetline CRL6-33	Northern Counties	H49/31D	1975
216	JTD396P	Daimler Fleetline CRL6-33	Northern Counties	H49/31D	1976

221-242

| | | Leyland Fleetline FE33ALR | Northern Counties | H49/31D | 1979-81 *233/5/7/8/42 are H49/33F |

221	XTE221V	226	XTE226V	231	MRJ231W	235	MRJ235W	239	MRJ239W
222	XTE222V	227	XTE227V	232	MRJ232W	236	MRJ236W	240	MRJ240W
223	XTE223V	228	XTE228V	233	MRJ233W	237	MRJ237W	241	MRJ241W
224	XTE224V	229	XTE229V	234	MRJ234W	238	MRJ238W	242	MRJ242W
225	XTE225V	230	XTE230V						

250	Q475MEV	Daimler Fleetline CRL6-33	Northern Counties(1984)	H49/31D	1972	
251	Q476MEV	Daimler Fleetline CRL6-33	Northern Counties(1984)	H49/31D	1972	
252	Q552MEV	Daimler Fleetline CRL6-33	Northern Counties(1985)	H49/31D	1972	
253	Q553MEV	Daimler Fleetline CRL6-33	Northern Counties(1985)	H49/31D	1972	
254	Q554MEV	Daimler Fleetline CRL6-33	Northern Counties(1985)	H49/31D	1972	
256	A110FDL	Leyland Olympian ONLXB/1R	Eastern Coach Works	DPH45/32F	1984	Ex Southern Vectis, 1991
257	B185BLG	Leyland Olympian ONLXB/1R	Eastern Coach Works	H45/32F	1984	Ex Crosville Wales, 1991
258	B189BLG	Leyland Olympian ONLXB/1R	Eastern Coach Works	H45/32F	1984	Ex Crosville Wales, 1991
259	B183BLG	Leyland Olympian ONLXB/1R	Eastern Coach Works	H45/32F	1984	Ex Crosville Wales, 1990
260	B184BLG	Leyland Olympian ONLXB/1R	Eastern Coach Works	H45/32F	1984	Ex Crosville Wales, 1990
262	H262GEV	Leyland Olympian ONCL10/1RZ	Leyland	H47/32F	1989	
263	H263GEV	Leyland Olympian ONCL10/1RZ	Leyland	H47/32F	1989	
264	H264GEV	Leyland Olympian ONCL10/1RZ	Leyland	H47/32F	1989	
265	H265GEV	Leyland Olympian ONCL10/1RZ	Leyland	H47/32F	1989	
281	MUH281X	Leyland Olympian ONLXB/1R	Eastern Coach Works	H45/32F	1982	Ex National Welsh, 1991
282	MUH285X	Leyland Olympian ONLXB/1R	Eastern Coach Works	H45/32F	1982	Ex National Welsh, 1991
283	MUH283X	Leyland Olympian ONLXB/1R	Eastern Coach Works	H45/32F	1982	Ex National Welsh, 1991
284	MUH286X	Leyland Olympian ONLXB/1R	Eastern Coach Works	H45/32F	1982	Ex National Welsh, 1991
301	YUM401S	Bristol VRT/SL3/6LXB	Eastern Coach Works	H43/31F	1978	Ex West Riding, 1992
302	YUM515S	Bristol VRT/SL3/6LXB	Eastern Coach Works	H43/31F	1978	Ex West Riding, 1992
303	YUM516S	Bristol VRT/SL3/6LXB	Eastern Coach Works	H43/31F	1978	Ex West Riding, 1992
304	DWY146T	Bristol VRT/SL3/6LXB	Eastern Coach Works	H43/31F	1979	Ex West Riding, 1992
305	DGR477S	Bristol VRT/SL3/6LXB	Eastern Coach Works	H43/31F	1979	Ex West Riding, 1992
307	WTU473W	Bristol VRT/SL3/6LXB	Eastern Coach Works	H43/31F	1980	Ex Rhondda, 1992
309	WTU474W	Bristol VRT/SL3/6LXB	Eastern Coach Works	H43/31F	1981	Ex Rhondda, 1992

The majority of the Leyland Olympians with Southend have been acquired second-hand, though four, including 262, H262GEV seen here were delivered new. The X1 London commuter service on which it was seen is being progressively re-stocked with coaches liveried with Green Line or London Coachlink names. *Colin Lloyd*

124

Showing the London Coachlink scheme is 447, H47MJN, a Leyland Olympian with Leyland bodywork previously in the Colchester fleet. The vehicle was photographed in Southend bus station. *BBP*

The standard Southend Transport livery is seen on Bristol VR 305, DGR477S, one of five to have joined the fleet in 1992 from West Riding. *David Cole*

Several Express Travel vehicles passed to Southend Transport during 1995 and are now being painted into Green Line livery for London commuter services. Passing along Buckingham Palace Road when heading for Windsor is 569, F425UVW. *Colin Lloyd*

351	YBF686S	Bristol VRT/SL3/501	Eastern Coach Works	H43/31F	1978	Ex PMT, 1992
352	FTU380T	Bristol VRT/SL3/501	Eastern Coach Works	H43/31F	1979	Ex PMT, 1992
381	BUH233V	Bristol VRT/SL3/6LXB	Eastern Coach Works	H43/31F	1980	Ex Rhondda, 1992
382	GTX751W	Bristol VRT/SL3/501(6LXB)	Eastern Coach Works	H43/31F	1981	Ex National Welsh, 1992
401	LHG440T	Bristol VRT/SL3/501(6LXB)	Eastern Coach Works	H43/31F	1978	Ex Ribble, 1992
402	LHG441T	Bristol VRT/SL3/501(6LXB)	Eastern Coach Works	H43/31F	1978	Ex Ribble, 1992
403	LHG447T	Bristol VRT/SL3/501(6LXB)	Eastern Coach Works	H43/31F	1978	Ex Ribble, 1992
404	LHG448T	Bristol VRT/SL3/501(6LXB)	Eastern Coach Works	H43/31F	1978	Ex Ribble, 1992
446	F246MTW	Leyland Olympian ONCL10/1RZ	Leyland	DPH43/29F	1988	Ex Colchester, 1994
447	H47MJN	Leyland Olympian ON2R50C13Z4	Leyland	DPH43/29F	1991	Ex Colchester, 1993
546	A246SVW	Leyland Tiger TRCTL11/3RP	Duple Caribbean	C57F	1984	
547	A247SVW	Leyland Tiger TRCTL11/3RP	Duple Caribbean	C57F	1984	
548	A248SVW	Leyland Tiger TRCTL11/3RP	Duple Caribbean	C57F	1984	
549	A249SVW	Leyland Tiger TRCTL11/3RP	Duple Caribbean	C57F	1984	
551	B100XTW	Leyland Tiger TRCTL11/3RP	Duple Caribbean	C57F	1984	
553	A141EPA	Leyland Tiger TRCTL11/2R	Plaxton Paramount 3200 E	C51F	1984	Ex Kentish Bus, 1990
555	A144EPA	Leyland Tiger TRCTL11/2R	Plaxton Paramount 3200 E	C51F	1984	Ex Kentish Bus, 1990
556	A156EPA	Leyland Tiger TRCTL11/3R	Plaxton Paramount 3200 E	C57F	1984	Ex Kentish Bus, 1990
557	B83SWX	Leyland Tiger TRCTL11/3R	Plaxton Paramount 3200 II	C57F	1985	Ex Yorkshire Voyager, 1992
558	B84SWX	Leyland Tiger TRCTL11/3R	Plaxton Paramount 3200 II	C57F	1985	Ex Yorkshire Voyager, 1992
559	B85SWX	Leyland Tiger TRCTL11/3R	Plaxton Paramount 3200 II	C53F	1985	Ex Yorkshire Voyager, 1992
563	A124EPA	Leyland Tiger TRCTL11/2R	Plaxton Paramount 3200 E	C51F	1984	Ex Kentish Bus, 1990
565	H845AHS	Volvo B10M-60	Plaxton Paramount 3500 III	C53F	1991	Ex Express Travel, 1995
566	H566MPD	Volvo B10M-60	Plaxton Paramount 3500 III	C53F	1991	Ex Express Travel, 1995
567	H567MPD	Volvo B10M-60	Plaxton Paramount 3500 III	C53F	1991	Ex Express Travel, 1995
568	H372PHK	Volvo B10M-60	Plaxton Paramount 3500 III	C53F	1991	Ex Express Travel, 1995
569	F425UVW	Volvo B10M-60	Plaxton Paramount 3200 III	C53F	1991	Ex Express Travel, 1995
570	F467UVW	Volvo B10M-60	Plaxton Paramount 3200 III	C53F	1991	Ex Express Travel, 1995
571	NXI9006	Volvo B10M-60	Plaxton Paramount 3200 III	C53F	1991	Ex Express Travel, 1995
572	F572UPB	Volvo B10M-60	Plaxton Paramount 3200 III	C53F	1991	Ex Express Travel, 1995

Latest arrivals with Southend are four Dennis Lance SLF chassis with Robert Wright bodywork. Produced at Ballymena in Northern Ireland, the model seen here is known as the Endeavour. Essex County Council funding supported the purchase of these vehicles. *BBP*

706	TPL292S	Leyland National 10351A/1R		B41F	1977	Ex County, 1989
707	TPL293S	Leyland National 10351A/1R		B41F	1977	Ex County, 1989
709	JBO345N	Leyland National 10351/2R		B41F	1975	Ex Cardiff Bus, 1991
710	JBO352N	Leyland National 10351/2R		B41F	1975	Ex Cardiff Bus, 1991
711	JBO349N	Leyland National 10351/2R		B41F	1975	Ex Cardiff Bus, 1991
713	LPB218P	Leyland National 10351/1R		B41F	1975	Ex London Country SW, 1989
714	NPK241R	Leyland National 10351A/1R		B41F	1977	Ex London Country SW, 1989
716	GGE156T	Leyland National 10351A/1R		B41F	1978	Ex Blackpool, 1991
717	GGE158T	Leyland National 10351A/1R		B41F	1978	Ex Blackpool, 1991
718	GGE161T	Leyland National 10351A/1R		B41F	1978	Ex Blackpool, 1991
719	GGE162T	Leyland National 10351A/1R		B41F	1978	Ex Blackpool, 1991
723	GGE167T	Leyland National 10351A/1R		B41F	1978	Ex Blackpool, 1991
725	GGE172T	Leyland National 10351A/1R		B41F	1978	Ex Blackpool, 1991
745	PJI3745	Leyland National 10351A/1R (DAF)		B41F	1978	Ex Blackpool, 1991
751	JTU586T	Leyland National 10351B/1R (6HLX)		B41F	1978	Ex Crosville Wales, 1991
761	M761JPA	Dennis Lance SLF 11SDA3201	Wright Endeavour	B39F	1994	
762	M762JPA	Dennis Lance SLF 11SDA3201	Wright Endeavour	B39F	1994	
763	M763JPA	Dennis Lance SLF 11SDA3201	Wright Endeavour	B39F	1994	
764	M764JPA	Dennis Lance SLF 11SDA3201	Wright Endeavour	B39F	1995	

Livery: Blue, white and red (buses); two-tone green (Green Line coaches)

Previous Registrations:

A110FDL	A701DDL, WDL748	NXI9006	F451PSL
F425UVW	F449PSL, NXI9004	PJI3745	GGE170T
F467UVW	F450PSL, NXI9005	Q475MEV	GHJ377L
F572UPB	F452PSL, NXI9007	Q476MEV	GHJ374L
H372PHK	H844AHS, NXI9003	Q552MEV	GHJ379L
H566MPD	H843AHS, NXI9002	Q553MEV	GHJ375L
H567MPD	H842AHS, NXI9001	Q554MEV	GHJ376L

On order: 4 Dennis Lance/East Lancashire double-deck buses.

SOVEREIGN / BTS
CAMBRIDGE COACH SERVICES

Sovereign Bus & Coach Co Ltd, Babbage Road, Stevenage, Hertfordshire, SG1 2EQ
BTS Coaches Ltd, Station Road, Borehamwood, Hertfordshire, WD6 1HB
Cambridge Coach Services Ltd, Kings Hedges Road, Impington,
Cambridge, CB4 4PQ

Depots : Station Road, Borehamwood(BTS); Venture Garage, Pinner Road, Harrow (Sovereign Harrow); Kings Hedges Road, Impington(Cambridge Coach Services); Swanland Road, North Mymms (Sovereign and Welwyn & Hatfield Line); Sandridge Gate Business Centre, St Albans (Sovereign) and Babbage Road, Stevenage (Soverign).

These three operations which are subsidiaries of Blazefield Holdings Ltd share a common fleet numbering system. As such, the fleet is shown contiguously and details of the allocation of vehicles to operations is given at the end.

32	BPF132Y	Leyland Olympian ONTL11/1R	Roe		H43/29F	1983	Ex London Country NE, 1989
33	BPF133Y	Leyland Olympian ONTL11/1R	Roe		H43/29F	1983	Ex London Country NE, 1989
37	BPF137Y	Leyland Olympian ONTL11/1R	Roe		H43/29F	1983	Ex London Country NE, 1989
38	A138DPE	Leyland Olympian ONTL11/1R	Roe		H43/29F	1983	Ex London Country NE, 1989
39	A139DPE	Leyland Olympian ONTL11/1R	Roe		H43/29F	1983	Ex Keighley & District, 1993
40	A140DPE	Leyland Olympian ONTL11/1R	Roe		H43/29F	1983	Ex Keighley & District, 1994

101-105		Volvo B10B-58		Wright Endurance	DP49F	1995	
101	M101UKX	**102**	M102UKX	**103**	M103UKX	**104**	M104UKX	**105**	M105UKX

201-207		Leyland Lynx LX2R11C15Z4S		Leyland Lynx	B49F	1989	
201	G201URO	**203**	G203URO	**205**	G205URO	**206**	G206URO	**207**	G207URO
202	G202URO	**204**	G204URO						

213	F203MBT	Leyland Lynx LX112TL11ZR1R	Leyland Lynx		B51F	1989	Ex Keighley & District, 1993
214	F204MBT	Leyland Lynx LX112TL11ZR1R	Leyland Lynx		B51F	1989	Ex Keighley & District, 1993
215	F205MBT	Leyland Lynx LX112TL11ZR1R	Leyland Lynx		B47F	1989	Ex Keighley & District, 1992
216	F206MBT	Leyland Lynx LX112TL11ZR1R	Leyland Lynx		B51F	1989	Ex Keighley & District, 1993

Opposite: **Two Sovereign vehicles are illustrated here. The upper picture shows a Mercedes-Benz 811D - 443, L3SBC the first of the 1993 delivery and one of five with Select index marks from DVLA. The lower picture shows 102, M102UKX. This is a Volvo B10B with Wrights Endurance bodywork. The Volvo B10B is the successor to the Lynx.** *Tony Wilson*

Sovereign, BTS and Cambridge Coach services are all part of Blazefield Holdings Ltd which also own several fleets in Yorkshire. Transferred from Harrogate & District in 1995 was 284, G384MWX, seen at Hatfield with a dedicated livery for the 734 Sovereign service to St Albans.
Richard Godfrey

Jetlink livery is worn by Sovereign 327, H327UWR, a Volvo B10M with Plaxton Paramount 3500 bodywork. It is seen at Stevenage bus station in August 1995, and was part of the Wallace Arnold touring fleet when new. *Colin Lloyd*

217	F207MBT	Leyland Lynx LX112TL11ZR1R	Leyland Lynx	B49F	1989	Ex Keighley & District, 1993	
218	F208MBT	Leyland Lynx LX112TL11ZR1R	Leyland Lynx	B51F	1989	Ex Harrogate & District, 1993	
220	E420EBH	Leyland Lynx LX112TL11ZR1R	Leyland Lynx	B51F	1988	Ex County, 1990	
240	E840EUT	Leyland Lynx LX112TL11ZR1R	Leyland Lynx	B51F	1987	Ex County, 1990	
258	F358JVS	Leyland Lynx LX112TL11ZR1R	Leyland Lynx	B49F	1988	Ex Jubilee, Stevenage, 1989	
259	F359JVS	Leyland Lynx LX112TL11ZR1R	Leyland Lynx	B49F	1988	Ex County, 1990	
271	E371YRO	Leyland Lynx LX112TL11ZR1R	Leyland Lynx	B51F	1987	Ex County, 1990	
284	G384MWX	Leyland Lynx LX112L10ZR1R	Leyland Lynx	DP47F	1990	Ex Harrogate & District, 1995	

301-308

	Volvo B10M-62		Plaxton Premiére 350	C52F	1994

301	M301BAV	303	M303BAV	305	M305BAV	307	M307BAV	308	M308BAV
302	M302BAV	304	M304BAV	306	M306BAV				

319	G519LWU	Volvo B10M-61	Plaxton Paramount 3500 III	C50F	1990	Ex Wallace Arnold, 1994
321	F421DUG	Volvo B10M-60	Plaxton Paramount 3500 III	C50F	1989	Ex Wallace Arnold, 1993
324	F424DUG	Volvo B10M-60	Plaxton Paramount 3500 III	C50F	1989	Ex Wallace Arnold, 1992
325	F425DUG	Volvo B10M-60	Plaxton Paramount 3500 III	C50F	1989	Ex Wallace Arnold, 1992
326	E362NEG	Volvo B10M-61	Plaxton Paramount 3200 III	C53F	1988	Ex Premier Travel, 1994
327	H627UWR	Volvo B10M-60	Plaxton Paramount 3500 III	C50F	1991	Ex Wallace Arnold, 1993
328	H628UWR	Volvo B10M-60	Plaxton Paramount 3500 III	C50F	1991	Ex Wallace Arnold, 1993
329	H629UWR	Volvo B10M-60	Plaxton Paramount 3500 III	C50F	1991	Ex Wallace Arnold, 1994
347	H647UWR	Volvo B10M-61	Plaxton Paramount 3200 III	C50F	1991	Ex Wallace Arnold, 1994
349	YXI2749	Volvo B10M-61	Plaxton Paramount 3500 III	C51FT	1989	Ex Rover, Bromsgrove, 1992
350	D350KVE	Volvo B10M-61	Van Hool Alizée	C53FL	1987	Ex Premier Travel, 1990
351	D351KVE	Volvo B10M-61	Van Hool Alizée	C53F	1987	Ex Premier Travel, 1990
354	TXI5497	Volvo B10M-61	Berkhof Esprite 350	C49FT	1984	Ex Keighley & District, 1994
358	E358NEG	Volvo B10M-61	Plaxton Paramount 3200 III	C53F	1988	Ex Premier Travel, 1994
359	E359NEG	Volvo B10M-61	Plaxton Paramount 3200 III	C53F	1988	Ex Premier Travel, 1994
360	E360NEG	Volvo B10M-61	Plaxton Paramount 3200 III	C53F	1988	Ex Premier Travel, 1994
362	G92RGG	Volvo B10M-60	Plaxton Paramount 3500 III	C49FT	1990	Ex Keighley & District, 1995
363	E363NEG	Volvo B10M-61	Plaxton Paramount 3200 III	C53F	1988	Ex Premier Travel, 1994
374	YXI2747	Volvo B10M-61	Van Hool Alizée	C53F	1985	Ex Rover, Bromsgrove, 1992

Cambridge Coach Services added eight Plaxton Premiére 350 coaches to their fleet at the end of 1994. Seen in Cambridge is 307, M307BAV. Cambridge Coach Services controls the associated Bus and Coach Investments ltd which uses the Rover fleetname, operating from a base in Bromsgrove. *Paul Wigan*

395	G95RGG	Volvo B10M-60		Plaxton Paramount 3500 III	C53F	1990	Ex Park's, 1993
396	G96RGG	Volvo B10M-60		Plaxton Paramount 3500 III	C53F	1990	Ex Park's, 1991
397	G97RGG	Volvo B10M-60		Plaxton Paramount 3500 III	C53F	1990	Ex Park's, 1991
398	G98RGG	Volvo B10M-60		Plaxton Paramount 3500 III	C53F	1990	Ex Park's, 1991

403-424
Mercedes-Benz 811D — Reeve Burgess Beaver — B31F — 1990-91

403	H403FGS	408	H408FGS	413	H413FGS	418	H418FGS	422	H422FGS
404	H404FGS	409	H409FGS	415	H415FGS	419	H419FGS	423	H423FGS
406	H406FGS	410	H410FGS	417	H417FGS	421	H421FGS	424	H424FGS
407	H407FGS	411	H411FGS					

433-454
Mercedes-Benz 811D — Plaxton Beaver — B31F — 1993-94

433	K3SBC	443	L3SBC	446	L946HTM	449	L949MBH	452	L952MBH
434	K4SBC	444	L944HTM	447	L947HTM	450	L950MBH	453	L953MBH
435	K5SBC	445	L945HTM	448	L948HTM	451	L951MBH	454	L954MBH
442	L2SBC						

455-461
Mercedes-Benz 811D — Plaxton Beaver — B31F — 1995

455	M455UUR	457	M457UUR	459	M459UUR	460	M460UUR	461	M461UUR
456	M456UUR	458	M458UUR					

521	FUG321T	Leyland National 10351B/1R		B44F	1979	Ex Keighley & District, 1994
525	FUG325T	Leyland National 10351B/1R		B44F	1979	Ex Keighley & District, 1995
543	DNW843T	Leyland National 10351B/1R		B44F	1979	Ex Keighley & District, 1994
604	YYG104S	Leyland National 11351A/1R		B49F	1978	Ex Skipton Busways, 1992
606	YEV306S	Leyland National 11351A/1R		B49F	1977	Ex Thamesway, 1991
641	VNO741S	Leyland National 11351A/1R		B49F	1977	Ex Thamesway, 1991
658	WJN558S	Leyland National 11351A/1R		B49F	1978	Ex Thamesway, 1991
664	VKE564S	Leyland National 11351A/1R		B49F	1977	Ex Hampshire Bus, 1992
692	EUM892T	Leyland National 11351A/1R		B49F	1979	Ex Skipton Busways, 1992
699	AYJ99T	Leyland National 11351A/1R		B52F	1979	Ex Harrogate & District, 1994

901-917 — Mercedes-Benz 709D — Reeve Burgess Beaver — B23F* — 1989 — *916/7 are DP23F 912-5 ex County, 1991

901	G901UPP	905	G905UPP	909	G909UPP	912	G912UPP	915	G915UPP
902	G902UPP	906	G906UPP	910	G910UPP	913	G913UPP	916	G916UPP
903	G903UPP	907	G907UPP	911	G911UPP	914	G914UPP	917	G917UPP
904	G904UPP	908	G908UPP						

920-931 — Mercedes-Benz 709D — Reeve Burgess Beaver — B23F — 1990

920	H920FGS	922	H922FGS	925	H925FGS	927	H927FGS	930	H930FGS
921	H921FGS	923	H923FGS	926	H926FGS	929	H929FGS	931	H931FGS

990	K390SLB	Mercedes-Benz 709D	Plaxton Beaver	B23F	1993
991	K391SLB	Mercedes-Benz 709D	Plaxton Beaver	B23F	1993
992	K392SLB	Mercedes-Benz 709D	Plaxton Beaver	B23F	1993
993	K393SLB	Mercedes-Benz 709D	Plaxton Beaver	B23F	1993

L139-152 — Leyland Olympian ON2R50C13Z4 — Northern Counties Palatine — H47/30F — 1991

L139	H139GGS	L142	H142GGS	L145	H145GGS	L148	H148GGS	L151	H151GGS
L140	H140GGS	L143	H143GGS	L146	H146GGS	L149	H149GGS	L152	H152GGS
L141	H141GGS	L144	H144GGS	L147	H147GGS	L150	H150GGS		

RM104	LDS280A	AEC Routemaster R2RH	Park Royal	H36/28R	1961	Ex Southend, 1994

RML2265-2756 — AEC Routemaster R2RH1 — Park Royal — H40/32R — 1965-68 On loan from LRT

2265	CUV265C	2487	JJD487D	2582	JJD582D	2659	SMK659F	2686	SMK686F
2322	CUV322C	2527	JJD527D	2598	JJD598D	2663	SMK663F	2694	SMK694F
2341	CUV341C	2538	JJD538D	2627	NML627E	2668	SMK668F	2719	SMK719F
2404	JJD404D	2563	JJD563D	2633	NML633E	2674	SMK674F	2756	SMK756F
2443	JJD443D	2569	JJD569D						

T57	WYV57T	Leyland Titan TNLXB2RRSp	Park Royal	H44/28F	1979	Ex London Buses, 1994
T277	GYE277W	Leyland Titan TNLXB2RRSp	Leyland	H44/28F	1981	Ex London Buses, 1992
T620	NUW620Y	Leyland Titan TNLXB2RRSp	Leyland	H44/28F	1983	Ex London Buses, 1993
T706	OHV706Y	Leyland Titan TNLXB2RRSp	Leyland	H44/28F	1983	Ex London Buses, 1993
T777	OHV777Y	Leyland Titan TNLXB2RRSp	Leyland	H44/28F	1983	Ex London Buses, 1992

Previous Registrations:

LDS280A	VLT104		TXI5497	B592XNO	YXI2749	F885RFP
MIB920	B31MKP		YXI2747	B490UNB		

Opertaions:
BTS Coaches: L139-152, RM104, RML2265-2756, T57-777 (T620 & T706 on extended loan to Sovereign)
Cambridge Coach Services: 301-8, 319, 321/4/5/9, 347, 350/1, 362, 395-8, 881
Rover: 326/49/54/9/60/3/74
Sovereign (Harrow): 411/3/5/7-9/21-4/35/55-61, 902-3/9, 925-7/9-31
Welwyn & Hatfield Line: 433/4, 664, 901/2/4/5/6/8, 992/3
Sovereign Buses: remainder.

Liveries: Cream and blue (Sovereign); cream and red (Welwyn & Hatfield Line); Red and yellow (BTS); grey and blue (Cambridge Coach Services and Rover)

Named vehicles: 301 *Sidney Sussex College*; 302 *Gonville & Caius*; 303 *Pembroke*; 304 *Clare*; 305 *Selwyn*; 306 *Robinson*; 307 *Newnham*; 308 *Magdalene*; 321 *Corpus Christi*; 324 *Trinity*; 325 *Girton*; 327 *Ray Freeman*; 329 *Lucy Cavendish*; 350 *St Johns*; 351 *Homerton*; 395 *Churchill*; 396 *Jesus*; 397 *Fitzwilliam*; 398 *Downing*.

Three vehicles from Blazefield operators are shown here. 905, G905UPP is a Mercedes-Benz 709D with Reeve Burgess Beaver bodywork and used by Welwyn-Hatfield Line, an operation which is part of the Sovereign company. In Sovereign livery is 454, L954MBH, similar to 905 above, but the longer and more powerful 811 version. This is seen in Welwyn Garden City. The lower picture shows BTS' Routemaster RML2663, SMK663F on LRT service 13. Two of these Routemasters are currently on long term loan to the Sovereign operation.
Richard Godfrey

Photographed in Wreningham, Spratts RCS754 features a 1994 Berkhof Excellence 2000 body on a 1992 Scania K113 that only ran for a few days before its original body was destroyed by fire. The Berkhof Excellence is produced at Valkenswaard in the Netherlands, one of three plants operated by Berkhof in that country. *David Donati*

Stephensons brought south a trio of Bristol VRs which were previously with Bluebird Buses in Scotland until 1994. Seen in Stratford is PHH407R. *BBP*

SPRATTS

Spratts Coaches (East Anglian & Continental) Ltd, Wreningham, Norfolk, NR16 1AZ

Reg	Chassis	Body	Seats	Year	History
RGS598R	Bedford YMT	Duple Dominant	C57F	1977	Ex Eagre, Gainsborough, 1995
TYE708S	Bedford YMT	Duple Dominant II	C53F	1977	Ex Grey Green, London, 1981
BWE193T	Bedford YMT	Duple Dominant II	C53F	1979	Ex Smith, Alcester, 1983
BWE194T	Bedford YMT	Duple Dominant II	C53F	1979	Ex Smith, Alcester, 1983
NRY22W	Bedford YLQ	Duple Dominant II	C45F	1980	
HIL7394	Bedford YNT	Duple Dominant IV	C49DL	1982	Ex ?, 1994
HIL7240	Bova EL26/281	Bova Europa	C49FT	1982	Ex Crusader, Clacton, 1984
HIL6327	DAF SB2300DHS585	Berkhof Esprite 340	C57F	1985	Ex Limebourne, 1988
HIL6328	DAF SB2300DHS585	Berkhof Esprite 340	C57F	1985	Ex Limebourne, 1988
C357FBO	Bedford YNV Venturer	Plaxton Paramount 3200 II	C57F	1985	Ex Gregory, Netherton, 1994
HIL7477	Scania K112CRS	Van Hool Alizée	C49FT	1985	
HIL7478	Scania K92CRS	Berkhof Esprite 340	C53F	1986	Ex The Kings Ferry, Gillingham, 1987
HIL6919	Bedford YMPS	Plaxton Paramount 3200 II	C35F	1986	Ex Coachmaster, Coulsdon, 1987
HIL7391	Bedford YNV Venturer	Plaxton Paramount 3200 II	C57F	1987	
E99ODH	Bova FHD12.280	Bova Futura	C49DL	1987	Ex Happy Times, Wednesfield, 1995
E48YDO	Mercedes-Benz 609D	Advanced Vehicle Bodies	C26F	1988	Ex Brown, Barway, 1994
F569MCH	Mercedes-Benz 609D	Advanced Vehicle Bodies	C24F	1989	Ex NPT, Bilsthorpe, 1992
HIL7479	Scania K92CRB	Van Hool Alizée	C53F	1988	Ex Harry Shaw, Coventry, 1991
CJS447	Scania K113CRB	Van Hool Alizée	C49FT	1989	Ex Elite, Stockport, 1992
RCS754	Scania K113CRB	Berkhof Excellence 2000HL(1994)	C49FT	1992	Ex The Kings Ferry, 1994

Livery: White and blue

Previous Registrations:

CJS447	G999HKW	HIL6919	C535JTG	HIL7477	C22YEX	
F569MCH	F552HRC, A5NPT	HIL7240	AVG870X, CJS447, BAR906X	HIL7478	C593KVW	
HIL6327	B686BTW	HIL7391	D422KVF	HIL7479	684DYX, E648NHP	
HIL6328	B689BTW	HIL7394	CTM791X	RCS754	J3KFC	

STEPHENSONS

Stephensons Coaches Ltd, Riverside, South Street, Rochford, Essex, SS4 1BS

	Reg	Chassis	Body	Seats	Year	History
	JTD393P	Daimler Fleetline CRL6	Northern Counties	H49/31F	1976	Ex Transit, 1994
	KOU796P	Bristol VRT/SL3/6LXB	Eastern Coach Works	H43/31F	1976	Ex City of Nottingham, 1994
	PHH407R	Bristol VRT/SL3/6LXB	Eastern Coach Works	H43/31F	1976	Ex Bluebird, 1994
w	PHH408R	Bristol VRT/SL3/6LXB	Eastern Coach Works	H43/31F	1976	Ex Bluebird, 1994
	OTO151R	Bristol VRT/SL3/501	Eastern Coach Works	H43/31F	1976	Ex Bluebird, 1994
	WWY120S	Bristol VRT/SL3/6LXB	Eastern Coach Works	H43/31F	1977	Ex Aintree Coachlines, 1992
	TPE155S	Bristol VRT/SL3/6LXB	Eastern Coach Works	H43/31F	1977	Ex The Bee Line, 1992
	YBF682S	Bristol VRT/SL3/6LXB	Eastern Coach Works	H43/31F	1978	Ex Fletcher, Offerton, 1994
	JMB328T	Leyland Leopard PSU3E/4R	Duple Dominant II Express	DP53F	1978	Ex Dalybus, Eccles, 1994
	ABV881V	Ford R1114	Duple Dominant II	C53F	1980	Ex Lloyd, Liverpool, 1994
	GAO628V	Bedford YMT	Unicar	C53F	1980	Ex Lloyd, Liverpool, 1994
	FTO558V	Bedford YMT	Plaxton Supreme IV Express	C53F	1979	Ex Booth, Eccles, 1995
	FAD272Y	Leyland Royal Tiger B50	Roe Doyen	C50F	1983	Ex Cheltenham & Gloucester, 1993
	SMW56Y	Dennis Dominator DDA164	Northern Counties	H43/31F	1983	Ex Thamesdown, 1995
	B431LRA	MCW Metroliner DR130/6	MCW	CH55/17FT	1985	Ex Maun, Sutton-in-Ashfield, 1995
	C340GFJ	Ford Transit 190	Robin Hood	B16F	1986	Ex Sleeman, High Wycombe, 1995
	OIB5401	Leyland Royal Tiger RTC	Leyland Doyen	C53F	1987	Ex Rossendale, 1993
	OIB5402	Leyland Royal Tiger RTC	Leyland Doyen	C53F	1987	Ex Rossendale, 1993
	D208NON	Freight Rover Sherpa	Carlyle	B18F	1987	Ex O'Brien, Canvey, 1995
	E94OUH	Freight Rover Sherpa	Carlyle Citybus 2	B20F	1987	Ex O'Brien, Canvey, 1995
	F484KDB	Mazda E2200	Made-to-Measure	M14	1989	Ex Kindserve, Huddersfield, 1995

Livery: White and pale green; white, orange & green (buses)

Previous Registration:

B431LRA	B233XEU, 899DXV	MSL21X	JSR42X, MSV533	OIB5402	D387VAO
FAD272Y	DAD218Y, YJV806	OIB5401	D892PNB		

Two examples of Scania K113s with bodywork from associated companies. Jonckheere Bus and Coach with its factory in Roeselare, Belgium is now part of the Berkhof group, though the Deauville range continues. Below is HSK845, a split-screen Deauville P599 model while above is a Berkhof Excellence 2000 body. The 1000LA bendi-bus model is a common sight in mainland Europe, and ought to suit UK passengers in preference to double-deck coaches for commuter services.

SUPREME

Abridge Enterprises Ltd, 303 London Road, Hadleigh, Benfleet, Essex SS7 2BN

Depot: Stock Road, Prittlewell, Southend and Guildford Road, Southend.

LGA18P	Leyland Atlantean AN68/1R	Roe	H43/33F	1975	Ex Graham's, Paisley, 1982
VGD779R	Leyland Atlantean AN68A/1R	Roe	H43/33F	1977	Ex Graham's, Paisley, 1982
BFR304R	Leyland Atlantean AN68A/2R	East Lancashire	H50/36F	1977	Ex Sheffield Omnibus, 1994
OKW504R	Leyland Fleetline FE30AGR	MCW	H44/27D	1977	Ex Carterton Coaches, 1994
SDA620S	Leyland Fleetline FE30AGR	Park Royal	H44/33F	1977	Ex Carterton Coaches, 1994
PTD671S	Leyland National 11351A/1R		B49F	1978	Ex White, Heathfield, 1995
OEM787S	Leyland Atlantean AN68A/1R	MCW	H43/32F	1978	Ex Sheffield Omnibus, 1994
XRF24S	Leyland Atlantean AN68A/1R	East Lancashire	H43/32F	1978	Ex Sheffield Omnibus, 1994
XRF25S	Leyland Atlantean AN68A/1R	East Lancashire	H43/32F	1978	Ex Sheffield Omnibus, 1994
URF673S	Bristol VRT/SL3/6LXB	Eastern Coach Works	H43/31F	1978	Ex Swallow, Rainham, 1994
BTU375S	Bristol VRT/SL3/6LXB	Eastern Coach Works	H43/31F	1978	Ex Swallow, Rainham, 1994
CWU139T	Leyland Fleetline FE30AGR	Roe	H44/33F	1978	Ex Yorkshire Rider, 1994
GHB85W	Bristol VRT/SL3/6LXB	East Lancashire	H44/32F	1981	Ex Beeston, 1995
HSK836	Volvo B10M-61	Plaxton P'mount 3500 III(1990)	C53F	1983	
HSK834	Volvo B10M-61	Jonckheere Jubilee P599	C49FT	1988	
HSK835	Volvo B10M-61	Jonckheere Jubilee P599	C49FT	1988	
HSK843	MAN 16-290	Jonckheere Deauville P599	C49FT	1989	
HSK844	Volvo B9M	Jonckheere Deauville P599	C37FT	1989	
HSK845	Scania K113CRB	Jonckheere Deauville P599	C51FT	1989	Ex Swallow, Rainham, 1992
HSK855	MAN 16-290	Jonckheere Deauville P599	C51FT	1990	
HSK856	MAN 16-290	Jonckheere Deauville P599	C51FT	1990	
HSK857	EOS E180Z	EOS 100	C53F	1990	
HSK858	EOS E180Z	EOS 100	C53F	1990	
HSK859	EOS E180Z	EOS 100	C53F	1990	
HSK860	EOS E180Z	EOS 100	C53F	1990	
HSK892	MAN 16-290	Jonckheere Deauville P599	C51FT	1990	Ex Dunn-Line, Nottingham, 1995
H10SUP	MAN 16-290	Jonckheere Deauville P599	C51FT	1991	
H20SUP	MAN 16-290	Jonckheere Deauville P599	C51FT	1991	
J2SUP	EOS E180Z	EOS 100	C53F	1991	
J3SUP	EOS E180Z	EOS 100	C53F	1991	
K3SUP	Scania K113CRB	Plaxton Premiére 350	C49FT	1993	Ex Dunn-Line, Nottingham, 1995
K4SUP	MAN 16-290	Jonckheere Deauville P599	C51FT	1993	
K5SUP	MAN 16-363	Jonckheere Deauville P599	C51FT	1993	
K6SUP	MAN 16-290	Jonckheere Deauville P599	C51FT	1993	
K459PNR	Toyota Coaster HDB30R	Caetano Optimo II	C18F	1993	Ex Charter Coach, Great Oakley, 1994
K707RNR	Volvo B10M-61	Caetano Algarve II	C49FT	1993	Ex Charter Coach, Great Oakley, 1994
K708RNR	Volvo B10M-61	Caetano Algarve II	C49FT	1993	Ex Charter Coach, Great Oakley, 1994
L100SUP	Volvo B9M	Berkhof Excellence 1000HL	C37F	1994	
L200SUP	Scania K113CRB	Berkhof Excellence 2000HL	C51FT	1994	
L300SUP	Volvo B9M	Berkhof Excellence 1000HL	C37F	1994	
L67YJF	Toyota Hiace	Caetano	M11	1990	Ex Caetano demonstrator, 1994
M24THJ	Volkswagen Caravelle	Volkswagen	M8	1995	
M256TAK	Scania K113TRB	Irizar Century	C49FT	1995	
M257TAK	Scania K113TRB	Irizar Century	C49FT	1995	
M258TAK	Scania K113TRB	Irizar Century	C49FT	1995	
M259TAK	Scania K113TRB	Irizar Century	C49FT	1995	

Livery: White, blue and red

Previous Registrations:

HSK834	E697NNH	HSK845	F909YNV	HSK859	G441NVV
HSK835	E696NNH	HSK855	G369RNH	HSK860	G442NVV
HSK836	MRP840Y	HSK856	G370RNH	HSK892	G169RBD
HSK843	F918YNV	HSK857	G439NVV	K3SUP	K991HVO
HSK844	F919YNV	HSK858	G438NVV		

THAMESWAY

Thamesway Ltd, Office 24, Eastgate Business Centre, Basildon,
Essex, SS14 1EB

Depots and outstations: Cherrydown, Basildon; North Rd, Brentwood; London Rd, Hadleigh; Morson Road, Ponders End.

A subsidiary of FirstBus plc

201	C201HJN	Mercedes-Benz L608D	Reeve Burgess	B20F	1985	Ex Eastern National, 1990
202	C696ECV	Mercedes-Benz L608D	Reeve Burgess	DP19F	1985	Ex Western National, 1993
203	C963GCV	Mercedes-Benz L608D	Reeve Burgess	DP19F	1986	Ex Western National, 1994
204	C978GCV	Mercedes-Benz L608D	PMT	B20F	1986	Ex Western National, 1994
206	C957GAF	Mercedes-Benz L608D	Reeve Burgess	B20F	1986	Ex Western National, 1994
207	C699ECV	Mercedes-Benz L608D	Reeve Burgess	DP19F	1985	Ex Western National, 1994
208	C491HCV	Mercedes-Benz L608D	Reeve Burgess	DP19F	1986	Ex Western National, 1994
209	C967GCV	Mercedes-Benz L608D	Reeve Burgess	DP19F	1986	Ex Western National, 1994

230-234

		Mercedes-Benz L608D	Reeve Burgess	B20F	1986	Ex Eastern National, 1990

230	D230PPU	231	D231PPU	232	D232PPU	233	D233PPU	234	D234PPU

245-260

		Mercedes-Benz 709D	Reeve Burgess Beaver	B23F	1988-89	Ex Eastern National, 1990

245	F245MVW	249	F249NJN	252	F252NJN	255	F255RHK	258	F258RHK
246	F246MVW	250	F250NJN	253	F253RHK	256	F256RHK	259	F259RHK
247	F247NJN	251	F251NJN	254	F254RHK	257	F257RHK	260	F260RHK
248	F248NJN								

261	D764KWT	Mercedes-Benz 609D	Robin Hood	B20F	1987	Ex SWT, 1994

301-356

		Mercedes-Benz 709D	Reeve Burgess Beaver	B23F	1991	

301	H301LPU	313	H314LJN	324	H331LJN	335	H344LJN	346	H356LJN
302	H302LPU	314	H315LJN	325	H332LJN	336	H345LJN	347	H357LJN
303	H303LPU	315	H317LJN	326	H334LJN	337	H346LJN	348	H358LJN
304	H304LPU	316	H319LJN	327	H335LJN	338	H347LJN	349	H359LJN
305	H305LPU	317	H321LJN	328	H336LJN	339	H348LJN	350	H361LJN
306	H306LPU	318	H322LJN	329	H337LJN	340	H349LJN	351	H362LJN
307	H307LJN	319	H324LJN	330	H338LJN	341	H351LJN	352	H363LJN
308	H308LJN	320	H326LJN	331	H339LJN	342	H352LJN	353	H364LJN
309	H310LJN	321	H327LJN	332	H341LJN	343	H353LJN	354	H365LJN
310	H311LJN	322	H329LJN	333	H342LJN	344	H354LJN	355	H366LJN
311	H312LJN	323	H330LJN	334	H343LJN	345	H355LJN	356	H367LJN
312	H313LJN								

357-387

		Mercedes-Benz 709D	Reeve Burgess Beaver	B23F	1991	

357	H368OHK	364	H375OHK	370	H381OHK	376	H387OHK	382	H393OHK
358	H369OHK	365	H376OHK	371	H382OHK	377	H388OHK	383	H394OHK
359	H370OHK	366	H377OHK	372	H383OHK	378	H389OHK	384	H395OHK
360	H371OHK	367	H378OHK	373	H384OHK	379	H390OHK	385	H396OHK
361	H372OHK	368	H379OHK	374	H385OHK	380	H391OHK	386	H397OHK
362	H373OHK	369	H380OHK	375	H386OHK	381	H392OHK	387	H398OHK
363	H374OHK								

388-395

		Mercedes-Benz 709D	Reeve Burgess Beaver	B23F	1991	Ex Eastern National, 1992

388	H388MAR	390	H390MAR	392	H392MAR	394	H394MAR	395	H395MAR
389	H389MAR	391	H391MAR	393	H393MAR				

396	K396KHJ	Mercedes-Benz 709D	Plaxton Beaver	B23F	1993
397	K397KHJ	Mercedes-Benz 709D	Plaxton Beaver	B23F	1993
398	K398KHJ	Mercedes-Benz 709D	Plaxton Beaver	B23F	1993

With the majority of Ford Transits now replaced, those minibuses that remain in the Thamesway fleet are almost all Mercedes-Benz examples. Above is 42, B42AAF, an early L608D van conversion while below is 314, H314LJN, now repainted in the new purple and yellow livery, and a Mercedes-Benz 709D based Reeve Burgess Beaver. *Colin Lloyd*

Newly delivered to Thamesway are the first of a batch of Volvo B10Ms with Plaxton Premier 320 bodywork for use on the City Saver service between Southend and London. This service uses coaches in a yellow, orange and blue livery. Photographed in the City on its first day was 603, N603APU. *Colin Lloyd*

501-507

Leyland Tiger TRCTL11/3RZ　Plaxton Paramount 3200 III　C53F　1986　Ex Shearings, 1992

501	D588MVR	503	D592MVR	505	D597MVR	506	D598MVR	507	D601MVR
502	D590MVR	504	D596MVR						

511	ATH110T	Leyland Leopard PSU5C/4R	Duple 320(1989)	C53F	1978	Ex United Welsh Coaches, 1992
512	B336BGL	Leyland Tiger TRCTL11/3RH	Duple Caribbean 2	C48FT	1983	Ex Western National, 1992
513	B337BGL	Leyland Tiger TRCTL11/3RH	Duple Caribbean 2	C48FT	1983	Ex Western National, 1992
514	E675UNE	Leyland Tiger TRCTL11/3RZ	Plaxton Paramount 3200 III	C53F	1988	Ex Shearings, 1993
515	E677UNE	Leyland Tiger TRCTL11/3RZ	Plaxton Paramount 3200 III	C53F	1988	Ex Shearings, 1993
516	F771GNA	Leyland Tiger TRCTL11/3ARZA	Plaxton Paramount 3200 III	C53F	1989	Ex Shearings, 1993
517	J45SNY	Leyland Tiger TRCL10/3ARZM	Plaxton 321	C50F	1991	Ex Bebb, Llantwit Fardre, 1993
518	J46SNY	Leyland Tiger TRCL10/3ARZM	Plaxton 321	C50F	1991	Ex Bebb, Llantwit Fardre, 1993
519	J48SNY	Leyland Tiger TRCL10/3ARZM	Plaxton 321	C50F	1991	Ex Bebb, Llantwit Fardre, 1993
520	J54SNY	Leyland Tiger TRCL10/3ARZM	Plaxton 321	C50F	1991	Ex Bebb, Llantwit Fardre, 1993
521	F613XWY	Leyland Tiger TRCTL11/3R	Plaxton Paramount 3200 E	C53F	1988	Ex Yorkshire Rider, 1994
522	F614XWY	Leyland Tiger TRCTL11/3R	Plaxton Paramount 3200 E	C53F	1988	Ex Yorkshire Rider, 1994

601-620

Volvo B10M-62　Plaxton Premiére 320　C53F　1995-96

601	N601APU	605	N605APU	609	N609APU	613	N613APU	617	N617APU
602	N602APU	606	N606APU	610	N610APU	614	N614APU	618	N618APU
603	N603APU	607	N607APU	611	N611APU	615	N615APU	619	N619APU
604	N604APU	608	N608APU	612	N612APU	616	N616APU	620	N620APU

705	C483BFB	Ford Transit 190	Dormobile	B16F	1985	Ex Badgerline, 1991

800-804

Mercedes-Benz 811D　Reeve Burgess Beaver　B23F　1989　Ex Eastern National, 1990

800	F800RHK	801	F801RHK	802	F802RHK	803	F803RHK	804	F804RHK

805-811

Mercedes-Benz 811D　Plaxton Beaver　B31F　1992

805	K805DJN	807	K807DJN	809	K809DJN	810	K810DJN	811	K811DJN
806	K806DJN	808	K808DJN						

Forming part of the 1995 Badgerline order are twenty-seven Dennis Darts with Plaxton Pointer bodies. Seen here is 932, M932TEV seen at Romford Station. Thamesway are now part of FirstBus following the merger of Badgerline Holdings and GRT plc. Full details of all FirstBus fleets may be found in sister publication The FirstBus Bus Handbook. *Tony Wilson*

901-917
Dennis Dart 9SDL3016   Plaxton Pointer   B35F   1993

901	K901CVW	905	K905CVW	909	K909CVW	912	K912CVW	915	K915CVW
902	K902CVW	906	K906CVW	910	K910CVW	913	K913CVW	916	K916CVW
903	K903CVW	907	K907CVW	911	K911CVW	914	K914CVW	917	K917CVW
904	K904CVW	908	K908CVW						

918-943
Dennis Dart 9.8SDL3035   Plaxton Pointer   B39F   1994

918	M918TEV	924	M924TEV	930	M930TEV	935	M935TEV	940	M940TEV
919	M919TEV	925	M925TEV	931	M931TEV	936	M936TEV	941	M941TEV
920	M920TEV	926	M926TEV	932	M932TEV	937	M937TEV	942	M942TEV
921	M921TEV	927	M927TEV	933	M933TEV	938	M938TEV	943	M943TEV
922	M922TEV	928	M928TEV	934	M934TEV	939	M939TEV		
923	M923TEV	929	M929TEV						

1001	H101KVX	Leyland Olympian ON2R50C13Z4	Leyland	H47/31F	1990
1002	H102KVX	Leyland Olympian ON2R50C13Z4	Leyland	H47/31F	1990
1003	H103KVX	Leyland Olympian ON2R50C13Z4	Leyland	H47/31F	1990
1004	H104KVX	Leyland Olympian ON2R50C13Z4	Leyland	H47/31F	1990

1400-1424
Leyland Lynx LX112L10ZR1R   Leyland Lynx   B49F   1988   Ex Eastern National, 1990

1400	E400HWC	1409	F409LTW	1412	F412MNO	1419	F419MWC	1422	F422MJN
1404	F404LTW	1410	F410MNO	1417	F417MWC	1420	F420MJN	1423	F423MJN
1405	F405LTW	1411	F411MNO	1418	F418MWC	1421	F421MJN	1424	F424MJN
1406	F406LTW								

1601	L601MWC	Volvo B6-9.9M	Northern Counties Paladin	B40F	1993

1803-1871 — Leyland National 11351A/1R — B49F — 1977-78 Ex Eastern National, 1990

1803	TJN502R	1830	VNO732S	1840	WJN560S	1853	YEV311S	1868	YEV326S
1821	VNO744S	1835	VAR895S	1845	WJN565S	1854	YEV312S	1869	YEV327S
1822	VNO745S	1837	VAR897S	1846	WJN566S	1857	YEV315S	1871	YEV329S
1823	VAR900S	1839	WJN559S	1847	YEV305S	1864	YEV322S		

1875-1922 — Leyland National 11351A/1R — B49F — 1978-79 Ex Eastern National, 1990

1876	BNO666T	1886	BNO676T	1894	BNO684T	1904	DAR126T	1912	DAR134T
1878	BNO668T	1887	BNO677T	1895	BNO685T	1906	DAR128T	1913	JHJ139V
1879w	BNO669T	1888w	BNO678T	1896	DAR118T	1907	DAR129T	1915	JHJ141V
1881	BNO671T	1889	BNO679T	1897	DAR119T	1908	DAR130T	1918	JHJ145V
1882	BNO672T	1891w	BNO681T	1898	DAR120T	1909	DAR131T	1919	JHJ146V
1884	BNO674T	1893w	BNO683T	1903	DAR125T	1911	DAR133T	1920w	JHJ148V

2202	FDZ984	Leyland Tiger TRCTL11/3R	Duple Goldliner	C48FT	1982	Ex Western National, 1994
3110	XHK215X	Bristol VRT/SL3/6LXB	Eastern Coach Works	H43/31F	1981	Ex Eastern National, 1990
3113	XHK218X	Bristol VRT/SL3/6LXB	Eastern Coach Works	H43/31F	1981	Ex Eastern National, 1990
4000	XHK235X	Leyland Olympian ONLXB/1R	Eastern Coach Works	H45/32F	1981	Ex Eastern National, 1990
4001	XHK236X	Leyland Olympian ONLXB/1R	Eastern Coach Works	H45/32F	1981	Ex Eastern National, 1990
4002	XHK237X	Leyland Olympian ONLXB/1R	Eastern Coach Works	H45/32F	1981	Ex Eastern National, 1990
4003	B698BPU	Leyland Olympian ONLXB/1R	Eastern Coach Works	H45/32F	1984	Ex Eastern National, 1991
4004	B699BPU	Leyland Olympian ONLXB/1R	Eastern Coach Works	H45/32F	1984	Ex Eastern National, 1992
4005	C711GEV	Leyland Olympian ONLXB/1R	Eastern Coach Works	H45/32F	1984	Ex Eastern National, 1991
4006	C712GEV	Leyland Olympian ONLXB/1R	Eastern Coach Works	H45/32F	1985	Ex Eastern National, 1991
4009	C409HJN	Leyland Olympian ONLXB/1RH	Eastern Coach Works	DPH42/30F	1985	Ex Eastern National, 1990
FRS21	E962SVP	Freight Rover Sherpa	Carlyle Citybus 2	B18F	1988	Ex District Bus, Wickford, 1995
FRS22	E509TOV	Freight Rover Sherpa	Carlyle Citybus 2	B18F	1988	Ex District Bus, Wickford, 1995
FRS23	F105SOG	Freight Rover Sherpa	Carlyle Citybus 2	B18F	1988	Ex District Bus, Wickford, 1995
FRS24	F892XOE	Freight Rover Sherpa	Carlyle Citybus 2	B18F	1989	Ex District Bus, Wickford, 1995
IMB26	F995XOV	Iveco Daily 49.10	Carlyle Dailybus 2	B23F	1990	Ex District Bus, Wickford, 1995
IMB27	F996XOV	Iveco Daily 49.10	Carlyle Dailybus 2	B23F	1990	Ex District Bus, Wickford, 1995
IMB28	G148GOL	Iveco Daily 49.10	Carlyle Dailybus 2	B23F	1991	Ex District Bus, Wickford, 1995
IMB29	G145GOL	Iveco Daily 49.10	Carlyle Dailybus 2	B23F	1991	Ex District Bus, Wickford, 1995
FRS30	D873LWR	Freight Rover Sherpa	Dormobile	B20F	1987	Ex District Bus, Wickford, 1995

Livery: Canary yellow and purple; Yellow and orange (City Saver) 501-21

Previous Registrations:

ATH110T	AFH192T, MKH487A, AEP253T, 999BCY, ATH58T, 278TNY
FDZ984	OHM831Y

Four Leyland Olympians new to Thamesway are numbered in the 1000 series, while those acquired from elsewhere are numbered in the 4000 series. Seen in New Barnet is 1003, H103KVX.
Malc McDonald

TOWLER

Alan C Towler, Church Road, Emneth,
Wisbech, Cambridge PE14 8AA

GNG710N	Bristol VRT/SL2/6LX	Eastern Coach Works	H43/31F	1974	Ex The Bee Line, 1993
GNJ574N	Bristol VRT/SL2/6LX	Eastern Coach Works	H43/31F	1974	Ex Brighton & Hove, 1990
NPD690W	Bedford YNT	Plaxton Supreme IV	C53F	1981	Ex Safeguard, Guildford, 1986
PAY7W	Bedford YMT	Duple Dominant IV	C53F	1981	Ex Kinch, Mountsorrell, 1984
RSE156W	Bedford YMT	Duple Dominant IV	C53F	1981	Ex Hawkes, Waunarlwydd, 1994
TPM616X	Bedford YNT	Plaxton Supreme VI	C53F	1982	Ex Gastonia, Cranleigh, 1985
UFX629X	Bristol LHS6L	Plaxton Supreme V	C35F	1982	Ex Derby, 1987
D217OOJ	Freight Rover Sherpa	Carlyle	B18F	1987	Ex Bee Line Buzz, 1992
131HUO	Leyland Tiger TRCL10/3ARZM	Jonckheere Jubilee P599	C51FT	1988	Ex Gillespie, Kelty, 1992
A16ATC	DAF SB2305DHTD585	Duple 340	C53FT	1988	Ex Selwyn Hughes, Llanfair Caereinion, 1995
E905LVE	Volkswagen LT55	Optare City Pacer	B25F	1988	Ex Cambus, 1993

Livery: Cream, green and orange

Previous Registrations:

131HUO	E686NNH	A16ATC	E594LVH

Representing the Towler fleet is E905LVE, a Volkswagen LT55 with Optare City Pacer bodywork. New to Cambus, it is seen working for its current owner in Kings Lynn. *Paul Wigan*

UNIVERSITYBUS

Universitybus Ltd, University of Hertfordshire, College Lane, Hatfield,
Hertfordshire AL10 9AB

Depot : BAe, Comet Way, Hatfield

OV304	H748CBP	Mercedes-Benz 811D	Phoenix	B33F	1990	
OV305	H749CBP	Mercedes-Benz 811D	Phoenix	B33F	1991	
OV306	H840NOC	Dennis Dart 9.8SDL3004	Carlyle Dartline	B40F	1990	Ex Dennis demonstrator, 1991
OV307	H849NOC	Dennis Dart 9.8SDL3004	Carlyle Dartline	B43F	1990	Ex Carlyle demonstrator, 1991
OV309	THX204S	Leyland National 10351A/2R		B36D	1978	Ex London Buses, 1992
OV310	THX216S	Leyland National 10351A/2R		B36D	1978	Ex London Buses, 1992
OV311	THX261S	Leyland National 10351A/2R	East Lancs Greenway(1993)	B41F	1978	Ex London Buses, 1992
OV313	THX122S	Leyland National 10351A/2R		B39D	1977	Ex Blue Triangle, Rainham, 1993
OV314	THX243S	Leyland National 10351A/2R		B39D	1978	Ex Blue Triangle, Rainham, 1993
OV315	G472PGE	Leyland Lynx LX112L10ZR1R	Leyland	B51F	1989	Ex Whitelaw, Stonehouse, 1993
OV316	JND257V	Leyland Leopard PSU5C/4R	Duple Dominant II	C53F	1980	Ex Whitelaw, Stonehouse, 1993
OV321	GNF15V	Leyland Titan TNTL11/1RF	Park Royal	H47/26F	1980	Ex Blue Triangle, 1994
OV323	M47HUT	Bluebird CSRE2700	Bluebird Q-Bus	B51F	1994	
OV324	M48HUT	Bluebird CSRE2700	Bluebird Q-Bus	B51F	1994	
OV325	M49HUT	Bluebird CSRE2700	Bluebird Q-Bus	B51F	1994	
OV326	M51HUT	Bluebird CSRE2700	Bluebird Q-Bus	B51F	1994	
	EUI4415	Volvo B10M-61	Berkhof Everest 365	C49F	1983	Ex Time Travel, Thornton Heath, 1995
	B761OPJ	Mercedes-Benz L608D	Reeve Burgess	C21F	1994	Ex Chivers, Elstead, 1995
	B49FFE	Mercedes-Benz L608D	Reeve Burgess	C23F	1994	Ex ??, 1995
	F930TBP	Mercedes-Benz 609D	Mercedes-Benz	C24F	1989	Ex van, 1995
	M255UKX	Mercedes-Benz OH1416	Wright Urbanranger	B47F	1995	
	M527UGS	Mercedes-Benz OH1416	Wright Urbanranger	B47F	1995	
	M146VVS	Dennis Dart 9.8SDL3054	Wright Handy-bus	B42F	1995	
	M148VVS	Dennis Dart 9.8SDL3054	Wright Handy-bus	B42F	1995	
	N421ENM	Dennis Dart 9.8SDL3054	Marshall C37	B40F	1995	
	N422ENM	Dennis Dart 9.8SDL3054	Marshall C37	B40F	1995	
	N423ENM	Dennis Dart 9.8SDL3054	Marshall C37	B40F	1995	
	N424ENM	Dennis Dart 9.8SDL3054	Marshall C37	B40F	1995	

Livery: White, black and grey

Previous Registrations: EUI4415   BDV862Y

Universitybus'
Leyland Lynx,
G472PGE, is seen
here at St Albans
rail station. The UH
symbol indicates the
University of
Hertfordshire, the
owners of the
Universitybus
operation. *BBP*

Recently delivered to Universitybus were two Mercedes-Benz OH1416 with Wright's Urbanranger body. One of these is seen in St Albans while working service 602 to Watford Junction rail station. Universitybus was the first customer for this competitively priced vehicle. *Colin Lloyd*

Originally with Greater Manchester, until it passed to London Buses several years ago, Titan GNF15V, is now the sole remaining double deck bus in the Universitybus fleet. It was photographed in Watford. *BBP*

Viscount operates Leyland Olympians with Leyland, Northern Counties and Eastern Coach Works bodies. Shown here are B4, H474CEG an all-Leyland example new to Viscount in 1990, and B10, F510NJE, one of six Northern Counties-bodied examples inherited from Cambus when the Peterborough operations were separated in 1989. The latter picture was taken in Huntingdon as B10 sets out on its return journey. *Lee Whitehead/Paul Wigan*

VISCOUNT

Viscount Bus and Coach Co Ltd, 351 Lincoln Road, Peterborough,
Cambridgeshire, PE1 2PG

Depots: Wisbech Road, March and Lincoln Road, Peterborough. Outstations: Crowland; Market Deeping; Stamford and Wisbech.

A subsidiary of Cambus Holdings Ltd.

B1	VEX291X	Bristol VRT/SL3/6LXB	Eastern Coach Works	DPH41/25F	1981	Ex Cambus, 1989
B2	E502LFL	Leyland Olympian ONLXCT/1RH	Optare	DPH43/27F	1988	Ex Cambus, 1989
B3	H473CEG	Leyland Olympian ON2R50G13Z4	Leyland	H47/31F	1990	
B4	H474CEG	Leyland Olympian ON2R50G13Z4	Leyland	H43/27F	1990	
B5	H475CEG	Leyland Olympian ON2R50G13Z4	Leyland	H47/31F	1990	

B6-B11

		Leyland Olympian ONLXB/1R	Northern Counties	H45/30F	1988	Ex Cambus, 1989

B6	F506NJE	B8	F508NJE	B9	F509NJE	B10	F510NJE	B11	F511NJE
B7	F507NJE								

B12	A561KWY	Leyland Olympian ONLXB/1R	Eastern Coach Works	H45/32F	1983	Ex Selby & District, 1995
B36	DEX227T	Bristol VRT/SL3/6LXB	Eastern Coach Works	H43/31F	1979	Ex Cambus, 1989
B37	HAH237V	Bristol VRT/SL3/6LXB	Eastern Coach Works	H43/31F	1979	Ex Cambus, 1989
B38	YNG208S	Bristol VRT/SL3/6LXB	Eastern Coach Works	H43/31F	1978	Ex Cambus, 1989
B39	PWY39W	Bristol VRT/SL3/6LXB	Eastern Coach Works	H43/31F	1980	Ex York City & District, 1990
B40	PWY40W	Bristol VRT/SL3/6LXB	Eastern Coach Works	H43/31F	1980	Ex York City & District, 1990

B41-B52

		Bristol VRT/SL3/6LXB	Eastern Coach Works	H43/31F	1977-81	Ex Cambus, 1989

B41	WPW201S	B44	RAH264W	B47	KVF247V	B49	KVF249V	B51	VEX301X
B42	WPW202S	B45	KVF245V	B48	KVF248V	B50	KVF250V	B52	VEX299X
B43	VPW85S	B46	KVF246V						

B57	BFX570T	Bristol VRT/SL3/6LXB	Eastern Coach Works	H43/31F	1979	Ex Wilts & Dorset, 1993
B58	VAH278X	Bristol VRT/SL3/6LXB	Eastern Coach Works	H43/31F	1981	Ex Cambus, 1989
B59	VAH279X	Bristol VRT/SL3/6LXB	Eastern Coach Works	H43/31F	1981	Ex Cambus, 1989
B60	VAH280X	Bristol VRT/SL3/6LXB	Eastern Coach Works	H43/31F	1981	Ex Cambus, 1989

Still a dominant feature of double-deck bus operation is the Bristol VR with many late examples now moving between fleets as the youngest VRs are now 13 years old. Photographed in Peterborough was B47, KVF247V, a veteran which originated with Eastern Counties. All six of the KVF batch were allocated to Peterborough with Eastern Counties and they have remained there.
Richard Godfrey.

B66-B73 Bristol VRT/SL3/6LXB Eastern Coach Works H43/31F 1979-81 Ex York City & District, 1990

B66	LWU466V	**B68**	LWU468V	**B70**	LWU470V	**B72**	SUB792W	**B73**	SUB793W
B67	LWU467V	**B69**	FWR219T	**B71**	SUB791W				

B74-B80 Bristol VRT/SL3/6LXB Eastern Coach Works H43/31F 1981 Ex Keighley & District, 1990

B74	SUB790W	**B76**	PWY46W	**B78**	PWY48W	**B79**	PWY49W	**B80**	PWY50W
B75	PWY45W	**B77**	PWY47W						

FLF453 JAH553D Bristol FLF6G Eastern Coach Works H38/32F 1966 Ex Cambus, 1989

S1-7 Optare MetroRider Optare B29F 1992-93 Ex Cambus, 1993

1	K391KUA	**3**	K393KUA	**5**	J805DWW	**6**	J806DWW	**7**	J807DWW
2	K392KUA	**4**	K975HUB						

S8	M808WWR	Optare MetroRider	Optare	B27F	1995
S9	M809WWR	Optare MetroRider	Optare	B27F	1995
S10	M810WWR	Optare MetroRider	Optare	B27F	1995

S71-S77 Iveco 59-12 Marshall C31 B25F 1992-93

S71	K171CAV	**S73**	K173CAV	**S75**	K175CAV	**S76**	K176CAV	**S77**	K177CAV
S72	K172CAV	**S74**	K174CAV						

WM1	E664RVP	MCW MetroRider MF150/17	MCW	B25F	1987	On loan from West Midlands Travel
WM2	D642NOE	MCW MetroRider MF150/4	MCW	B25F	1987	On loan from West Midlands Travel
WM7	D647NOE	MCW MetroRider MF150/4	MCW	B25F	1987	On loan from West Midlands Travel
WM9	D645NOE	MCW MetroRider MF150/4	MCW	B25F	1987	On loan from West Midlands Travel
WM10	E657RVP	MCW MetroRider MF150/17	MCW	B25F	1987	On loan from West Midlands Travel
WM12	D631NOE	MCW MetroRider MF150/4	MCW	B25F	1987	On loan from West Midlands Travel
WM13	D603NOE	MCW MetroRider MF150/4	MCW	B25F	1987	On loan from West Midlands Travel
WM15	D640NOE	MCW MetroRider MF150/4	MCW	B25F	1987	On loan from West Midlands Travel
WM16	D604NOE	MCW MetroRider MF150/4	MCW	B25F	1987	On loan from West Midlands Travel
WM17	D605NOE	MCW MetroRider MF150/4	MCW	B25F	1987	On loan from West Midlands Travel

Livery: White, yellow, blue and grey; red, cream and maroon (Peterborough Bus Company) B37/57, S2/3/9/10.

Named Vehicles: B3 *Sir Henry Royce Bt*; B4 *John Clare*; B5 *Katharine of Aragon*; B6 *Red Poll*; B7 *Viscount Crowland*; B8 *Owen Palmer*; B11 *Evelyn Glennie OBE*; B12 *Robin Redbreast*; B55 *Red Admiral*; B75 *Scarlett O'Hara*; FLF453 *Old Scarlett*; S2 *Redwing*; S4 *Redstart*; S8 *Sir William Laxton*; S9 *Red Setter*; S10 *Red Arrows.*

Viscount currently operate several buses on loan from West Midlands Travel's large hire fleet. Seen at Peterborough with Viscount names is WM1, E664RVP, a MCW MetroRider.
Lee Whitehead

WATSON ENTERPRISES

Viking Bland Ltd, 56 Lampits Hill, Corringham, Essex RM18 7HH

Depot: Unit 2, Thurrock Park Way, Tilbury

7042EL	Kässbohrer Setra S215HD	Kässbohrer	C49FT	1985	Ex Brooks, Reading, 1989
HIL2833	Volvo C10M-70	Ramseier & Jenser	C49F	1985	Ex Park's, 1991
F26YBO	Kässbohrer Setra S215HR	Kässbohrer Rational	C49FT	1987	Ex Bebb, Llantwit Fardre, 1991
HIL2838	Kässbohrer Setra S215HD	Kässbohrer	C49FT	1987	Ex Draper, Sidcup, 1991
K596VBC	Toyota Coaster HDB30R	Caetano Optimo II	C18F	1993	

Livery: White

Previous Registrations:

7042EL	From new		HIL2833	C346GSD	HIL2838	E186EPF

The silver, black and red livery of Watson Enterprises is shown on 7042EL, a Kässbohrer Setra 215.
This vehicle was new to Trevor Carnell, the innovative coach operator who sadly died earlier in 1995.
Colin Lloyd

WAYLANDS

WF & MA Berry, 4 Well Terrace, Beccles, Norfolk, NR34 0HR

Depot: Ellough Industrial Estate, Beccles

WHJ869S	Ford Transit 160	Ford	M6	1977	Ex private owner, 1990
B163TNE	Ford Transit 160	Deansgate	M12	1985	Ex Wheatley, Barrowash, 1994
C117KMA	Mercedes-Benz L608D	PMT Handforth	C21F	1986	Ex Smithyman, Maltby, 1994
C247OFE	Mercedes-Benz L608D	Reeve Burgess	B20F	1986	Ex RoadCar, 1995
C248OFE	Mercedes-Benz L608D	Reeve Burgess	B20F	1986	Ex RoadCar, 1995
D768JUB	Freight Rover Sherpa	Dormobile	B20F	1986	Ex Yorkshire Rider, 1990
D774PTU	Freight Rover Sherpa	Dormobile	B16F	1986	Ex Dighton, Ipswich, 1994
D204NON	Freight Rover Sherpa	Carlyle	B18F	1987	Ex RoadCar, 1994
F623FNA	Mercedes-Benz 609D	Made-to-Measure	C24F	1988	Ex Pride of the Road, 1994
F596CDT	Freight Rover Sherpa	Carlyle Citybus 2	B20F	1988	Ex RoadCar, 1994
F207CNG	Ford Transit VE6	Ford	M8	1989	Ex private owner, 1990
F52UBX	Renault Trafic	Cymric	M14	1989	Ex private owner, 1992
F715UBX	Renault Trafic	Cymric	M14	1989	Ex Charter Hire, Cardiff, 1992
F783LJR	Toyota Coaster HB31R	Caetano Optimo	C21F	1989	Ex ?, 1995
G277TST	Freight Rover Sherpa	Dormobile	B20F	1989	Ex Alexander's, Aberdeen, 1991
G363PNS	Ford Transit VE6	Dormobile	B16F	1989	Ex Neil, Duxford, 1994
G432VJV	Mercedes-Benz 208D	Devon Conversions	M8	1990	Ex Ryder Rentals, 1994
J281RNE	Mercedes-Benz 609D	Made-to-Measure	C20F	1992	Ex Cygnus, Paisley, 1994
J35UTG	Leyland DAF 400	Carlyle Citybus 2	B20F	1992	Ex Bebb, Llantwit Fardre, 1994
K4WMS	Renault Master T35D	Cymric	M16	1992	
L4WMS	Renault Master T35D	Cymric	M16	1994	
M4WMS	Renault Master T35D	Cymric	M16	1994	
M242AEX	Mercedes-Benz 711D	Marshall C19	B29F	1995	
N4WMS	Renault Master T35D	Cymric	M16	1995	

Livery:

Seen in Lambeth Road is Duple-bodied Bova A14BUS of West's Coaches. This example features the Calypso design that resembles aspects of the Caribbean model. *Colin Lloyd*

WEST'S

West's Coaches Ltd, 198/200 High Road, Woodford Green, Essex, IG8 8EF

JFP177V	Ford R1114	Duple Dominant II	C53F	1980	
LUE260V	Ford R1114	Duple Dominant II	C46F	1980	
KGA56Y	Bova EL26/581	Bova Europa	C53F	1982	Ex Henry Crawford, Neilston, 1987
A15BUS	Bova EL28/581	Duple Calypso	C53F	1984	Ex Blue Iris, Nailsea, 1988
A14BUS	Bova EL28/581	Duple Calypso	C53F	1984	Ex Antler, Rugeley, 1988
D869NVS	Freight Rover Sherpa	Dormobile	B16F	1986	Ex London Country NW, 1988
E667YDT	MCW MetroRider MF150/88	MCW	B23F	1988	
F711CWJ	MCW MetroRider MF150/97	MCW	B23F	1988	
F712CWJ	MCW MetroRider MF150/97	MCW	B23F	1988	
F713CWJ	MCW MetroRider MF150/110	MCW	B23F	1988	
F714CWJ	MCW MetroRider MF150/110	MCW	B23F	1988	
F715CWJ	MCW MetroRider MF150/110	MCW	B23F	1988	
F718CWJ	MCW MetroRider MF150/110	MCW	B23F	1988	
F719CWJ	MCW MetroRider MF150/110	MCW	B23F	1988	
F367CHE	MCW MetroRider MF150/110	MCW	B23F	1988	
A10BUS	DAF SB220LC550	Optare Delta	B47F	1989	
A12BUS	DAF SB2305DHS585	Caetano Algarve	C53F	1989	Ex Abbeyways, Halifax, 1991
A16BUS	Volvo B10M-60	Plaxton Paramount 3500 III	C53F	1989	Ex Park's, 1992
A18BUS	Volvo B10M-60	Plaxton Paramount 3500 III	C53F	1989	Ex Essex Coachways, Bow, 1994
F814TMD	Volvo B10M-60	Plaxton Paramount 3500 III	C53F	1989	Ex Lacey, Barking, 1994
A19BUS	DAF SB3000DKV601	Caetano Algarve	C49FT	1989	Ex Ace, Mansfield, 1993
H20BUS	Leyland Swift LBM6T/2RA	Wadham Stringer Vanguard II	B39F	1991	
J6BUS	Dennis Dart 9SDL3011	Wright Handy-bus	B35F	1992	
J9BUS	Dennis Dart 9.8SDL3012	Wright Handy-bus	DP40F	1992	
J12BUS	Dennis Dart 9.8SDL3017	Wright Handy-bus	B40F	1992	
K2BUS	Dennis Dart 9.8SDL3017	Wright Handy-bus	B40F	1992	
K5BUS	DAF SB220LC550	Optare Delta	B49F	1993	

Previous Registrations:

A10BUS	G259EHD	A15BUS	A321HFP	A19BUS	G949VBC
A12BUS	F233RJX	A16BUS	F972HGE	H20BUS	H550AMT, A19BUS
A14BUS	B127DHL	A18BUS	F813TMD		

Livery: White, red and yellow

West's K2BUS, a Dennis Dart with Wright Handy-bus bodywork is seen at Traps Hill, Loughton while operating the Chingford circular. It is now one of four similar buses in the fleet. *Richard Godfrey*

Go Whippet operate a varied collection of vehicles on their services in the Cambridge area. Representing them are OCU781R with a Scania BR111DH underframe and MCW Metropolitan body from a batch of 164 supplied to London Transport. It is now converted to single-door and was photographed as it left Cambridge bus station for St Ives.

Photographed at Bar Hill while heading for Huntingdon is FEW224Y. It is one of five DAF MB200s with Plaxton Paramount 3200 Express bodies in the fleet. The picture shows a non-standard express entrance arrangement and destination display used by Go Whippet. This operator also has five Volvo Citybuses, the double-deck version of the B10M. Three have Northern Counties bodies while the other two, like E441ADV seen here were built by Alexander. E441ADV is seen at St Ives, and was previously operated by Filer of Ilfracombe and was unusual for a small operator in rural Devon.
Paul Wigan

WHIPPET

Whippet Coaches Ltd, Cambridge Road, Fenstanton, Cambridgeshire

Depots : Fairways Depot, Potton Road, Biggleswade and Cambridge Road, Fenstanton. **Outstations** : Village Hall Car Park, Gamlingay; Old Railway Station Yard, Graffham; Manor Farm, Hurleditch Road, Onwell and Back Lane, Ringstead.

KJD271P	Scania BR111DH	MCW Metropolitan	H45/32F	1976	Ex London Transport, 1984
LEW971P	Leyland Atlantean AN68/1R	Roe	H45/34F	1976	
OCU781R	Scania BR111DH	MCW Metropolitan	H45/29D	1976	Ex Reading, 1989
OUC109R	Scania BR111DH	MCW Metropolitan	H43/32F	1976	Ex London Transport, 1983
OUC123R	Scania BR111DH	MCW Metropolitan	H43/29D	1976	Ex London Transport, 1985
WKH424S	Scania BR111DH	MCW Metropolitan	H44/30F	1977	Ex Camm, Nottingham, 1989
WKH426S	Scania BR111DH	MCW Metropolitan	O44/30F	1977	Ex Camm, Nottingham, 1989
EAV811V	Leyland Atlantean AN68A/2R	Northern Counties	H47/36F	1980	
EAV812V	Volvo B58-56	Duple Dominant	B63F	1980	
RDS82W	Volvo B58-56	Duple Dominant	DP53F	1980	Ex Skill's, Sheffield, 1991
FCY290W	Bedford YMQ	Duple Dominant	B45F	1981	Ex Hedingham & District, 1992
FCY292W	Bedford YMQ	Duple Dominant	B45F	1981	Ex Hedingham & District, 1992
FCY293W	Bedford YMQ	Duple Dominant	B45F	1981	Ex Hedingham & District, 1992
REG870X	Volvo B58-56	Duple Dominant	B63F	1981	
KYN283X	Leyland Titan TNLXB2RRSp	Leyland	H44/30F	1981	Ex London Buses, 1993
KYN296X	Leyland Titan TNLXB2RRSp	Leyland	H44/30F	1981	Ex London Buses, 1993
VAV161X	Volvo B10M-61	Plaxton Supreme VI Express	C57F	1982	
EEW113Y	DAF MB200DKFL600	Plaxton Paramount 3200 E	C57F	1983	
FEW224Y	DAF MB200DKFL600	Plaxton Paramount 3200 E	C57F	1983	
FEW225Y	DAF MB200DKFL600	Plaxton Paramount 3200 E	C57F	1983	
FEW226Y	DAF MB200DKFL600	Plaxton Paramount 3200 E	C53F	1983	
FEW227Y	DAF MB200DKFL600	Plaxton Paramount 3200 E	C53F	1983	
A807REW	DAF MB200DKFL600	Duple Caribbean	C55F	1984	
B102EFL	DAF SB2300DHS585	Plaxton Paramount 3500 II	C53F	1985	
B103EFL	DAF SB2300DHS585	Plaxton Paramount 3500 II	C53F	1985	
GIL2968	Volvo B10M-61	Plaxton Paramount 3200 II	C57F	1985	Ex Reliance, Gravesend, 1991
C189MFL	DAF MB230DKFL615	Plaxton Paramount 3500 II	C53F	1986	
C43NEW	DAF MB230DKVL615	Plaxton Paramount 3500 II	C53F	1986	
D850AAV	Leyland Atlantean AN68/2L	Willowbrook	H49/37D	1987	
E893HEG	DAF SB2305DHS585	Plaxton Paramount 3500 III	C53F	1987	
E441ADV	Volvo Citybus B10M-50	Alexander RV	DPH47/35F	1988	Ex Filer, Ilfracombe, 1991
E176OEW	Volvo Citybus B10M-50	Alexander RV	DPH47/35F	1988	
E177OEW	DAF SB2305DHS585	Duple 340	C55F	1988	
E178OEW	DAF SB2305DHS585	Duple 340	C55F	1988	
F693PAY	Volvo B10M-61	Plaxton Paramount 3200 III	C53F	1989	
F694PAY	Volvo B10M-61	Plaxton Paramount 3500 III	C53F	1989	
G823UMU	Volvo Citybus B10M-50	Northern Counties	DPH45/35F	1989	
G824UMU	Volvo Citybus B10M-50	Northern Counties	DPH45/35F	1989	
H303CAV	Volvo Citybus B10M-50	Northern Counties	DPH45/35F	1990	
J722KBC	Volvo B10M-60	Plaxton Paramount 3200 III	C53F	1992	
J723KBC	Volvo B10M-60	Plaxton Paramount 3200 III	C53F	1992	
PIW4798	OCC Omni	OCC	B12F	1994	
M150EAV	OCC Omni	OCC	B12F	1995	
M589SDC	OCC Omni	OCC	B21F	1995	

Livery: Two-tone blue and cream

Previous Registration:

GIL2968	B169WKO	PIW4798	?

Windmill Coaches have built a fleet of Bova Futura coaches. Typical is L425OWF seen in Victoria Street in April 1995. Windmill are now owned by, though operated separately from, Crusader Holidays. *Colin Lloyd*

Motts Travel used the Yellow Bus name for their stage carriage operations, much of which passed to The Shires in the summer of 1995. Coach operations as well as some contracts continue, as does 90WFC, a Volvo B10M with Jonckheere Deauville bodywork. The vehicle was photographed while parked at the Epsom Derby. *BBP*

WINDMILL COACHES

Staines Crusader Coaches, 105 London Road, Copford, Colchester, Essex CO6 1LH

WGE37S	Bedford YMT	Plaxton Supreme	C53F	1978	Ex Robinson, Seaview, 1990
G421WFP	Bova FHD12.290	Bova Futura	C51FT	1990	
H423EUT	Bova FHD12.290	Bova Futura	C51FT	1991	
K424GHE	Bova FHD12.290	Bova Futura	C51FT	1995	
L425OWF	Bova FHD12.290	Bova Futura	C51FT	1994	

Livery: White and orange

YELLOW BUS / MOTTS

Motts Coaches (Aylesbury) Ltd, 15 Station Road, Stoke Mandeville,
Buckinghamshire, HP22 5UL

8	UKE830X	Leyland Leopard PSU3G/4R	Eastern Coach Works B51	DP49F	1982	Ex East Kent, 1991
13	KON323P	Leyland Fleetline FE30ALR(6LXG) MCW		H43/33F	1976	Ex West Midlands Travel, 1989
107	EHS107T	Leyland Leopard PSU3E/4R	Duple Dominant	B55F	1978	Ex Glyn Williams, Crosskeys, 1993
151	MUS151P	Leyland Leopard PSU3C/4R	Duple Dominant	B53F	1976	Ex Glyn Williams, Crosskeys, 1993
283	SUR283R	Leyland Leopard PSU3C/4R	Plaxton Supreme III	C53F	1977	Ex Clarke, Southall, 1987
368	OWG368X	Leyland Leopard PSU3F/4R	Plaxton Bustler	DP53F	1982	Ex South Yorkshire's Transport, 1991
463	OJD463R	Leyland Fleetline FE30AGR	Park Royal	H44/24D	1977	Ex London Buses, 1992
539	CUB539Y	MCW Metrobus DR102/32	MCW	H46/30F	1983	Ex Centrewest, 1994
540	CUB540Y	MCW Metrobus DR102/32	MCW	H46/30F	1983	Ex Centrewest, 1994
	6601MT	Volvo B10M-61	Jonckheere Jubilee P50	C51FT	1983	Ex Telling's, Byfleet, 1987
	SJI8286	Volvo B10M-61	Jonckheere Jubilee P90	CH46/13FT	1984	
	5705MT	Volvo B10MT-53	Van Hool Astral	CH55/12FT	1985	Ex Harris, Armadale, 1988
	4932PH	DAF SB2300DHTD585	Plaxton Paramount 3200 II	C53FL	1985	
	278CFC	Volvo B10MT-53	Jonckheere Jubilee P95	CH54/13DT	1985	Ex Flight's, Birmingham, 1989
	KSK966	DAF SB2300DHTD585	Plaxton Paramount 3200 II	C53F	1986	Ex Smith, Alcester, 1987
	KSK967	DAF SB2305DHTD585	Plaxton Paramount 3200 III	C53F	1987	Ex Smith, Alcester, 1988
	D407ERE	Freight Rover Sherpa	PMT Bursley	B18F	1987	Ex PMT, 1995
	5812MT	Volvo B10M-61	Jonckheere Jubilee P50	C51FT	1987	
	CSU960	Volvo B10M-61	Plaxton Paramount 3500 III	C49FT	1988	Ex Selwyn, Runcorn, 1989
	6957MT	Volvo B10M-61	Jonckheere Jubilee P99	C51FT	1988	Ex Morriston Coaches, Swansea, 1991
	4442MT	Aüwaerter Neoplan N122/3	Aüwaerter Skyliner	CH51/20CT	1988	Ex London Coaches, 1994
	F600DWB	Mercedes-Benz 609D	Whittaker Europa	C24F	1988	Ex Telford, Highworth, 1993
	F952RNV	Volvo B10M-61	Jonckheere Deauville P599	C51FT	1988	Ex Sunseeker Tours, Torquay, 1991
	9920MT	Volvo B10M-60	Jonckheere Deauville P599	C48FT	1989	Ex Antler, Rugeley, 1992
	F648PLW	Mercedes-Benz 609D	Reeve Burgess Beaver	C23F	1989	Ex Advance, Hemel Hempstead, 1991
	SIB6724	MAN 16.290	Jonckheere Deauville	C51FT	1989	Ex Shaw Hadwin, Silverdale, 1994
	6247MT	Volvo B10M-60	Jonckheere Deauville P599	C47FT	1989	
	5723MT	Volvo B10M-60	Jonckheere Deauville P599	C47FT	1989	
	90WFC	Volvo B10M-60	Jonckheere Deauville P599	C51FT	1990	
	H65XBD	Volvo B10M-60	Jonckheere Deauville P599	C51FT	1991	
	K229WNH	MAN 11.190	Jonckheere Deauville	C34FT	1992	Ex Jones, Newton Aycliffe, 1994
	K729GBE	Mercedes-Benz 814D	Autobus Classique 2	C25F	1993	Ex Classic, West Pelton, 1995
	K266OGA	Volvo B10M-61	Jonckheere Deauville	C53FT	1992	Ex Henry Crawford, Neilston, 1995
	K914RGE	Volvo B10M-61	Jonckheere Deauville	C53F	1993	Ex Clarkes of London, 1995

Livery: Yellow

Previous Registrations:

278CFC	C712GOP	6247MT	F902YNV	CSU960	E486BFM
4442MT	E93VWA	6601MT	ONV649Y	KSK966	C782MVH
4932PH	C460JCP	6957MT	E209GNV	KSK967	D289XCX
5705MT	B421CGG	90WFC	G380RNH	SIB6724	F957RNV, 525XPD
5723MT	F903YNV	9920MT	F103CBD	SJI8286	A384UNH, 4442MT
5812MT	D100DNV				

17EJU	Shorey	1482PP	Galloway	A101EPA	The Shires
25CTM	Seamarks	1754PP	Galloway	A110FDL	Southend
46AEW	Lodge's	2086PP	Galloway	A113EPA	The Shires
62CBK	Kenzie's	2267MK	Seamarks	A115EPA	The Shires
90WFC	Motts	2513PP	Rex Motor Services	A121EPA	The Shires
98TNO	Simmonds	2583KP	Buffalo	A122PAR	Hedingham
100BGO	Coach Services	2917MK	Seamarks	A124EPA	Southend
114RVX	Crusader	2942FH	Harris Bus	A128NAR	Fords Coaches
114UPH	Biss Brothers	2997HL	Buffalo	A136EPA	The Shires
125LUP	Biss Brothers	3196DD	Emblings	A138DPE	Sovereign
129SDV	Hedingham	3990ME	Sanders Coaches	A139DPE	Sovereign
131HUO	Towler	4011LJ	Crusader	A140DPE	Sovereign
149GJF	Semmence	4092PP	Galloway	A141DPE	The Shires
152EPA	The Shires	4442MT	Motts	A141EPA	Southend
153WAR	Richmond's	4512UR	Simmonds	A142DPE	The Shires
166UMB	Simmonds	4750WY	Great Yarmouth	A143DPE	The Shires
219GRA	Beestons	4932PH	Motts	A143EPA	The Shires
221GRA	Beestons	4940VF	Simmonds	A144EPA	Southend
222GRA	Beestons	5048PP	Galloway	A149FPG	The Shires
226LRB	Beestons	5228NW	Classic Coaches	A150EPA	The Shires
229LRB	Hedingham	5280NW	Classic Coaches	A151EPA	The Shires
238JUO	Charles Cook	538ELX	Simmonds	A151FPG	The Shires
239LYC	Richmond's	5516PP	Galloway	A152FPG	The Shires
256JPA	Simmonds	5611PP	Galloway	A153EPA	The Shires
259VYC	Sanders Coaches	5705MT	Motts	A153FPG	The Shires
264KTA	Classic Coaches	5723MT	Motts	A154FPG	The Shires
275FUM	Richmond's	5812MT	Motts	A155EPA	The Shires
278CFC	Motts	5970FH	Harris Bus	A155FPG	The Shires
354TRT	Sanders Coaches	6037PP	Galloway	A156EPA	Southend
403NMM	Richmond's	6101MV	Seamarks	A157EPA	The Shires
426YRA	Richmond's	6149KP	Eastern Counties	A197RUR	Felix
429UFM	The Shires	6220WY	Great Yarmouth	A202LCL	Neaves
430UFM	The Shires	6247MT	Motts	A211JDX	Chambers
436VVT	Lodge's	6306FH	Harris Bus	A246SVW	Southend
438XYA	Richmond's	6539FN	Caroline Seagull	A247SVW	Southend
460UEV	Simmonds	6541FN	Caroline Seagull	A248SVW	Southend
522FN	Caroline Seagull	6543FN	Caroline Seagull	A249SVW	Southend
523FN	Caroline Seagull	6544FN	Caroline Seagull	A250SVW	Colchester
524FN	Bordacoach	6545FN	Caroline Seagull	A266BTY	Semmence
526FN	Caroline Seagull	6546FN	Caroline Seagull	A301KFP	Semmence
530MUY	County	6547FN	Caroline Seagull	A331VHB	Hedingham
531FN	Caroline Seagull	6601MT	Motts	A486FPV	Hedingham
535FN	Caroline Seagull	6920MX	Eastern Counties	A487FPV	Hedingham
536FN	Caroline Seagull	6957MT	Motts	A561KWY	Viscount
537FN	Caroline Seagull	7042EL	Watson	A583MEH	Semmence
538FN	Caroline Seagull	7178KP	Buffalo	A660KUM	Eastern National
556EHN	Biss Brothers	7236PW	Simmonds	A663KUM	Eastern National
559ABX	Richmond's	7463RU	Cedric's	A665KUM	Eastern National
570EFJ	Classic Coaches	7694VC	Eastern Counties	A668KUM	Eastern National
572CNW	Classic Coaches	7968FH	Harris Bus	A681KDV	Cambus
574CNW	Classic Coaches	8333UR	Simmonds	A683KDV	Cambus
593FGF	Richmond's	8552PE	J B S	A694OHJ	Eastern National
648EAU	Richmond's	8726FH	Prestwood Travel	A698EAU	The Shires
649ETF	Richmond's	9242FH	Harris Bus	A699EAU	The Shires
668PTM	Richmond's	9349KP	Buffalo	A709KRT	Hedingham
686CXV	Cedar Coaches	9383MX	Simmonds	A807REW	Whippet
696BTV	Biss Brothers	9569KM	Seamarks	A819XMK	Simmonds
713WAF	Cedar Coaches	9683ML	Seamarks	AAL551A	Lodge's
729KTO	Richmond's	9920MT	Motts	ABD253B	Classic Coaches
753LNU	Richmond's	9983PW	Simmonds	ABV881V	Stephensons
759KFC	Hedingham	A10BUS	West's	ACP832V	Graham's
760BUS	Rover Bus Services	A12APT	APT	AEG121Y	Luckybus
784EYB	Fargo Coachlines	A12BUS	West's	AFH194T	Beestons
820KPO	Fords Coaches	A14BUS	West's	AFJ759T	Galloway
827APT	APT	A15BUS	West's	AJD24T	Neaves
848FXN	Marshall's	A16APT	APT	ANO271S	Eastern National
851FYD	Richmond's	A16BUS	West's	ANW710C	Classic Coaches
856GKH	Lamberts	A16ETC	Towler	APH511T	Neaves
892LTV	Richmond's	A18BUS	West's	APM111T	Prestwood Travel
1230HN	J B S	A19BUS	West's	APM117T	Prestwood Travel
1245FH	Harris Bus	A20APT	APT	APT42S	APT
1273LJ	Coach Services	A22UBD	Sanders Coaches	APT416B	APT
1404FM	Marshall's	A33UGA	Semmence	APW942S	Sanders Coaches
1440PP	Galloway	A62OJX	Don's	ARP612X	The Shires

Reg	Operator	Reg	Operator	Reg	Operator
ARP613X	The Shires	BAZ6877	APT	BVG219T	Eastern Counties
ARP614X	The Shires	BAZ7296	Airport Coaches	BVG220T	Eastern Counties
ARP615X	The Shires	BAZ7336	Airport Coaches	BVG221T	Eastern Counties
ARP616X	The Shires	BAZ7349	Airport Coaches	BVG222T	Eastern Counties
ARP617X	The Shires	BAZ7384	County	BVG223T	Eastern Counties
ARP618X	The Shires	BAZ7385	County	BVG224T	Eastern Counties
ARP619X	The Shires	BAZ7386	County	BVG225T	Eastern Counties
ARP620X	The Shires	BAZ8576	Golden Boy	BVP809V	Colchester
ATH110T	Thamesway	BBM53A	Galloway	BVP810V	Colchester
ATL312X	Sanders Coaches	BCJ733V	Hedingham	BVP812V	Colchester
AUD460R	Fords Coaches	BCL213T	Cambus	BVP821V	Colchester
AUD461R	Hedingham	BCL216T	Eastern Counties	BVV542T	The Shires
AUP714S	NIBS	BCL217T	Eastern Counties	BVV545T	The Shires
AYG848S	Eastern National	BDZ5198	Jacksons	BVV547T	The Shires
AYG850S	Eastern National	BEP963V	Eastern National	BVV548T	The Shires
AYJ99T	Sovereign	BEV105X	Hedingham	BWE193T	Spratts
B23XKX	Coach Services	BFL503V	Lamberts	BWE194T	Spratts
B49FFE	Universitybus	BFR301R	Bordacoach	BWK9T	Sanders Coaches
B63APP	Red Rose	BFR304R	Supreme	BXI3079	Semmence
B82NDX	Ipswich	BFS18L	Enterprise	C25KAV	Kenzie's
B83SWX	Southend	BFS19L	Enterprise	C28RFL	Kenzie's
B84SWX	Southend	BFS21L	Enterprise	C38WBF	Flying Banana
B85SWX	Southend	BFX570T	Viscount	C41HHJ	Colchester
B97PLU	Caroline Seagull	BHK710X	Hedingham	C43NEW	Whippet
B100XTW	Southend	BIL4419	NIBS	C46DUR	Galloway
B102EFL	Whippet	BIL4539	NIBS	C57WBF	Flying Banana
B103EFL	Whippet	BIL4710	NIBS	C72HDT	Semmence
B114LDX	Ipswich	BIL6538	NIBS	C106SDX	Ipswich
B115LDX	Ipswich	BIL7894	NIBS	C107HGL	Eastern National
B116LDX	Ipswich	BIL8430	Sanders Coaches	C107SDX	Ipswich
B117LDX	Ipswich	BIL8949	Sanders Coaches	C108SDX	Ipswich
B124BOO	Hedingham	BIL9406	NIBS	C109SDX	Ipswich
B134YSL	Enterprise	BNO664T	Eastern National	C110SDX	Ipswich
B163TNE	Lamberts	BNO666T	Thamesway	C111SDX	Ipswich
B183BLG	Southend	BNO668T	Thamesway	C112SDX	Ipswich
B184BLG	Southend	BNO669T	Thamesway	C113SDX	Ipswich
B185BLG	Southend	BNO670T	Shorey	C114HUH	Flying Banana
B189BLG	Southend	BNO671T	Thamesway	C117EMG	Simmonds
B192BPP	Chambers	BNO672T	Thamesway	C117KMA	Waylands
B201GNL	Flying Banana	BNO674T	Thamesway	C130GHS	Lodge's
B204GNL	Flying Banana	BNO675T	Eastern National	C130HJN	Eastern National
B220JPH	Morley's	BNO676T	Thamesway	C134USS	Sanders Coaches
B251DNV	Hallmark	BNO677T	Thamesway	C141KFL	Fords Coaches
B261KPF	County	BNO678T	Thamesway	C147SPB	The Shires
B262LPH	The Shires	BNO679T	Thamesway	C148SPB	The Shires
B270LPH	The Shires	BNO680T	Eastern National	C149SPB	The Shires
B271LPH	The Shires	BNO681T	Thamesway	C163JTW	Golden Boy
B272LPH	The Shires	BNO683T	Thamesway	C180KHG	Buffalo
B273AMG	Hedingham	BNO684T	Thamesway	C189MFL	Whippet
B273LPH	The Shires	BNO685T	Thamesway	C201HJN	Thamesway
B284KPF	The Shires	BNO700T	Hedingham	C202HJN	Eastern National
B292KPF	The Shires	BNO703T	Hedingham	C203HJN	Eastern National
B293KPF	The Shires	BPF132Y	Sovereign	C204HJN	Eastern National
B336BGL	Thamesway	BPF133Y	Sovereign	C205HJN	Eastern National
B337BGL	Thamesway	BPF135Y	The Shires	C206HJN	Eastern National
B345RVF	Coach Services	BPF136Y	The Shires	C207HJN	Eastern National
B387UEX	Beestons	BPF137Y	Sovereign	C208HJN	Eastern National
B420NJF	Flying Banana	BPL460T	The Shires	C210HJN	Eastern National
B423CMC	Graham's	BPL462T	The Shires	C212HJN	Eastern National
B431LRA	Stephensons	BPL463T	The Shires	C215HJN	Eastern National
B512JJR	Semmence	BPL464T	The Shires	C217HJN	Eastern National
B513JJR	Semmence	BPL465T	The Shires	C220HJN	Eastern National
B670EHL	Sanders Coaches	BPL466T	The Shires	C220VCT	Sanders Coaches
B689BPU	Eastern National	BPL467T	The Shires	C223HJN	Eastern National
B691BPU	Eastern National	BPL468T	The Shires	C230HCV	Eastern National
B696WAR	Eastern National	BPL469T	The Shires	C231HCV	Eastern National
B697WAR	Eastern National	BPL470T	The Shires	C232HCV	Eastern National
B698BPU	Thamesway	BPL471T	The Shires	C238HNO	Fargo Coachlines
B699BPU	Thamesway	BPL473T	The Shires	C245OFE	Jacksons
B711EOF	Beestons	BRC836T	Hedingham	C247OFE	Waylands
B761OPJ	Universitybus	BRC839T	Hedingham	C248OFE	Waylands
B792MGV	Chambers	BRF691T	Eastern Counties	C249SPC	The Shires
B817BPP	Seamarks	BTU375S	Supreme	C253SPC	County
B891MAB	Marshall's	BTX152T	The Shires	C254SPC	County
B897AGJ	Jacksons	BTX39V	Morley's	C255SPC	County
BAR103X	Hedingham	BUH233V	Southend	C260SPC	County
BAZ6869	The Shires	BVG218T	Eastern Counties	C263SPC	County

C265SPC	County	C721BEX	Eastern Counties	C990GCV	Eastern National
C307CRH	Flying Banana	C722BEX	Eastern Counties	C995ERO	Fords Coaches
C316URF	Flying Banana	C723BEX	Eastern Counties	CAH885Y	Ambassador Travel
C324YPW	J B S	C724BEX	Eastern Counties	CAH886Y	Ambassador Travel
C326DND	Simmonds	C725BEX	Eastern Counties	CAV312V	Emblings
C333HHB	Enterprise	C725FKE	Eastern Counties	CBD779K	The Shires
C336SFL	Cambus	C726BEX	Eastern Counties	CBD897T	The Shires
C340GFJ	Stephensons	C726FKE	Eastern Counties	CBD898T	The Shires
C357FBO	Spratts	C727BEX	Eastern Counties	CBD899T	The Shires
C407HJN	Eastern National	C727FKE	Eastern Counties	CBD900T	The Shires
C408HJN	Eastern National	C728BEX	Eastern Counties	CBD904T	The Shires
C409HJN	Thamesway	C741BEX	Eastern Counties	CBE882X	Semmence
C410HJN	Eastern National	C742BEX	Eastern Counties	CBV9S	Buckinghamshire
C412HJN	Eastern National	C743BEX	Eastern Counties	CBV10S	APT
C413HJN	Eastern National	C744BEX	Eastern Counties	CBV19S	Buckinghamshire
C414HJN	Eastern National	C745BEX	Eastern Counties	CBV305S	Hedingham
C415HJN	Eastern National	C746BEX	Eastern Counties	CBV306S	Hedingham
C416HJN	Eastern National	C747BEX	Eastern Counties	CBV307S	Hedingham
C417HJN	Eastern National	C748BEX	Eastern Counties	CBV308S	Hedingham
C418HJN	Eastern National	C749BEX	Eastern Counties	CBV309S	Hedingham
C419HJN	Eastern National	C750BEX	Eastern Counties	CCL774T	Eastern Counties
C421HJN	Eastern National	C751BEX	Eastern Counties	CCL775T	Eastern Counties
C430BHY	Flying Banana	C752BEX	Eastern Counties	CCL776T	Eastern Counties
C431BHY	Flying Banana	C753BEX	Eastern Counties	CCL778T	Eastern Counties
C441HHL	Charles Cook	C754BEX	Eastern Counties	CDO999V	Belle Coaches
C445LGN	Caroline Seagull	C755BEX	Eastern Counties	CEV89T	Hedingham
C447NNV	Buckinghamshire	C756BEX	Eastern Counties	CEW205V	Emblings
C448NNV	Buckinghamshire	C757BEX	Eastern Counties	CFM345S	Hedingham
C482BHY	Eastern National	C764NRC	Amos Coaches	CFM347S	Hedingham
C483BFB	Thamesway	C815FMC	Coach Services	CFM349S	Beestons
C484BHY	Eastern National	C854AOW	The Lutonians	CFM355S	Beestons
C485BHY	Eastern National	C892BEX	Eastern Counties	CHK312X	Fords Coaches
C486BHY	Eastern National	C893BEX	Eastern Counties	CHK571T	Lamberts
C489BHY	Eastern National	C894BEX	Eastern Counties	CJH115V	Osborne's
C491HCV	Thamesway	C895BEX	Eastern Counties	CJH141V	Osborne's
C493BHY	Eastern National	C896BEX	Eastern Counties	CJH143V	Hedingham
C494BHY	Eastern National	C897BEX	Eastern Counties	CJO470R	Eastern Counties
C495BHY	Eastern National	C898BEX	Eastern Counties	CJO471R	Eastern Counties
C496BHY	Eastern National	C899BEX	Eastern Counties	CJO472R	Eastern Counties
C502DYM	The Shires	C902BEX	Eastern Counties	CJS447	Spratts
C503DYM	The Shires	C903BEX	Eastern Counties	CKC312L	Eastern Counties
C504DYM	The Shires	C905BEX	Eastern Counties	CKM140Y	Semmence
C506DYM	The Shires	C906BEX	Eastern Counties	CKM141Y	Semmence
C509DYM	The Shires	C907BEX	Eastern Counties	CKX392T	Fords Coaches
C517DND	Great Yarmouth	C908BEX	Eastern Counties	CPE480Y	Prestwood Travel
C525EWR	Luckybus	C909BEX	Eastern Counties	CPU125X	Osborne's
C535TJF	Flying Banana	C910BEX	Eastern Counties	CPV2T	Simmonds
C566NHJ	NIBS	C912BEX	Eastern Counties	CRO689L	Beestons
C637BEX	Eastern Counties	C913BEX	Eastern Counties	CSK282	Angian
C638BEX	Eastern Counties	C914BEX	Eastern Counties	CSU960	Motts
C652BEX	Eastern Counties	C916BEX	Eastern Counties	CUB539Y	Motts
C658KVW	Fords Coaches	C917BEX	Eastern Counties	CUB540Y	Motts
C668WRT	Chambers	C919BEX	Eastern Counties	CUV265C	B T S
C678ECV	Eastern National	C952YAH	Eastern Counties	CUV322C	B T S
C684ECV	Eastern National	C957GAF	Thamesway	CUV341C	B T S
C685ECV	Eastern National	C957YAH	Eastern Counties	CVA108V	Sanders Coaches
C687ECV	Eastern National	C958YAH	Eastern Counties	CVE12V	Kenzie's
C688ECV	Eastern National	C959YAH	Eastern Counties	CVE7V	Kenzie's
C695ECV	Eastern National	C960YAH	Eastern Counties	CVF28T	Great Yarmouth
C696ECV	Thamesway	C961YAH	Eastern Counties	CVF29T	Great Yarmouth
C697ECV	Eastern National	C963GCV	Thamesway	CVF30T	Great Yarmouth
C698ECV	Eastern National	C964GCV	Eastern National	CVF31T	Great Yarmouth
C699ECV	Thamesway	C965YAH	Eastern Counties	CWU139T	Supreme
C700ECV	Eastern National	C966YAH	Eastern Counties	CYD133S	Sanders Coaches
C707OPN	Fargo Coachlines	C967GCV	Thamesway	CYH770V	Reg's
C711BEX	Eastern Counties	C967YAH	Eastern Counties	D21RPP	The Shires
C711GEV	Thamesway	C970YAH	Eastern Counties	D21XPF	Belle Coaches
C712BEX	Eastern Counties	C972YAH	Eastern Counties	D22XPF	Belle Coaches
C712GEV	Thamesway	C975YAH	Eastern Counties	D23RPP	The Shires
C713BEX	Eastern Counties	C978GCV	Thamesway	D25RPP	The Shires
C714BEX	Eastern Counties	C979HOX	Coach Services	D26RPP	The Shires
C715BEX	Eastern Counties	C979YAH	Eastern Counties	D30BEW	Kenzie's
C716BEX	Eastern Counties	C980YAH	Eastern Counties	D31CFL	Kenzie's
C717BEX	Eastern Counties	C981YAH	Eastern Counties	D42PGJ	The Lutonians
C718BEX	Eastern Counties	C982YAH	Eastern Counties	D43DNH	Flying Banana
C719BEX	Eastern Counties	C983YAH	Eastern Counties	D43RWC	Colchester
C720BEX	Eastern Counties	C984YAH	Eastern Counties	D45OKH	County

Reg	Operator	Reg	Operator	Reg	Operator
D46OKH	County	D164VRP	Buckinghamshire	D554HNW	County
D54TLV	Challenger	D169NON	Challenger	D566NDA	Red Rose
D66ONS	Fords Coaches	D172LTA	Chambers	D576VBV	Hedingham
D69YRF	The Lutonians	D173NON	Challenger	D584MVR	Hedingham
D70TLV	Flying Banana	D175NON	Challenger	D588MVR	Thamesway
D81NWW	Seamarks	D176LTA	Chambers	D590MVR	Thamesway
D101VRP	Buckinghamshire	D177VRP	Buckinghamshire	D592MVR	Thamesway
D102SPP	Cedar Coaches	D179LTA	Flying Banana	D596MVR	Thamesway
D102VRP	Buckinghamshire	D181VRP	Buckinghamshire	D597MVR	Thamesway
D103VRP	Buckinghamshire	D183VRP	Buckinghamshire	D598MVR	Thamesway
D104VRP	Buckinghamshire	D188NON	Challenger	D600MVR	Hedingham
D105VRP	Buckinghamshire	D192NON	Challenger	D601MVR	Thamesway
D106VRP	Buckinghamshire	D192VRP	Buckinghamshire	D603ACW	The Shires
D107VRP	Buckinghamshire	D197NON	Challenger	D603NOE	Viscount
D108VRP	Buckinghamshire	D203NON	Rules	D604AFR	Great Yarmouth
D109VRP	Buckinghamshire	D203RGH	Luckybus	D604NOE	Viscount
D110VRP	Buckinghamshire	D204NON	Waylands	D605AFR	Great Yarmouth
D111TFT	The Lutonians	D207MKK	Seamarks	D605NOE	Viscount
D111VRP	Buckinghamshire	D208NON	Stephensons	D606AFR	Great Yarmouth
D111WCC	Challenger	D210GLJ	The Lutonians	D609PJN	Jacksons
D112VRP	Buckinghamshire	D211LWX	Chambers	D610AFR	Great Yarmouth
D112WCC	Challenger	D212LWX	Chambers	D613YCX	Belle Coaches
D113VRP	Buckinghamshire	D213OOJ	Challenger	D616YCX	Semmence
D114TFT	The Lutonians	D217NUR	Waylands	D624KJT	Sanders Coaches
D114VRP	Buckinghamshire	D217OOJ	Towler	D631NOE	Viscount
D115VRP	Buckinghamshire	D218OOJ	Challenger	D632NOE	Cambus
D116VRP	Buckinghamshire	D226OOJ	Challenger	D640NOE	Viscount
D116WCC	Challenger	D228OOJ	Challenger	D642DRT	Chambers
D117VRP	Buckinghamshire	D230PPU	Thamesway	D642NOE	Viscount
D118VRP	Buckinghamshire	D231PPU	Thamesway	D645NOE	Viscount
D119VRP	Buckinghamshire	D232HMT	Hedingham	D647NOE	Viscount
D120VRP	Buckinghamshire	D232PPU	Thamesway	D648NOE	Cambus
D121EFH	Luckybus	D233PPU	Thamesway	D694MAG	Sanders Coaches
D121VRP	Buckinghamshire	D234PPU	Thamesway	D755MUR	The Shires
D122VRP	Buckinghamshire	D245OOJ	Challenger	D756MUR	The Shires
D123VRP	Buckinghamshire	D251OOJ	Challenger	D757MUR	The Shires
D124VRP	Buckinghamshire	D272HFX	Coach Services	D758LEX	Eastern Counties
D125VRP	Buckinghamshire	D301PEV	Harris Bus	D758MUR	The Shires
D126VRP	Buckinghamshire	D302PEV	Harris Bus	D759LEX	Eastern Counties
D127NON	Challenger	D303PEV	Harris Bus	D759MUR	The Shires
D127VRP	Buckinghamshire	D304PEV	Harris Bus	D761MUR	The Shires
D128VRP	Buckinghamshire	D342JUM	APT	D762MUR	The Shires
D128WCC	Challenger	D345WPE	Hedingham	D763MUR	The Shires
D129DRV	County	D350KVE	Cambridge CS	D764KWT	Thamesway
D129SHE	Sanders Coaches	D351KVE	Cambridge CS	D764MUR	The Shires
D129VRP	Buckinghamshire	D352KVA	The Lutonians	D764TDV	Lodge's
D130VRP	Buckinghamshire	D369JUM	Enterprise	D765MUR	The Shires
D131VRP	Buckinghamshire	D377JUM	Beestons	D767MUR	The Shires
D131WCC	Challenger	D401ASF	Eastern Counties	D768JUB	Waylands
D132VRP	Buckinghamshire	D407ASF	Eastern Counties	D768MUR	The Shires
D133VRP	Buckinghamshire	D407ERE	Motts	D769MUR	The Shires
D134TFT	The Lutonians	D415ASF	Eastern Counties	D770MUR	The Shires
D134VRP	Buckinghamshire	D417ASF	Eastern Counties	D772PTU	The Lutonians
D134WCC	Challenger	D425ASF	Eastern Counties	D774PTU	Waylands
D135VRP	Buckinghamshire	D430ASF	Eastern Counties	D779NUD	Eastern Counties
D136VRP	Buckinghamshire	D441CEW	Sanders Coaches	D814BVT	Red Rose
D136XVW	Hedingham	D447FSP	Luckybus	D820PUK	Challenger
D137VRP	Buckinghamshire	D447PGH	Sanders Coaches	D823UBH	Rover Bus Services
D137XVW	Hedingham	D459POO	Golden Boy	D850AAV	Whippet
D138NON	Challenger	D472RVS	The Shires	D869NVS	West's
D138VRP	Buckinghamshire	D493YLN	The Lutonians	D873LWR	Thamesway
D139VRP	Buckinghamshire	D494YLN	The Lutonians	D934EBP	The Shires
D140VRP	Buckinghamshire	D495RNM	The Shires	D989JYG	Luckybus
D141VRP	Buckinghamshire	D497RNM	The Shires	DAL771J	Rules
D142VRP	Buckinghamshire	D498RNM	The Shires	DAR118T	Thamesway
D143VRP	Buckinghamshire	D499RNW	The Shires	DAR119T	Thamesway
D144VRP	Buckinghamshire	D501MJA	Red Rose	DAR120T	Thamesway
D145VRP	Buckinghamshire	D508WNV	Marshall's	DAR121T	Eastern National
D147VRP	Buckinghamshire	D510NDA	The Lutonians	DAR125T	Thamesway
D148VRP	Buckinghamshire	D510PPU	Eastern National	DAR126T	Thamesway
D155NON	The Lutonians	D511PPU	Eastern National	DAR128T	Thamesway
D155VRP	Buckinghamshire	D512PPU	Eastern National	DAR129T	Thamesway
D156VRP	Buckinghamshire	D519FYL	The Shires	DAR130T	Thamesway
D157NON	Challenger	D526MJO	Airport Coaches	DAR131T	Thamesway
D161NON	Challenger	D527MJO	Airport Coaches	DAR133T	Thamesway
D162NON	Challenger	D529NDA	The Lutonians	DAR134T	Thamesway
D164NON	Challenger	D534KGL	Eastern National	DBH452X	Hedingham

DBU889	Felix	E134KRP	Belle Coaches	E565BNK	County
DBV28W	Cambus	E176OEW	Whippet	E581TYG	Lamberts
DDA66	Shorey	E177OEW	Whippet	E600WDV	Chambers
DDX741T	County	E178OEW	Whippet	E633SEL	Chambers
DEX226T	Eastern Counties	E199UWT	Cedric's	E657RVP	Viscount
DEX227T	Viscount	E218ARM	Semmence	E661AWJ	The Shires
DEX228T	Cambus	E218OEG	Fargo Coachlines	E662AWJ	The Shires
DEX229T	Eastern Counties	E221LER	Felix	E663AWJ	The Shires
DEX230T	Eastern Counties	E226WKW	Rex Motor Services	E663YDT	Lodge's
DEX231T	Cambus	E233WKW	Rex Motor Services	E664KCX	Cedar Coaches
DFK214	Beestons	E237VOM	Flying Banana	E664RVP	Viscount
DGR477S	Southend	E240NSE	Rover Bus Services	E667YDT	West's
DHE695V	Sanders Coaches	E256PEL	Don's	E668UNE	Hedingham
DHE699V	Galloway	E290OMG	County	E674NNV	Belle Coaches
DJA551T	Coach Services	E296VOM	County	E675UNE	Thamesway
DJI1594	Sanders Coaches	E305EVW	Harris Bus	E677UND	Semmence
DMJ305X	Buffalo	E306EVW	Harris Bus	E677UNE	Thamesway
DNG232T	Cambus	E323OMG	The Shires	E700EHJ	County
DNG233T	Buckinghamshire	E331DRO	The Shires	E701EHJ	County
DNG234T	Cambus	E332DRO	The Shires	E701TNG	Eastern Counties
DNG236T	Eastern Counties	E333DRO	The Shires	E702TNG	Eastern Counties
DNK431T	Hedingham	E334DRO	The Shires	E731DNM	The Shires
DNW843T	Sovereign	E335DRO	The Shires	E743OEW	Felix
DPH501T	The Shires	E336DRO	The Shires	E750VWT	Cambus
DPW781T	Eastern Counties	E337DRO	The Shires	E758JAY	Don's
DPW782T	Eastern Counties	E338DRO	The Shires	E786MEU	Graham's
DSK648	Simmonds	E339MMM	Simmonds	E787DNG	Sanders Coaches
DSU733	County	E340DRO	The Shires	E816UKW	Enterprise
DWP3S	Lamberts	E341DRO	The Shires	E832EUT	Coach Services
DWU294T	Hedingham	E342DRO	The Shires	E836FRP	Hallmark
DWU298T	Eastern National	E343DRO	The Shires	E837FRP	Hallmark
DWY146T	Southend	E343SWY	County	E840EUT	Sovereign
E23FLD	Enterprise	E344DRO	The Shires	E851PEX	Eastern Counties
E34MCE	Kenzie's	E345DRO	The Shires	E852PEX	Eastern Counties
E40OAH	Great Yarmouth	E346DRO	The Shires	E853PEX	Eastern Counties
E41OAH	Great Yarmouth	E347DRO	The Shires	E854PEX	Eastern Counties
E42OAH	Great Yarmouth	E347SWY	County	E855PEX	Eastern Counties
E42RDW	Cambus	E348DRO	The Shires	E856GFV	Felix
E43OAH	Great Yarmouth	E348SWY	County	E856PEX	Eastern Counties
E43RDW	Cambus	E349DRO	The Shires	E859AKN	Harris Bus
E44OAH	Great Yarmouth	E349SWY	County	E872EHK	Fargo Coachlines
E44RDW	Cambus	E350SWY	County	E881YKY	The Shires
E45OAH	Great Yarmouth	E352NEG	County	E882YKY	The Shires
E45RDW	Cambus	E353DHK	Fargo Coachlines	E893HEG	Whippet
E46RDW	Cambus	E353NEG	County	E901LVE	Prestwood Travel
E46RVG	Great Yarmouth	E354NEG	County	E902LVE	Prestwood Travel
E47RVG	Great Yarmouth	E355NEG	County	E905LVE	Towler
E48MRP	The Shires	E357NEG	Biss Brothers	E911LVE	Cambus
E48RVG	Great Yarmouth	E358NEG	Sovereign	E912LVE	Cambus
E48YDO	Spratts	E371YRO	Sovereign	E913NEW	Cambus
E49RVG	Great Yarmouth	E400HWC	Thamesway	E940CJN	Biss Brothers
E64BVS	The Shires	E401HWC	Eastern National	E962SVP	Thamesway
E66BVS	The Shires	E408YLG	Richmond's	E965PME	The Shires
E66MVV	Buckinghamshire	E420EBH	Sovereign	E966PME	The Shires
E67MVV	Buckinghamshire	E432KRT	Lodge's	E969PME	The Shires
E68MVV	Buckinghamshire	E441ADV	Whippet	E970NMK	The Shires
E69MVV	Buckinghamshire	E445TYG	County	E970PME	The Shires
E70MVV	Buckinghamshire	E448TYG	County	E970SVP	The Lutonians
E71MVV	Buckinghamshire	E449TYG	County	E971DNK	The Shires
E72MVV	Buckinghamshire	E451TYG	County	E972DNK	The Shires
E73MVV	Buckinghamshire	E452TYG	County	E973DNK	The Shires
E79HVX	Hedingham	E454TYG	The Shires	E974DNK	The Shires
E83DRY	Belle Coaches	E455TYG	County	E975DNK	The Shires
E84DRY	Belle Coaches	E461TEW	Cambus	E976DNK	The Shires
E87KGV	Chambers	E473YWJ	Airport Coaches	E977DNK	The Shires
E94OUH	Stephensons	E478CNM	The Shires	E978DNK	The Shires
E99ODH	Spratts	E479CNM	The Shires	E979DNK	The Shires
E105GOO	Crusader	E484CNM	The Shires	E980DNK	The Shires
E105SOG	Thamesway	E486CNM	The Shires	E981DNK	The Shires
E106GOO	Crusader	E500LFL	Cambus	E984DNK	The Shires
E107GOO	Crusader	E501LFL	Cambus	E985DNK	The Shires
E108GOO	Crusader	E502LFL	Viscount	E986DNK	The Shires
E114KDX	Ipswich	E509TOV	Thamesway	E987DNK	The Shires
E115KDX	Ipswich	E519PWR	Enterprise	E988DNK	The Shires
E116KDX	Ipswich	E530VKH	Richmond's	E989DNK	The Shires
E117KDX	Ipswich	E558CGJ	APT	E990DNK	The Shires
E118KFV	County	E564BNK	County	E991DNK	The Shires

E989DNK	The Shires	F72SMC	Buzz	F260RHK	Thamesway
E990DNK	The Shires	F73SMC	Buzz	F268CEY	The Shires
E991DNK	The Shires	F74SMC	Buzz	F269CEY	The Shires
E992DNK	The Shires	F75SMC	Buzz	F269GUD	Sanders Coaches
E992JOO	Hallmark	F76SMC	Buzz	F287FGL	The Shires
E993DNK	The Shires	F77SMC	Buzz	F300MNK	The Shires
E994DNK	The Shires	F78SMC	Buzz	F301MNK	The Shires
E995DNK	The Shires	F78VWK	Jacksons	F301RMH	Felix
E996DNK	The Shires	F79SMC	Buzz	F302MNK	The Shires
E997DNK	The Shires	F81ODX	Ipswich	F303MNK	The Shires
E998DNK	The Shires	F81WBD	Fargo Coachlines	F303RMH	Jacksons
E999DNK	The Shires	F82WBD	Fargo Coachlines	F305RMH	Simmonds
EAC878T	Sanders Coaches	F94CBD	Beestons	F310OVW	Harris Bus
EAV810V	Buffalo	F96CBD	Hallmark	F312PEV	Harris Bus
EAV811V	Whippet	F100BPW	Ambassador Travel	F313TLU	Cedric's
EAV812V	Whippet	F101AVG	Eastern Counties	F314RHK	Harris Bus
EBZ6531	County	F101BPW	Ambassador Travel	F314RMH	The Shires
ECT999V	Semmence	F102AVG	Eastern Counties	F321SMD	Jacksons
EDV505D	Classic Coaches	F103AVG	Eastern Counties	F358EKL	The Lutonians
EDV546D	Classic Coaches	F104AVG	Eastern Counties	F358JVS	Sovereign
EEW113Y	Whippet	F105AVG	Eastern Counties	F359GKN	Buckinghamshire
EGV190T	Coach Services	F106CCL	Ambassador Travel	F359JVS	Sovereign
EGV719T	Belle Coaches	F107NRT	Cambus	F365BUA	Buzz
EHE234V	Eastern Counties	F108NRT	Cambus	F367CHE	West's
EHL336	Classic Coaches	F115JGS	County	F370BUA	Seamarks
EHS107T	Motts	F121TRU	The Shires	F373MUT	Coach Services
EIJ4016	Cedric's	F122TRU	The Shires	F400PUR	The Shires
EJR791	Emblings	F123TRU	The Shires	F401PUR	The Shires
ELA389T	Coach Services	F124TRU	The Shires	F402LTW	Eastern National
EMB363S	Beestons	F125TRU	The Shires	F402PUR	The Shires
ENM10T	Neaves	F128TRU	The Shires	F403LTW	Eastern National
EON825V	Colchester	F145SPV	Hedingham	F403PUR	The Shires
EON826V	Colchester	F146SPV	Hedingham	F404LTW	Thamesway
EON829V	Colchester	F147SPV	Hedingham	F404PUR	The Shires
EPC906V	Galloway	F148SPV	Hedingham	F405LTW	Thamesway
EPD505V	The Shires	F150LTW	Hedingham	F406LTW	Thamesway
EPD512V	The Shires	F151KGS	The Shires	F407LTW	Eastern National
EPD514V	The Shires	F151NPU	Hedingham	F408LTW	Eastern National
EPD515V	The Shires	F152KGS	The Shires	F409LTW	Thamesway
EPD517V	The Shires	F153KGS	The Shires	F410MNO	Thamesway
EPD521V	The Shires	F154DKV	County	F411MNO	Thamesway
EPD523V	The Shires	F154KGS	The Shires	F412MNO	Thamesway
EPH27V	Semmence	F155KGS	The Shires	F413MNO	Eastern National
EPM126V	Rules	F167SMT	Cambus	F414MNO	Eastern National
EPM140V	Prestwood Travel	F168SMT	Cambus	F415MWC	Eastern National
EPM144V	Prestwood Travel	F171SMT	Cambus	F416MWC	Eastern National
EPM146V	Prestwood Travel	F183UEE	Simmonds	F417MWC	Thamesway
EPP819Y	Seamarks	F203MBT	Sovereign	F418MWC	Thamesway
EPW928Y	Caroline Seagull	F204MBT	Sovereign	F419MWC	Thamesway
ERP550T	The Shires	F205MBT	Sovereign	F420MJN	Thamesway
ESU913	Cambus	F206MBT	Sovereign	F421DUG	Cambridge CS
ESU920	Cambus	F207CNG	Waylands	F421MJN	Thamesway
ETC760B	Don's	F207MBT	Sovereign	F422MJN	Thamesway
ETO182L	NIBS	F208MBT	Sovereign	F423MJN	Thamesway
EUB552Y	Semmence	F218RJX	Belle Coaches	F424DUG	Cambridge CS
EUI4415	Universitybus	F220PPV	Ipswich	F424MJN	Thamesway
EUM892T	Sovereign	F243RRT	Chambers	F425DUG	Cambridge CS
EWR166T	Beestons	F245MTW	Colchester	F425MJN	Eastern National
EWR651Y	Eastern National	F245MVW	Thamesway	F425UVW	Southend
EWR652Y	Eastern National	F246HNE	Chambers	F426MJN	Eastern National
EWR653Y	Eastern National	F246MTW	Southend	F427MJN	Eastern National
EWW213T	Osborne's	F246MVW	Thamesway	F428MJN	Eastern National
EWW946Y	Eastern National	F247NJN	Thamesway	F429MJN	Eastern National
EYH693V	Fords Coaches	F248NJN	Thamesway	F464NRT	Hedingham
F24WNH	Belle Coaches	F249NJN	Thamesway	F466TJV	Belle Coaches
F26YBO	Watson	F250NJN	Thamesway	F467UVW	Southend
F36DAV	Kenzie's	F251ACC	The Shires	F484KDB	Stephensons
F37DAV	Richmond's	F251NJN	Thamesway	F506NJE	Viscount
F39EEG	Kenzie's	F252NJN	Thamesway	F506OYW	The Shires
F52UBX	Waylands	F252OFP	Cambus	F507NJE	Viscount
F61RKX	Rover Bus Services	F253RHK	Thamesway	F508NJE	Viscount
F61SMC	County	F254RHK	Thamesway	F509NJE	Viscount
F62MTM	Richmond's	F255RHK	Thamesway	F510NJE	Viscount
F62SMC	County	F256RHK	Thamesway	F511NJE	Viscount
F63SMC	County	F257RHK	Thamesway	F512NJE	Cambus
F67NLH	Jacksons	F258RHK	Thamesway	F513NJE	Cambus
F71SMC	Buzz	F259RHK	Thamesway	F514NJE	Cambus

Reg	Operator	Reg	Operator	Reg	Operator
F515NJE	Cambus	F892XOE	Thamesway	G55GEX	Great Yarmouth
F516NJE	Cambus	F900RDX	Coach Services	G58BEL	The Shires
F517NJE	Cambus	F930TBP	Universitybus	G92RGG	Cambridge CS
F554TLW	The Shires	F947NER	Cambus	G93ERP	Buckinghamshire
F569MCH	Spratts	F948NER	Cambus	G94ERP	Buckinghamshire
F572UPB	Southend	F952RNV	Motts	G95RGG	Cambridge CS
F596CDT	Waylands	F969GKJ	The Shires	G96ERP	Buckinghamshire
F598CET	The Shires	F976WEF	Chambers	G96RGG	Cambridge CS
F600DWB	Motts	F977APW	Graham's	G97ERP	Buckinghamshire
F607PBH	Charles Cook	F995XOV	Thamesway	G97RGG	Cambridge CS
F613XWY	Thamesway	F996XOV	Thamesway	G98NBD	Buckinghamshire
F614XWY	Thamesway	FAD272Y	Stephensons	G98RGG	Cambridge CS
F623FNA	Waylands	FAR601T	Fargo Coachlines	G99NBD	Buckinghamshire
F633LMJ	The Shires	FBJ713T	Rules	G100NBD	Buckinghamshire
F634LMJ	The Shires	FBZ2514	County	G101CJN	Crusader
F634UEF	The Shires	FCY285W	Hedingham	G102CJN	Crusader
F635LMJ	The Shires	FCY287W	Hedingham	G103CJN	Crusader
F636LMJ	The Shires	FCY288W	Hedingham	G103YNK	Cedar Coaches
F637LMJ	The Shires	FCY289W	Hedingham	G104CJN	Crusader
F638LMJ	The Shires	FCY290W	Whippet	G104SVM	Simmonds
F639LMJ	The Shires	FCY292W	Whippet	G107HNG	Ambassador Travel
F640LMJ	The Shires	FCY293W	Whippet	G108HNG	Ambassador Travel
F641LMJ	The Shires	FDX270T	Simmonds	G109HNG	Ambassador Travel
F642LMJ	The Shires	FDZ984	Thamesway	G111HNG	Ambassador Travel
F643LMJ	The Shires	FEV115Y	Hedingham	G118VDX	Ipswich
F644LMJ	The Shires	FEW224Y	Whippet	G119VDX	Ipswich
F648PLW	Motts	FEW225Y	Whippet	G120VDX	Ipswich
F657KNL	The Shires	FEW226Y	Whippet	G121VDX	Ipswich
F660KNL	The Shires	FEW227Y	Whippet	G122VDX	Ipswich
F678AWW	Buzz	FHJ565	Beestons	G123VDX	Ipswich
F693PAY	Whippet	FHV504	Harris Bus	G124VDX	Ipswich
F694PAY	Whippet	FIL2294	Lamberts	G129YEV	The Shires
F701MBC	Eastern Counties	FIL2296	Lamberts	G130YEV	The Shires
F702MBC	Eastern Counties	FIL2297	Lamberts	G131YWC	The Shires
F703MBC	Eastern Counties	FIL2833	Watson	G132YWC	The Shires
F704MBC	Eastern Counties	FIL2838	Watson	G145GOL	Thamesway
F705ENE	Emblings	FIL4033	Beestons	G146GOL	The Lutonians
F705MBC	Eastern Counties	FIL4034	Beestons	G148GOL	Thamesway
F706MBC	Eastern Counties	FIL4162	Beestons	G167XJF	Hallmark
F707MBC	Eastern Counties	FIL4163	Beestons	G171BLH	Luckybus
F708ENE	Coach Services	FIL4164	Beestons	G201URO	Sovereign
F708MBC	Eastern Counties	FIL4165	Beestons	G202URO	Sovereign
F709ENE	Coach Services	FIL4166	Beestons	G203URO	Sovereign
F709NJF	Eastern Counties	FIL4169	Beestons	G204URO	Sovereign
F710MBC	Eastern Counties	FIL4345	Beestons	G205URO	Sovereign
F711CWJ	West's	FIL4741	Beestons	G206URO	Sovereign
F712CWJ	West's	FIL4742	Beestons	G207URO	Sovereign
F713CWJ	West's	FIL4743	Beestons	G208CHN	Chambers
F714CWJ	West's	FIL6281	Watson	G221VDX	Ipswich
F715CWJ	West's	FIL7253	Buzz	G222VDX	Ipswich
F715PFP	Eastern Counties	FIL8613	Beestons	G223VDX	Ipswich
F715UBX	Waylands	FIL8614	Beestons	G224HCP	Belle Coaches
F718CWJ	West's	FIL8615	Beestons	G224VDX	Ipswich
F719CWJ	West's	FIL8693	Sanders Coaches	G228PGU	Graham's
F719PFP	Eastern Counties	FNJ993V	Fargo Coachlines	G276HDW	The Lutonians
F721PFP	Eastern Counties	FPP5T	Sanders Coaches	G277HDW	The Lutonians
F722PFP	Eastern Counties	FRP905T	Cambus	G277TST	Waylands
F722SML	Golden Boy	FSU379	Marshall's	G278WKX	Seamarks
F725MNB	Red Rose	FSU637	Lodge's	G281UMJ	The Shires
F727EKR	Red Rose	FTO551V	Sanders Coaches	G282UMJ	The Shires
F747XCS	The Shires	FTO557V	Sanders Coaches	G283UMJ	The Shires
F771GNA	Thamesway	FTO558V	Stephensons	G284UMJ	The Shires
F779LNB	Chambers	FTU380T	Southend	G285UMJ	The Shires
F781GNA	Hedingham	FUG321T	Sovereign	G286UMJ	The Shires
F791DWT	Seamarks	FUG325T	Sovereign	G287UMJ	The Shires
F795JKX	County	FUJ904V	Coach Services	G288UMJ	The Shires
F796JKX	County	FVG667T	Coach Services	G289UMJ	The Shires
F800RHK	Thamesway	FWR216T	Cambus	G290UMJ	The Shires
F801RHK	Thamesway	FWR217T	Cambus	G291UMJ	The Shires
F802RHK	Thamesway	FWR218T	Cambus	G292UMJ	The Shires
F803RHK	Thamesway	FWR219T	Viscount	G293UMJ	The Shires
F804RHK	Thamesway	FYX814W	County	G294UMJ	The Shires
F810TMD	Richmond's	G'97VMM	The Shires	G295UMJ	The Shires
F814TMD	West's	G40SAV	Kenzie's	G350GCK	Reg's
F849LHS	Harris Bus	G52GEX	Great Yarmouth	G360FOP	The Shires
F863FWB	Rex Motor Services	G53GEX	Great Yarmouth	G361FOP	The Lutonians
F880TNH	Beestons	G54GEX	Great Yarmouth	G363PNS	Waylands

Reg	Operator	Reg	Operator	Reg	Operator
G384MWX	Sovereign	G915UPP	Sovereign	GRF267V	Eastern Counties
G389LDT	Sanders Coaches	G916UPP	Sovereign	GRT520V	Coach Services
G395OWB	Great Yarmouth	G917UPP	Sovereign	GSL897N	Osborne's
G407DPD	Semmence	G918UPP	County	GSL898N	Buffalo
G421WFP	Windmill Cs	G919UPP	County	GSL899N	Osborne's
G432VJV	Waylands	G924WGS	County	GSL900N	Osborne's
G434ART	Rex Motor Services	G925WGS	County	GSL901N	Osborne's
G453SGB	Great Yarmouth	G926WGS	County	GSL902N	Osborne's
G456KNG	Great Yarmouth	G927WGS	County	GSL908N	Cedar Coaches
G457KNG	Great Yarmouth	G928WGS	County	GSU379	Boon's Tours
G458KNG	Great Yarmouth	G929WGS	County	GSU384	Marshall's
G468JNH	Beestons	G930WGS	County	GTM155T	Buffalo
G469LVG	Caroline Seagull	G931WGS	County	GTX751W	Southend
G470LVG	Caroline Seagull	G932WGS	County	GUG132N	NIBS
G472PGE	Universitybus	G954GRP	Coach Services	GUP743C	Kenzie's
G488KBD	Belle Coaches	G964WNR	Lodge's	GVF755T	Sanders Coaches
G512MNG	Ambassador Travel	G971TTM	Seamarks	GVS984V	Osborne's
G519LWU	Cambridge CS	G973LRP	Beestons	GVV889N	The Shires
G520LWU	Cambus	G995VEU	Airport Coaches	GVW894T	Hedingham
G525LWU	Cambus	GAG48N	Eastern Counties	GWO111W	Semmence
G526LWU	Cambus	GAO628V	Stephensons	GWT630	Classic Coaches
G527LWU	Cambus	GEG963W	Neaves	GYE277W	B T S
G541JBV	Reg's	GEX790Y	Fords Coaches	H2LWJ	Enterprise
G545JOG	County	GFH6V	Sanders Coaches	H10BCK	Hallmark
G603YUT	Hallmark	GGE156T	Southend	H10SUP	Supreme
G609MVG	Ambassador Travel	GGE158T	Southend	H20BUS	West's
G624WPB	Reg's	GGE161T	Southend	H20SUP	Supreme
G643YVS	Biss Brothers	GGE162T	Southend	H35DGD	The Shires
G645UPP	The Shires	GGE167T	Southend	H47MJN	Southend
G646UPP	The Shires	GGE172T	Southend	H48MJN	Colchester
G647UPP	The Shires	GGM84W	Hedingham	H48NDU	Hedingham
G648ONH	Rover Bus Services	GGM108W	Hedingham	H49MJN	Colchester
G648UPP	The Shires	GHB574V	The Shires	H65XBD	Motts
G649UPP	The Shires	GHB85W	Beestons	H101KVX	Thamesway
G650UPP	The Shires	GHM797N	NIBS	H101NVW	Hallmark
G651UPP	The Shires	GHM803N	NIBS	H102KVX	Thamesway
G652UPP	The Shires	GHV51N	Shorey	H103KVX	Thamesway
G653UPP	The Shires	GHV979N	Buffalo	H104KVX	Thamesway
G654UPP	The Shires	GHV999N	Shorey	H113DVM	Sanders Coaches
G655UPP	The Shires	GIL2968	Whippet	H139GGS	B T S
G656UPP	The Shires	GIL6253	The Shires	H140GGS	B T S
G657UPP	The Shires	GIL6949	The Shires	H140WMR	Airport Coaches
G697VAV	Emblings	GIL8487	The Shires	H141GGS	B T S
G706JAH	Eastern Counties	GIL8488	The Shires	H142GGS	B T S
G707JAH	Eastern Counties	GJI4481	Sanders Coaches	H143GGS	B T S
G708JAH	Eastern Counties	GMB387T	Beestons	H144GGS	B T S
G709JAH	Eastern Counties	GNF15V	Universitybus	H144NVW	Fargo Coachlines
G710JAH	Eastern Counties	GNG708N	Eastern Counties	H145GGS	B T S
G757VNR	Hallmark	GNG709N	Eastern Counties	H146GGS	B T S
G760VRT	Chambers	GNG710N	Towler	H147GGS	B T S
G805RNC	Graham's	GNG711N	Buckinghamshire	H148GGS	B T S
G818YJF	Enterprise	GNG713N	Eastern Counties	H149GGS	B T S
G823UMU	Whippet	GNG714N	Eastern Counties	H150GGS	B T S
G824UMU	Whippet	GNG715N	Eastern Counties	H151GGS	B T S
G828YJF	Enterprise	GNJ574N	Towler	H152GGS	B T S
G833RDS	Great Yarmouth	GNJ575N	Buckinghamshire	H160HJN	Hedingham
G834RDS	Great Yarmouth	GNK781T	Rules	H167EJU	Ambassador Travel
G839VAY	Belle Coaches	GNM235N	Caroline Seagull	H170DJF	Buffalo
G854VAY	Fords Coaches	GNN221N	Ambassador Travel	H176EJU	Ambassador Travel
G855KKY	Chambers	GNV332N	The Shires	H180HPV	Ipswich
G864XDX	Chambers	GNV334N	The Shires	H194TYC	Don's
G885VNA	Graham's	GNV653N	The Shires	H196GRO	The Shires
G896TGG	The Shires	GNV655N	The Shires	H197GRO	The Shires
G901UPP	Sovereign	GNV656N	The Shires	H198GRO	The Shires
G902UPP	Sovereign	GNV658N	The Shires	H199GRO	The Shires
G903UPP	Sovereign	GNV660N	The Shires	H201GRO	The Shires
G904UPP	Sovereign	GOE264V	Sanders Coaches	H202GRO	The Shires
G905UPP	Sovereign	GOI1294	Galloway	H203GRO	The Shires
G906UPP	Sovereign	GPV212T	Hedingham	H204DVM	Chambers
G907UPP	Sovereign	GPV685N	Hedingham	H225EDX	Ipswich
G908UPP	Sovereign	GRA841V	Eastern Counties	H226EDX	Ipswich
G909UPP	Sovereign	GRA842V	Eastern Counties	H227EDX	Ipswich
G910UPP	Sovereign	GRA843V	Eastern Counties	H231KBH	The Shires
G911UPP	Sovereign	GRA844V	Eastern Counties	H242MUK	The Shires
G912UPP	Sovereign	GRA845V	Eastern Counties	H243MUK	The Shires
G913UPP	Sovereign	GRA846V	Eastern Counties	H244MUK	The Shires
G914UPP	Sovereign	GRA847V	Eastern Counties	H245MUK	The Shires

H251GEV	County	H373OHK	Thamesway	H566MPD	Southend
H252GEV	County	H374OHK	Thamesway	H567MPD	Southend
H253GEV	County	H375OHK	Thamesway	H601OVW	Eastern National
H254GEV	County	H376OHK	Thamesway	H602OVW	Eastern National
H255GEV	County	H377OHK	Thamesway	H603OVW	Eastern National
H256GEV	County	H378OHK	Thamesway	H604OVW	Eastern National
H257GEV	County	H379OHK	Thamesway	H605OVW	Eastern National
H258GEV	County	H379TNG	Ambassador Travel	H606OVW	Eastern National
H262GEV	Southend	H380OHK	Thamesway	H607OVW	Eastern National
H263GEV	Southend	H380TNG	Ambassador Travel	H607SWG	Marshall's
H264GEV	Southend	H381OHK	Thamesway	H608OVW	Eastern National
H265GEV	Southend	H381TNG	Ambassador Travel	H608SWG	Marshall's
H271CEW	Emblings	H382OHK	Thamesway	H609OVW	Eastern National
H301LPU	Thamesway	H383OHK	Thamesway	H611RAH	Eastern Counties
H302LPU	Thamesway	H384OHK	Thamesway	H612RAH	Eastern Counties
H303CAV	Whippet	H385HRY	Hallmark	H613RAH	Eastern Counties
H303LPU	Thamesway	H385OHK	Thamesway	H614CGG	The Shires
H304LPU	Thamesway	H386OHK	Thamesway	H614RAH	Eastern Counties
H305LPU	Thamesway	H387OHK	Thamesway	H615RAH	Eastern Counties
H306LPU	Thamesway	H388MAR	Thamesway	H616RAH	Eastern Counties
H307LJN	Thamesway	H388OHK	Thamesway	H617RAH	Eastern Counties
H308LJN	Thamesway	H389CFT	Beestons	H618RAH	Eastern Counties
H310LJN	Thamesway	H389MAR	Thamesway	H619RAH	Eastern Counties
H311LJN	Thamesway	H389OHK	Thamesway	H620RAH	Eastern Counties
H312LJN	Thamesway	H389SYG	Red Rose	H627UWR	Sovereign
H313LJN	Thamesway	H390MAR	Thamesway	H628UWR	Sovereign
H314LJN	Thamesway	H390OHK	Thamesway	H629UWR	Cambridge CS
H315LJN	Thamesway	H391MAR	Thamesway	H641UWE	The Shires
H317LJN	Thamesway	H391OHK	Thamesway	H642UWE	The Shires
H319LJN	Thamesway	H392MAR	Thamesway	H642UWR	Cambus
H321LJN	Thamesway	H392OHK	Thamesway	H643UWR	Cambus
H322LJN	Thamesway	H393MAR	Thamesway	H645UWR	Hedingham
H324LJN	Thamesway	H393OHK	Thamesway	H647UWR	Cambridge CS
H326LJN	Thamesway	H394MAR	Thamesway	H649UWR	Cambus
H327LJN	Thamesway	H394OHK	Thamesway	H652UWR	Cambus
H329LJN	Thamesway	H395MAR	Thamesway	H653UWR	Cambus
H330LJN	Thamesway	H395OHK	Thamesway	H668ATN	Red Rose
H331LJN	Thamesway	H396OHK	Thamesway	H733LOL	Red Rose
H332LJN	Thamesway	H397OHK	Thamesway	H748CBP	Universitybus
H334LJN	Thamesway	H398OHK	Thamesway	H749CBP	Universitybus
H335LJN	Thamesway	H402DEG	Cambus	H830YGA	Fords Coaches
H336LJN	Thamesway	H403DEG	Cambus	H833AHS	Ambassador Travel
H337LJN	Thamesway	H403ERP	Hallmark	H840NOC	Universitybus
H338LJN	Thamesway	H403FGS	Sovereign	H845AHS	Southend
H339LJN	Thamesway	H404FGS	Sovereign	H846UUA	Seamarks
H341LJN	Thamesway	H406FGS	Sovereign	H848AUS	The Shires
H342LJN	Thamesway	H406GAV	Cambus	H849NOC	Universitybus
H343LJN	Thamesway	H407ERO	The Shires	H854DAV	Emblings
H344LJN	Thamesway	H407FGS	Sovereign	H903AHS	County
H345LJN	Thamesway	H407GAV	Cambus	H920FGS	Sovereign
H346LJN	Thamesway	H408BVR	The Shires	H921FGS	Sovereign
H347LJN	Thamesway	H408ERO	The Shires	H922FGS	Sovereign
H348LJN	Thamesway	H408FGS	Sovereign	H922LOX	The Shires
H349LJN	Thamesway	H409BVR	The Shires	H923FGS	Sovereign
H351LJN	Thamesway	H409ERO	The Shires	H923LOX	The Shires
H352LJN	Thamesway	H409FGS	Sovereign	H925FGS	Sovereign
H353LJN	Thamesway	H410ERO	The Shires	H925LOX	The Shires
H354LJN	Thamesway	H410FGS	Sovereign	H926FGS	Sovereign
H355LJN	Thamesway	H411CJF	Fords Coaches	H926LOX	The Shires
H356LJN	Thamesway	H411FGS	Sovereign	H927FGS	Sovereign
H357LJN	Thamesway	H413FGS	Sovereign	H929FGS	Sovereign
H358LJN	Thamesway	H415FGS	Sovereign	H930FGS	Sovereign
H359LJN	Thamesway	H417FGS	Sovereign	H931FGS	Sovereign
H361LJN	Thamesway	H418FGS	Sovereign	H982KVX	Fargo Coachlines
H362LJN	Thamesway	H419FGS	Sovereign	HAH237V	Viscount
H363LJN	Thamesway	H421FGS	Sovereign	HAH238V	Eastern Counties
H364LJN	Thamesway	H422FGS	Sovereign	HAH239V	Eastern Counties
H365LJN	Thamesway	H423EUT	Windmill Cs	HAH240V	Eastern Counties
H366LJN	Thamesway	H423FGS	Sovereign	HAR116Y	Hedingham
H367LJN	Thamesway	H424FGS	Sovereign	HAX94W	Hedingham
H368OHK	Thamesway	H473CEG	Viscount	HBD913T	The Shires
H369OHK	Thamesway	H474CEG	Viscount	HBD918T	The Shires
H370GRY	County	H475CEG	Viscount	HBH411Y	Morley's
H370OHK	Thamesway	H475KSG	Felix	HC8936	Hallmark
H371OHK	Thamesway	H477LHJ	Harris Bus	HCL927Y	Ambassador Travel
H372OHK	Thamesway	H523SWE	The Shires	HCL957Y	Ambassador Travel
H372PHK	Southend	H533KSG	Flying Banana	HDT375	Richmond's

164

Reg	Operator	Reg	Operator	Reg	Operator
HDZ8354	County	J8BBC	Biss Brothers	J604WHJ	County
HEX47Y	Ambassador Travel	J8FTG	Sanders Coaches	J605WHJ	County
HEX52Y	Ambassador Travel	J9BUS	West's	J606WHJ	County
HFL14W	Kenzie's	J12BUS	West's	J607WHJ	County
HGA637T	Beestons	J20GSM	Belle Coaches	J608WHJ	County
HGG997T	Sanders Coaches	J31UTG	The Lutonians	J609WHJ	County
HHG193W	Reg's	J32UTG	The Lutonians	J610UTW	Eastern National
HHJ372Y	Eastern National	J35UTG	Waylands	J610WHJ	County
HHJ373Y	Eastern National	J42PAV	Kenzie's	J611UTW	Eastern National
HHJ375Y	Eastern National	J43UFL	Kenzie's	J611WHJ	County
HHJ376Y	Eastern National	J45SNY	Thamesway	J612UTW	Eastern National
HHJ381Y	Eastern National	J45UFL	Kenzie's	J612WHJ	County
HHJ382Y	Eastern National	J46SNY	Thamesway	J613UTW	Eastern National
HHT57N	Cedar Coaches	J46UFL	Kenzie's	J614UTW	Eastern National
HIB664	Simmonds	J48SNY	Thamesway	J615UTW	Eastern National
HIJ6931	Fargo Coachlines	J51GCX	Harris Bus	J616UTW	Eastern National
HIL3470	Rover Bus Services	J52GCX	Harris Bus	J617UTW	Eastern National
HIL4585	Emblings	J54SNY	Thamesway	J618UTW	Eastern National
HIL6244	Cedric's	J63GCX	Hallmark	J619UTW	Eastern National
HIL6245	Cedric's	J76VTG	Harris Bus	J61NTM	Simmonds
HIL6327	Spratts	J91WWC	Harris Bus	J620UTW	Eastern National
HIL6328	Spratts	J92YAR	Harris Bus	J621BVG	Eastern Counties
HIL6919	Spratts	J138OBU	Sanders Coaches	J621UTW	Eastern National
HIL7240	Spratts	J160LPV	Ipswich	J622BVG	Eastern Counties
HIL7391	Spratts	J171GGG	The Shires	J622UTW	Eastern National
HIL7394	Spratts	J201JRP	Buckinghamshire	J623BVG	Eastern Counties
HIL7467	The Shires	J202JRP	Buckinghamshire	J623UTW	Eastern National
HIL7477	Spratts	J203JRP	Buckinghamshire	J624BVG	Eastern Counties
HIL7478	Spratts	J204JRP	Buckinghamshire	J624UTW	Eastern National
HIL7479	Spratts	J208RVS	Seamarks	J625BVG	Eastern Counties
HIL7594	The Shires	J216XKY	Reg's	J625UTW	Eastern National
HIL7595	The Shires	J217XKY	Reg's	J626UTW	Eastern National
HIL7596	The Shires	J218NRT	Ipswich	J627UTW	Eastern National
HIL7597	The Shires	J220HDS	Felix	J628UTW	Eastern National
HJB464W	Hedingham	J228JDX	Ipswich	J629UTW	Eastern National
HLP10C	Classic Coaches	J245MFP	Hedingham	J630UTW	Eastern National
HNW366D	Classic Coaches	J281RNE	Waylands	J652DVG	Caroline Seagull
HOD55	Cedar Coaches	J295TWK	Hedingham	J702GWT	Cambus
HRO982V	Seamarks	J301WHJ	County	J702CWT	Cambus
HRP673N	The Shires	J302WHJ	County	J706CWT	Cambus
HRT530N	Amos Coaches	J303WHJ	County	J722KBC	Whippet
HSK834	Supreme	J304WHJ	County	J723KBC	Whippet
HSK835	Supreme	J305WHJ	County	J724KBC	Hedingham
HSK836	Supreme	J306WHJ	County	J739CWT	Cambus
HSK843	Supreme	J307WHJ	County	J740CWT	Cambus
HSK844	Supreme	J308WHJ	County	J741CWT	Cambus
HSK845	Supreme	J309WHJ	County	J742CWT	Cambus
HSK855	Supreme	J310WHJ	County	J743CWT	Cambus
HSK856	Supreme	J311WHJ	County	J744CWT	Cambus
HSK857	Supreme	J312WHJ	County	J788KHD	Hallmark
HSK858	Supreme	J313WHJ	County	J805DWW	Viscount
HSK859	Supreme	J314XVX	County	J806DWW	Viscount
HSK860	Supreme	J315XVX	County	J807DWW	Viscount
HSK892	Supreme	J316XVX	County	J811KHD	Galloway
HSV194	Cambus	J317XVX	County	J811KHD	Hallmark
HSV195	Cambus	J367BNW	Seamarks	J917HGD	The Shires
HSV196	Cambus	J392BNG	Belle Coaches	J933WHJ	County
HSV673	APT	J401XVX	County	J934WHJ	County
HTU154N	Emblings	J402XVX	County	J935WHJ	County
HTU164N	Beestons	J403XVX	County	J936WHJ	County
HUX15V	Sanders Coaches	J404WDA	Great Yarmouth	J937WHJ	County
HUX82V	Sanders Coaches	J404XVX	County	J938WHJ	County
HWJ933W	Cedric's	J408TEW	Cambus	J960DWX	Cambus
HWJ934W	Cedric's	J409TEW	Cambus	J961DWX	Cambus
IIB278	Rover Bus Services	J431HDS	Ambassador Travel	J962DWX	Cambus
IIL4579	The Shires	J432HDS	Ambassador Travel	JAH241V	Eastern Counties
IIL4580	The Shires	J437HDS	Ambassador Travel	JAH242V	Eastern Counties
IIL4821	The Shires	J438HDS	Ambassador Travel	JAH243V	Eastern Counties
IIL4822	The Shires	J447HDS	Cambus	JAH244V	Eastern Counties
IIL4823	The Shires	J448HDS	Cambus	JAH552D	Cambus
IIL4824	The Shires	J465NJU	Hallmark	JAH553D	Viscount
J2EST	Enterprise	J530FCL	Eastern Counties	JAR484Y	Amos Coaches
J2SUP	Supreme	J582WVX	Harris Bus	JAR495V	Hedingham
J3SUP	Supreme	J583WVX	Harris Bus	JBO345N	Southend
J6BUS	West's	J601WHJ	County	JBO349N	Southend
J7BBC	Biss Brothers	J602WHJ	County	JBO352N	Southend
J7FTG	Sanders Coaches	J603WHJ	County	JBO75W	County

Reg	Operator	Reg	Operator	Reg	Operator
JBO80W	County	JTD391P	Southend	K323CVX	County
JBY804	Kenzie's	JTD392P	Southend	K340HNG	Flying Banana
JCL808V	Eastern Counties	JTD393P	Stephensons	K390SLB	Sovereign
JCL809V	Eastern Counties	JTD396P	Southend	K390TCE	Cambus
JCY870	Classic Coaches	JTL805V	Sanders Coaches	K391KUA	Viscount
JDB797V	Marshall's	JTU586T	Southend	K391SLB	Sovereign
JDN506L	Sanders Coaches	JUB650V	Cambus	K392BVS	Felix
JEV245Y	Fords Coaches	JUS774N	Don's	K392KUA	Viscount
JFA450V	Belle Coaches	JVE370P	Emblings	K392SLB	Sovereign
JFP177V	West's	JVH378	Classic Coaches	K393KUA	Viscount
JFR397N	Morley's	JWT757V	Hedingham	K393SLB	Sovereign
JGA189N	Don's	JWT760V	Eastern National	K396KHJ	Thamesway
JGU938V	Sanders Coaches	JWV271W	Hedingham	K397KHJ	Thamesway
JGV336V	Semmence	K2APT	APT	K398KHJ	Thamesway
JGV929	Simmonds	K2BUS	West's	K405FHJ	County
JHJ139V	Thamesway	K3SBC	Sovereign	K406FHJ	County
JHJ140V	Eastern National	K3SUP	Supreme	K407FHJ	County
JHJ141V	Thamesway	K4SBC	Sovereign	K408FHJ	County
JHJ142V	Eastern National	K4SUP	Supreme	K409FHJ	County
JHJ145V	Thamesway	K4WMS	Waylands	K410FHJ	County
JHJ146V	Thamesway	K5BUS	West's	K411FHJ	County
JHJ147V	Eastern National	K5SBC	Sovereign	K412FHJ	County
JHJ148V	Thamesway	K5SUP	Supreme	K413FHJ	County
JHJ150V	Eastern National	K6SUP	Supreme	K414FHJ	County
JHK495N	Colchester	K8BUS	The Shires	K419FAV	Buckinghamshire
JHL983	Classic Coaches	K11BOO	Boon's Tours	K424GHE	Windmill Cs
JIL2760	Emblings	K25WND	The Shires	K426FAV	Buckinghamshire
JIL5623	Osborne's	K26HCL	Eastern Counties	K428FAV	Buckinghamshire
JIL5628	Osborne's	K26WND	The Shires	K447XPA	The Shires
JIL5655	Emblings	K27HCL	Eastern Counties	K448XPA	The Shires
JIL5660	Emblings	K27WND	The Shires	K457PNR	Cambus
JIL7539	Emblings	K28HCL	Eastern Counties	K458PNR	Cambus
JIL8238	Luckybus	K28WND	The Shires	K459PNR	Supreme
JIL9034	Rover Bus Services	K29HCL	Eastern Counties	K521RJX	Hallmark
JIW3696	County	K29WND	The Shires	K525RJX	Hallmark
JJD404D	B T S	K31VRY	Hallmark	K540OGA	Red Rose
JJD443D	B T S	K31WND	The Shires	K543OGA	The Shires
JJD487D	B T S	K32VRY	Hallmark	K550RJX	Boon's Tours
JJD527D	B T S	K32WND	The Shires	K578YOJ	The Shires
JJD538D	B T S	K49TER	Kenzie's	K579YOJ	The Shires
JJD563D	B T S	K51TER	Kenzie's	K580YOJ	The Shires
JJD569D	B T S	K52TER	Kenzie's	K596VBC	Watson
JJD582D	B T S	K53TER	Kenzie's	K622WOV	Harris Bus
JJD598D	B T S	K62KEX	Great Yarmouth	K623WOV	Harris Bus
JJF879V	Sanders Coaches	K63KEX	Great Yarmouth	K631GVX	Eastern National
JJT441N	Buckinghamshire	K95GEV	Harris Bus	K632GVX	Eastern National
JKV413V	Neaves	K96GEV	Harris Bus	K633GVX	Eastern National
JKV414V	Hedingham	K96OGA	Cambus	K634GVX	Eastern National
JKV420V	Semmence	K97GEV	Harris Bus	K635GVX	Eastern National
JKV422V	Semmence	K100LCT	Ipswich	K636GVX	Eastern National
JMB328T	Stephensons	K101VJU	Belle Coaches	K637GVX	Eastern National
JND257V	Universitybus	K110TCP	Galloway	K638GVX	Eastern National
JNG49N	Eastern Counties	K120TCP	Galloway	K639GVX	Eastern National
JNG50N	Eastern Counties	K122OCT	Harris Bus	K640GVX	Eastern National
JNG51N	Eastern Counties	K123OCT	Harris Bus	K641GVX	Eastern National
JNG52N	Eastern Counties	K129OCT	Boon's Tours	K642GVX	Eastern National
JNG54N	Eastern Counties	K171CAV	Viscount	K643GVX	Eastern National
JNG56N	Eastern Counties	K172CAV	Viscount	K644GVX	Eastern National
JNG57N	Eastern Counties	K173CAV	Viscount	K645GVX	Eastern National
JNG58N	Eastern Counties	K174CAV	Viscount	K646GVX	Eastern National
JNK551N	Sanders Coaches	K175CAV	Viscount	K707FNO	County
JNU137N	Eastern Counties	K176CAV	Viscount	K707RNR	Supreme
JOI9820	Rover Bus Services	K177CAV	Viscount	K708FNO	County
JOX467P	Ambassador Travel	K184GDU	The Shires	K708RNR	Supreme
JPE233V	The Shires	K198EVW	Hedingham	K709FNO	County
JPE234V	The Shires	K202FEH	The Shires	K710FNO	County
JPE236V	The Shires	K203FEH	The Shires	K711FNO	County
JPE237V	The Shires	K219PPV	Ipswich	K712FNO	County
JPL185K	Buzz	K226WNH	Hallmark	K729GBE	Motts
JRP796L	The Shires	K227WNH	Hallmark	K731JAH	Eastern Counties
JRP797L	The Shires	K229WNH	Motts	K732JAH	Eastern Counties
JRP798L	The Shires	K266OGA	Motts	K733JAH	Eastern Counties
JRP799L	The Shires	K318CVX	County	K734JAH	Eastern Counties
JRP800L	The Shires	K319CVX	County	K735JAH	Eastern Counties
JSC883E	Boon's Tours	K320CVX	County	K736JAH	Eastern Counties
JSC890E	Caroline Seagull	K321CVX	County	K737JAH	Eastern Counties
JTD388P	Southend	K322CVX	County	K738JAH	Eastern Counties

Reg	Operator	Reg	Operator	Reg	Operator
K739JAH	Eastern Counties	KKE734N	Eastern Counties	L73UNG	Ambassador Travel
K740JAH	Eastern Counties	KKU835P	Buffalo	L74UNG	Ambassador Travel
K741JAH	Eastern Counties	KKY841P	The Shires	L93OAR	Harris Bus
K742JAH	Eastern Counties	KNK539V	Neaves	L97PTW	Harris Bus
K743JAH	Eastern Counties	KNR310V	Semmence	L98PTW	Harris Bus
K744JAH	Eastern Counties	KNV509P	The Shires	L100BUS	Luckybus
K805DJN	Thamesway	KNV513P	The Shires	L100SUP	Supreme
K806DJN	Thamesway	KON323P	Motts	L109PVW	Crusader
K807DJN	Thamesway	KOO787V	Eastern National	L110PVW	Crusader
K808DJN	Thamesway	KOO789V	Eastern National	L110RWB	Marshall's
K809DJN	Thamesway	KOO790V	Eastern National	L111PVW	Crusader
K810DJN	Thamesway	KOO794V	Eastern National	L112PVW	Crusader
K811DJN	Thamesway	KOU796P	Stephensons	L121OWF	Enterprise
K878GOO	Cedric's	KPJ238W	County	L129GBA	Hallmark
K886BRW	Hallmark	KPJ239W	The Shires	L130GBA	Hallmark
K901CVW	Thamesway	KPJ241W	The Shires	L133HVS	The Shires
K902CVW	Thamesway	KPJ242W	The Shires	L161ADX	Ipswich
K903CVW	Thamesway	KPJ243W	The Shires	L162ADX	Ipswich
K904CVW	Thamesway	KPJ244W	County	L169ADX	Ipswich
K905CVW	Thamesway	KPJ245W	County	L181ADX	Ipswich
K906CVW	Thamesway	KPJ246W	County	L182ADX	Ipswich
K907CVW	Thamesway	KPJ247W	County	L183APV	Ipswich
K908CVW	Thamesway	KPJ248W	County	L184APV	Ipswich
K908RGE	Cedric's	KPJ249W	County	L198SCM	Felix
K909CVW	Thamesway	KPJ250W	County	L200BUS	Luckybus
K910CVW	Thamesway	KPJ251W	County	L200SUP	Supreme
K911CVW	Thamesway	KPJ252W	County	L207RNO	Hedingham
K911RGE	Cambus	KPJ254W	County	L208RNO	Hedingham
K912CVW	Thamesway	KPJ256W	County	L245PAH	Eastern Counties
K912RGE	Cambus	KPT800T	Sanders Coaches	L246PAH	Eastern Counties
K913CVW	Thamesway	KRP560V	The Shires	L247PAH	Eastern Counties
K914CVW	Thamesway	KRP563V	The Shires	L248PAH	Eastern Counties
K914RGE	Motts	KRP565V	The Shires	L249PAH	Eastern Counties
K915CVW	Thamesway	KRP566V	The Shires	L250PAH	Eastern Counties
K916CVW	Thamesway	KSK966	Motts	L251PAH	Eastern Counties
K917CVW	Thamesway	KSK967	Motts	L252PAH	Eastern Counties
K963HUB	Cambus	KSU369	Boon's Tours	L253PAH	Eastern Counties
K964HUB	Cambus	KSU412	Angian	L254PAH	Eastern Counties
K965HUB	Cambus	KSU473	Crusader	L255PAH	Eastern Counties
K966HUB	Cambus	KSU850P	Don's	L256PAH	Eastern Counties
K967HUB	Cambus	KUB550V	County	L257PAH	Eastern Counties
K968HUB	Cambus	KUB551V	County	L258PAH	Eastern Counties
K969HUB	Cambus	KUC228P	Osborne's	L259PAH	Eastern Counties
K970HUB	Cambus	KUC948P	Simmonds	L300BUS	Luckybus
K971HUB	Cambus	KVF245V	Viscount	L300SUP	Supreme
K972HUB	Cambus	KVF246V	Viscount	L305HPP	The Shires
K973HUB	Cambus	KVF247V	Viscount	L306HPP	The Shires
K974HUB	Cambus	KVF248V	Viscount	L307HPP	The Shires
K975HUB	Viscount	KVF249V	Viscount	L308HPP	The Shires
KAF577W	Buffalo	KVF250V	Viscount	L309HPP	The Shires
KAU574V	Sanders Coaches	KVG601V	Eastern Counties	L310HPP	The Shires
KAU575V	Sanders Coaches	KVG602V	Eastern Counties	L311HPP	The Shires
KBC2V	Osborne's	KVG603V	Eastern Counties	L312HPP	The Shires
KBH860V	Biss Brothers	KVG604V	Eastern Counties	L313HPP	The Shires
KBH861V	Biss Brothers	KVG606V	Eastern Counties	L314HPP	The Shires
KDH832V	Galloway	KVG607V	Eastern Counties	L315HPP	The Shires
KEP829X	Eastern National	KVG608V	Eastern Counties	L316HPP	The Shires
KGA56Y	West's	KVG609V	Eastern Counties	L326AUT	The Shires
KGS489Y	Hedingham	KWB695W	Coach Services	L327AUT	The Shires
KHB35W	Fargo Coachlines	KYN283X	Whippet	L328AUT	The Shires
KHJ786P	Hedingham	KYN296X	Whippet	L343FWF	Biss Brothers
KIA891	Simmonds	L2SBC	Sovereign	L355HFU	Simmonds
KIB5227	Rules	L3CED	Cedric's	L400BUS	Luckybus
KIW3769	Rover Bus Services	L3SBC	Sovereign	L415NHJ	County
KIW4388	Cedric's	L4WMS	Waylands	L425OWF	Windmill Cs
KIW4391	Cedric's	L21AHA	Eastern National	L475GOV	Harris Bus
KIW4981	Cedric's	L43MEH	The Shires	L476GOV	Harris Bus
KIW6416	Cedric's	L54REW	Kenzie's	L500BUS	Luckybus
KIW6511	County	L56REW	Kenzie's	L501MOO	County
KIW7813	Cedric's	L57REW	Kenzie's	L526EHD	Hallmark
KIW8513	County	L58TEW	Kenzie's	L530EHD	Hallmark
KJD12P	Charles Cook	L67UNG	Ambassador Travel	L531EHD	Hallmark
KJD271P	Whippet	L67YJF	Supreme	L600BUS	Luckybus
KJD89P	Simmonds	L68UNG	Ambassador Travel	L601MWC	Thamesway
KKE731N	Eastern Counties	L69UNG	Ambassador Travel	L613LVX	County
KKE732N	Eastern Counties	L71UNG	Ambassador Travel	L614LVX	County
KKE733N	Eastern Counties	L73NWU	Jacksons	L634ANX	Fargo Coachlines

L637ANX	Fargo Coachlines	L947HTM	Sovereign
L647MEV	Eastern National	L948HTM	Sovereign
L648MEV	Eastern National	L949MBH	Sovereign
L649MEV	Eastern National	L950MBH	Sovereign
L650MEV	Eastern National	L951MBH	Sovereign
L651MEV	Eastern National	L952MBH	Sovereign
L652MEV	Eastern National	L953MBH	Sovereign
L653MEV	Eastern National	L954MBH	Sovereign
L654MEV	Eastern National	L978UAH	Ambassador Travel
L655MEV	Eastern National	L979UAH	Ambassador Travel
L655MFL	Cambus	L980CRY	Simmonds
L656MEV	Eastern National	LAH817A	Sanders Coaches
L656MFL	Cambus	LAH894A	Caroline Seagull
L657MFL	Cambus	LBD837P	The Shires
L658MFL	Cambus	LBZ2940	Reg's
L659MFL	Cambus	LBZ2941	Reg's
L660MFL	Cambus	LBZ2942	Reg's
L661MFL	Cambus	LBZ2943	Reg's
L662MFL	Cambus	LBZ2944	Reg's
L663MFL	Cambus	LCW175W	Beestons
L664MFL	Cambus	LDS280A	B T S
L665MFL	Cambus	LDV398P	Beestons
L667MFL	Cambus	LDV847F	Classic Coaches
L668MFL	Cambus	LDW362P	Beestons
L668WFT	Fargo Coachlines	LDX75G	Ipswich
L669MFL	Cambus	LDZ3142	J B S
L705CNR	Osborne's	LER666P	Kenzie's
L706CNR	Osborne's	LEW16W	Kenzie's
L707CNR	Hallmark	LEW971P	Whippet
L713OVX	County	LGA18P	Supreme
L714OVX	County	LHG440T	Southend
L715OVX	County	LHG441T	Southend
L716OVX	County	LHG445T	APT
L717OVX	County	LHG447T	Southend
L718OVX	County	LHG448T	Southend
L722OVX	County	LIB1611	Rules
L723PHK	County	LIB226	Simmonds
L724PHK	County	LIL2288	Luckybus
L801KNO	County	LIW9272	Cedric's
L801MEV	Eastern National	LJI477	Fords Coaches
L802KNO	County	LJR284X	Lamberts
L802MEV	Eastern National	LLT345V	Eastern Counties
L803KNO	County	LMA413T	Hedingham
L803OPU	Eastern National	LNU581W	Sanders Coaches
L804KNO	County	LOD724P	Buckinghamshire
L804OPU	Eastern National	LOD725P	Buckinghamshire
L805OPU	Eastern National	LPB218P	Southend
L805OVX	County	LPF596P	Cedric's
L806OPU	Eastern National	LRA801P	Hedingham
L807OPU	Eastern National	LSU113	Crusader
L808OPU	Eastern National	LTG272X	Angian
L809OPU	Eastern National	LTG274X	Angian
L810OPU	Eastern National	LTG276X	Simmonds
L811OPU	Eastern National	LUA283V	Beestons
L812OPU	Eastern National	LUA289V	Osborne's
L813OPU	Eastern National	LUA716V	Eastern National
L814OPU	Eastern National	LUA717V	Eastern National
L815OPU	Eastern National	LUB514P	Buffalo
L816OPU	Eastern National	LUE260V	West's
L817OPU	Eastern National	LVS418V	Reg's
L818OPU	Eastern National	LWU466V	Viscount
L819OPU	Eastern National	LWU467V	Viscount
L820OPU	Eastern National	LWU468V	Viscount
L821OPU	Eastern National	LWU469V	Eastern National
L822OPU	Eastern National	LWU470V	Viscount
L832MWT	Ipswich	LXI2743	Buffalo
L834MWT	Seamarks	M2SOB	Simmonds
L863BEA	The Shires	M3SOB	Simmonds
L864BEA	The Shires	M4WMS	Waylands
L890UVE	NIBS	M7SLC	Lodge's
L891UVE	NIBS	M8CED	Cedric's
L922LJO	The Shires	M15CED	Cedric's
L923LJO	The Shires	M15HMC	Hallmark
L938ORC	Ambassador Travel	M16HMC	Hallmark
L944HTM	Sovereign	M38WUR	The Shires
L945HTM	Sovereign	M39WUR	The Shires
L946HTM	Sovereign	M41EPV	Ipswich

M41WUR	The Shires		
M42EPV	Ipswich		
M42WUR	The Shires		
M43WUR	The Shires		
M45WUR	The Shires		
M47WUR	The Shires		
M48HUT	Universitybus		
M49HUT	Universitybus		
M51HUT	Universitybus		
M52WEV	Harris Bus		
M59WEB	Kenzie's		
M61WEB	Kenzie's		
M61WER	Biss Brothers		
M62MOG	Red Rose		
M62WEB	Kenzie's		
M63WEB	Kenzie's		
M64WEB	Kenzie's		
M65WEB	Kenzie's		
M67WEB	Kenzie's		
M68XVF	Great Yarmouth		
M69XVF	Great Yarmouth		
M101UKX	Sovereign		
M102UKX	Sovereign		
M103UKX	Sovereign		
M104UKX	Sovereign		
M105UKX	Sovereign		
M121SKY	Biss Brothers		
M131SKY	Biss Brothers		
M136SKY	Simmonds		
M146VVS	Universitybus		
M148KJF	Marshall's		
M148VVS	Universitybus		
M150EAV	Whippet		
M150RBH	The Shires		
M151RBH	The Shires		
M152RBH	The Shires		
M153RBH	The Shires		
M154RBH	The Shires		
M156RBH	The Shires		
M157RBH	The Shires		
M158RBH	The Shires		
M159RBH	The Shires		
M160RBH	The Shires		
M166VJN	Eastern National		
M210VEV	Hedingham		
M211WHJ	Hedingham		
M212WHJ	Hedingham		
M213EDX	Ipswich		
M214EDX	Ipswich		
M215EDX	Ipswich		
M216EDX	Ipswich		
M231SGS	Seamarks		
M242AEX	Waylands		
M247SPP	The Shires		
M248SPP	The Shires		
M249SPP	The Shires		
M250SPP	The Shires		
M250TAK	Marshall's		
M251SPP	The Shires		
M254TAK	Marshall's		
M255TAK	Marshall's		
M255UKX	Universitybus		
M256TAK	Supreme		
M257TAK	Supreme		
M258TAK	Supreme		
M259TAK	Supreme		
M266VPU	County		
M267VPU	County		
M268VPU	County		
M269VPU	County		
M301BAV	Cambridge CS		
M302BAV	Cambridge CS		
M303BAV	Cambridge CS		
M304BAV	Cambridge CS		
M305BAV	Cambridge CS		
M306BAV	Cambridge CS		
M306VET	Fargo Coachlines		

Reg	Operator	Reg	Operator	Reg	Operator
M307BAV	Cambridge CS	M616RCP	Hallmark	M810WWR	Viscount
M307VET	Fargo Coachlines	M617RCP	Hallmark	M830RCP	Galloway
M308BAV	Cambridge CS	M618RCP	Hallmark	M832CVG	Lamberts
M308VET	Fargo Coachlines	M619RCP	Hallmark	M839RCP	Hallmark
M309VET	Fargo Coachlines	M640EPV	Ipswich	M841LFT	Hallmark
M310VET	Fargo Coachlines	M657VJN	Eastern National	M842LFT	Hallmark
M313VET	Boon's Tours	M658VJN	Eastern National	M848MOL	Red Rose
M321VET	Ambassador Travel	M659VJN	Eastern National	M889WAK	Airport Coaches
M322VET	Ambassador Travel	M660VJN	Eastern National	M918TEV	Thamesway
M330KRY	Ambassador Travel	M661VJN	Eastern National	M919TEV	Thamesway
M331KRY	Ambassador Travel	M662VJN	Eastern National	M920TEV	Thamesway
M332KRY	Ambassador Travel	M663VJN	Eastern National	M921TEV	Thamesway
M345UVX	Graham's	M664VJN	Eastern National	M922TEV	Thamesway
M360XEX	Eastern Counties	M665VJN	Eastern National	M923TEV	Thamesway
M361XEX	Eastern Counties	M667VJN	Eastern National	M924TEV	Thamesway
M362XEX	Eastern Counties	M668VJN	Eastern National	M925TEV	Thamesway
M363XEX	Eastern Counties	M669VJN	Eastern National	M926TEV	Thamesway
M364XEX	Eastern Counties	M670VJN	Eastern National	M927TEV	Thamesway
M365UCT	Golden Boy	M671VJN	Eastern National	M928TEV	Thamesway
M365XEX	Eastern Counties	M672VJN	Eastern National	M929TEV	Thamesway
M366XEX	Eastern Counties	M673VJN	Eastern National	M930TEV	Thamesway
M367XEX	Eastern Counties	M674VJN	Eastern National	M931TEV	Thamesway
M368XEX	Eastern Counties	M675VJN	Eastern National	M932TEV	Thamesway
M369XEX	Eastern Counties	M676VJN	Eastern National	M933TEV	Thamesway
M370XEX	Eastern Counties	M702RVS	Seamarks	M934TEV	Thamesway
M371XEX	Eastern Counties	M710OMJ	The Shires	M935TEV	Thamesway
M372XEX	Eastern Counties	M711OMJ	The Shires	M936TEV	Thamesway
M373XEX	Eastern Counties	M712OMJ	The Shires	M937TEV	Thamesway
M374HOX	Fargo Coachlines	M713OMJ	The Shires	M938TEV	Thamesway
M374XEX	Eastern Counties	M714OMJ	The Shires	M939TEV	Thamesway
M375YEX	Eastern Counties	M715OMJ	The Shires	M940TEV	Thamesway
M376YEX	Eastern Counties	M716OMJ	The Shires	M941TEV	Thamesway
M377YEX	Eastern Counties	M717OMJ	The Shires	M942TEV	Thamesway
M378YEX	Eastern Counties	M718OMJ	The Shires	M943TEV	Thamesway
M379YEX	Eastern Counties	M719OMJ	The Shires	M961ENH	J B S
M380YEX	Eastern Counties	M719UTW	County	M971CVG	Sanders Coaches
M384KVR	Flying Banana	M720OMJ	The Shires	M975WWR	Cambus
M384WET	Biss Brothers	M720UTW	County	M976WWR	Cambus
M441CVG	Lamberts	M721OMJ	The Shires	M977WWR	Cambus
M455UUR	Sovereign	M721UTW	County	M978WWR	Cambus
M456UUR	Sovereign	M722OMJ	The Shires	M979VWY	Cambus
M457UUR	Sovereign	M723OMJ	The Shires	MAU142P	NIBS
M458UUR	Sovereign	M724OMJ	The Shires	MBE616R	Fargo Coachlines
M459UUR	Sovereign	M725OMJ	The Shires	MBT551T	Simmonds
M460UUR	Sovereign	M725UTW	County	MBZ3733	Graham's
M461UUR	Sovereign	M726OMJ	The Shires	MBZ7136	Lodge's
M46WUR	The Shires	M726UTW	County	MBZ7141	NIBS
M46xxx	Supreme	M727OMJ	The Shires	MCA676T	Biss Brothers
M47HUT	Universitybus	M727UTW	County	MCL937P	Buckinghamshire
M486HBC	Fords Coaches	M728OMJ	The Shires	MCL938P	Eastern Counties
M501XWC	Harris Bus	M728UTW	County	MCL940P	Eastern Counties
M502XWC	Harris Bus	M729OMJ	The Shires	MCL941P	Eastern Counties
M503XWC	Harris Bus	M729UTW	County	MCL944P	Eastern Counties
M504XWC	Harris Bus	M730AOO	County	MDM282P	Buckinghamshire
M527UGS	Universitybus	M731AOO	County	MDW584P	Hedingham
M577JBC	Osborne's	M732AOO	County	MDX668V	Belle Coaches
M584ANG	Eastern Counties	M733AOO	County	MEB626	Emblings
M585ANG	Eastern Counties	M734AOO	County	MED406P	Bordacoach
M586ANG	Eastern Counties	M735AOO	County	MEL556P	Buckinghamshire
M587ANG	Eastern Counties	M736AOO	County	MEL559P	Buckinghamshire
M587BFL	Richmond's	M737AOO	County	MEV83V	Colchester
M588ANG	Eastern Counties	M738AOO	County	MEV84V	Colchester
M588BFL	Richmond's	M741KJU	Ambassador Travel	MEV85V	Colchester
M589ANG	Eastern Counties	M742KJU	Ambassador Travel	MEV86V	Colchester
M589SDC	Whippet	M743KJU	Ambassador Travel	MEV87V	Colchester
M590ANG	Eastern Counties	M759PVM	Beestons	MEX768P	Eastern Counties
M591ANG	Eastern Counties	M761JPA	Southend	MEX769P	Eastern Counties
M592ANG	Eastern Counties	M762JPA	Southend	MEX770P	Eastern Counties
M593ANG	Eastern Counties	M763JPA	Southend	MFA721V	Eastern National
M601RCP	Hallmark	M764JPA	Southend	MFK768V	Osborne's
M602RCP	Hallmark	M802RCP	Hallmark	MGR672P	Hedingham
M603RCP	Hallmark	M803RCP	Hallmark	MHJ729V	Eastern National
M604RCP	Hallmark	M804RCP	Hallmark	MHJ731V	Eastern National
M612RCP	Hallmark	M805RCP	Hallmark	MIB9067	Sanders Coaches
M613RCP	Hallmark	M806RCP	Hallmark	MIW2853	Lamberts
M614RCP	Hallmark	M808WWR	Viscount	MIW3561	Sanders Coaches
M615RCP	Hallmark	M809WWR	Viscount	MJB481	Lodge's

The latest arrival with Galloways of Mendlesham is N665JGV, a DAF SB220 with Ikarus Citibus bodywork. This the operators first new bus which is currently operating route 86, Ipswich to Stowmarket for Suffolk County Council. At it's maximum, the vehicle seats 51, though two are convertable to luggage racks. *Geoff Mills*

MJI2374	Jacksons	MRJ237W	Southend	N601APU	Thamesway
MJI3376	Jacksons	MRJ238W	Southend	N602APU	Thamesway
MJI3409	Marshall's	MRJ239W	Southend	N603APU	Thamesway
MJI4487	Angian	MRJ240W	Southend	N604APU	Thamesway
MJI6252	Marshall's	MRJ241W	Southend	N605APU	Thamesway
MJI6253	Marshall's	MRJ242W	Southend	N606APU	Thamesway
MJI7854	Seamarks	MRT9P	Ipswich	N607APU	Thamesway
MJI7855	Seamarks	MSK286	Hallmark	N608APU	Thamesway
MJI7856	Seamarks	MSK287	Hallmark	N609APU	Thamesway
MJI7857	Seamarks	MUA865P	Colchester	N610APU	Thamesway
MJI8660	Seamarks	MUD535W	Coach Services	N611APU	Thamesway
MJI8661	Seamarks	MUH281X	Southend	N612APU	Thamesway
MJI8662	Seamarks	MUH283X	Southend	N613APU	Thamesway
MJI8663	Seamarks	MUH284X	The Shires	N614APU	Thamesway
MKK458P	Hedingham	MUH285X	Southend	N615APU	Thamesway
MMJ538V	Coach Services	MUH286X	Southend	N616APU	Thamesway
MMJ547V	Sanders Coaches	MUH287X	The Shires	N617APU	Thamesway
MNH569V	The Shires	MUS151P	Motts	N618APU	Thamesway
MNH572V	The Shires	MVK538R	Boon's Tours	N619APU	Thamesway
MNH573V	The Shires	MXI8204	Cedric's	N620APU	Thamesway
MNH574V	The Shires	N190DBH	The Lutonians	N665JGV	Galloway
MNH577V	The Shires	N421ENM	Universitybus	N739AVW	County
MNH578V	The Shires	N422ENM	Universitybus	N740AVW	County
MNH579V	The Shires	N423ENM	Universitybus	N741AVW	County
MNK427V	Osborne's	N424ENM	Universitybus	N742AVW	County
MNK429V	Osborne's	N445XVA	Cambus	N743ANW	County
MNK430V	Osborne's	N446XVA	Cambus	N744AVW	County
MNM40V	Sanders Coaches	N447XVA	Cambus	N823APU	Eastern National
MOD569P	Hedingham	N448XVA	Cambus	N824APU	Eastern National
MPJ210L	County	N449XVA	Cambus	N825APU	Eastern National
MRB802P	Hedingham	N450XVA	Cambus	N826APU	Eastern National
MRJ231W	Southend	N451XVA	Cambus	N827APU	Eastern National
MRJ232W	Southend	N452XVA	Cambus	N828APU	Eastern National
MRJ233W	Southend	N518XER	Cambus	N829APU	Eastern National
MRJ234W	Southend	N519XER	Cambus	N830APU	Eastern National
MRJ235W	Southend	N520XER	Cambus	N990BWJ	Coach Services
MRJ236W	Southend	N597DWY	Sanders	NAH135P	Eastern Counties

Reg	Operator	Reg	Operator	Reg	Operator
NAH136P	Buckinghamshire	OEX794W	Eastern Counties	PBD40R	Harris Bus
NAH137P	Buckinghamshire	OEX796W	Eastern Counties	PBD43R	Harris Bus
NAH138P	Cambus	OFL113J	Emblings	PCL251W	Eastern Counties
NAH139P	Eastern Counties	OGR647	Sanders Coaches	PCL252W	Eastern Counties
NAH141P	Eastern Counties	OHE274X	Colchester	PCL253W	Eastern Counties
NBX862	Angian	OHE280X	Colchester	PCL254W	Eastern Counties
NCD553M	Hedingham	OHE934R	Galloway	PCL255W	Eastern Counties
NCK980J	Eastern Counties	OHV706Y	B T S	PCL256W	Eastern Counties
NDL652R	NIBS	OHV777Y	B T S	PCL257W	Eastern Counties
NDL869	Classic Coaches	OIB3510	County	PEB2R	Kenzie's
NDP38R	Morley's	OIB3520	County	PEX386R	Cambus
NER610M	Morley's	OIB3521	County	PEX610W	Eastern Counties
NFX446P	Hedingham	OIB3522	County	PEX613W	Eastern Counties
NHU2	Classic Coaches	OIB3523	County	PEX614W	Eastern Counties
NIB8459	The Shires	OIB5401	Stephensons	PEX615W	Eastern Counties
NIW4122	Don's	OIB5402	Stephensons	PEX616W	Eastern Counties
NJI9241	Belle Coaches	OJD126R	Hedingham	PEX617W	Eastern Counties
NJI9242	Belle Coaches	OJD141R	Buffalo	PEX618W	Buckinghamshire
NJI9243	Belle Coaches	OJD192R	Morley's	PEX619W	Buckinghamshire
NJI9244	Belle Coaches	OJD195R	Eastern Counties	PEX620W	Cambus
NJI9245	Belle Coaches	OJD212R	Beestons	PEX621W	Cambus
NJT34P	Buckinghamshire	OJD232R	Morley's	PEX622W	Buckinghamshire
NKE307P	Semmence	OJD261R	The Shires	PFL435R	Simmonds
NKY161	Don's	OJD357R	Shorey	PHG186T	Reg's
NLH288	Coach Services	OJD363R	The Shires	PHH407R	Stephensons
NMJ269V	Reg's	OJD368R	The Shires	PHH408R	Stephensons
NML627E	B T S	OJD414R	Buffalo	PHK387R	Hedingham
NML633E	B T S	OJD425R	The Shires	PHK620V	Osborne's
NNO63P	Boon's Tours	OJD448R	Bordacoach	PIA892	Shorey
NNO66P	Boon's Tours	OJD463R	Motts	PIJ3379	Ambassador Travel
NPD169L	The Shires	OJD468R	Buffalo	PIJ4317	Ambassador Travel
NPD690W	Towler	OJI4627	Belle Coaches	PIJ8513	Ambassador Travel
NPK241R	Southend	OJI4754	Belle Coaches	PIJ9274	Ambassador Travel
NPU974M	Eastern National	OJI4755	Belle Coaches	PIW4798	Whippet
NPU979M	Hedingham	OJI4756	Belle Coaches	PJE999J	Kenzie's
NPV308W	Belle Coaches	OJI4758	Belle Coaches	PJI3670	Beestons
NPV309W	Belle Coaches	OJR338	Rover Bus Services	PJI3671	Beestons
NRP581V	The Shires	OKW504R	Supreme	PJI3745	Southend
NRU307M	Buckinghamshire	OLN65P	Cedar Coaches	PJI4655	Don's
NRU310M	Buckinghamshire	OMA504V	County	PJI4712	Beestons
NRU311M	Buckinghamshire	ONH925V	The Shires	PJI4713	Beestons
NRY22W	Spratts	ONH927V	Cambus	PJI5637	Sanders Coaches
NRY333W	Neaves	ONH928V	The Shires	PJI7348	Sanders Coaches
NSJ19R	Morley's	ONH929V	The Shires	PJI8327	Sanders Coaches
NSJ21R	Morley's	ONN274M	Ambassador Travel	PJI8328	Sanders Coaches
NSJ3R	Cedar Coaches	ONN279M	Ambassador Travel	PJI8333	Enterprise
NSU113	Crusader	ONR79R	Fords Coaches	RJI8614	Sanders Coaches
NSU182	Jacksons	OPW179P	Cambus	PKE806M	Fords Coaches
NSV707	Classic Coaches	OPW180P	Cambus	PNK167R	Coach Services
NTC571R	Cedric's	OPW181P	Eastern Counties	PNW296W	Beestons
NUF990W	Semmence	OPW182P	Cambus	PPG3R	Belle Coaches
NUM341V	Cambus	ORP468M	The Shires	PPJ162W	Prestwood Travel
NUW620Y	B T S	OSR191R	Osborne's	PRC848X	Eastern Counties
NVD328P	Charles Cook	OSR192R	Jacksons	PRC850X	Eastern Counties
NXI9006	Southend	OSR194R	Jacksons	PRC851X	Eastern Counties
OAL631M	Ambassador Travel	OSU314	Semmence	PRC852X	Eastern Counties
OBN502R	Beestons	OTO151R	Stephensons	PRC853X	Eastern Counties
OBN503R	Charles Cook	OTO677W	Semmence	PRC854X	Eastern Counties
OCK985K	Eastern Counties	OUC109R	Whippet	PRC855X	Eastern Counties
OCK988K	Eastern Counties	OUC123R	Whippet	PRC857X	Eastern Counties
OCK994K	Eastern Counties	OUC49R	Buffalo	PRE205R	Emblings
OCK995K	Eastern Counties	OUD436M	Buckinghamshire	PRG124J	Fords Coaches
OCO117S	Harris Bus	OUD483T	The Shires	PRG127J	Fords Coaches
OCO118S	Harris Bus	OUD484T	The Shires	PRG134J	Fords Coaches
OCU781R	Whippet	OUD485T	The Shires	PRP802M	The Shires
OCY916R	The Shires	OUP683P	Eastern Counties	PRP803M	The Shires
ODL175R	Caroline Seagull	OVV518R	The Shires	PRP804M	The Shires
ODL176R	Caroline Seagull	OVV519R	The Shires	PRP805M	The Shires
ODL657R	Eastern Counties	OVV851R	The Shires	PRT700W	Belle Coaches
ODL658R	Eastern Counties	OVV852R	The Shires	PSU377	Rover Bus Services
ODL659R	Eastern Counties	OVV853R	The Shires	PTD671S	Supreme
ODU254P	Morley's	OVV855R	The Shires	PTT92R	Cambus
OEL233P	Eastern Counties	OWG368X	Motts	PTV597X	Semmence
OEL236P	Eastern Counties	OXK395	Angian	PUF131M	Colchester
OEM787S	Supreme	OYV703R	Belle Coaches	PUU970	Biss Brothers
OEX792W	Eastern Counties	PAY7W	Towler	PVF353R	Cambus
OEX793W	Eastern Counties	PBB760	Coach Services	PVF359R	Eastern Counties

Reg	Operator	Reg	Operator	Reg	Operator
PVF360R	Eastern Counties	RJI5721	Semmence	SJI1622	Sanders Coaches
PVF367R	Eastern Counties	RJI5723	Semmence	SJI1623	Sanders Coaches
PVF368R	Eastern Counties	RJI6861	The Shires	SJI1624	Sanders Coaches
PVF369R	Eastern Counties	RJI6862	The Shires	SJI1625	Sanders Coaches
PVF377	Sanders Coaches	RJI7972	Beestons	SJI1626	Sanders Coaches
PVG24W	Great Yarmouth	RJI7973	Beestons	SJI1627	Sanders Coaches
PVG25W	Great Yarmouth	RJI8604	Sanders Coaches	SJI1628	Sanders Coaches
PVG26W	Great Yarmouth	RJI8607	Sanders Coaches	SJI1629	Sanders Coaches
PVG27W	Great Yarmouth	RJR869Y	Enterprise	SJI1630	Sanders Coaches
PVV312	Semmence	RLJ93X	Simmonds	SJI1631	Sanders Coaches
PVV313	Semmence	RNK749M	Buffalo	SJI1632	Sanders Coaches
PWR443W	Cedric's	RNN982N	Ambassador Travel	SJI2954	Osborne's
PWR446W	Cedric's	RNN984N	Ambassador Travel	SJI4423	Beestons
PWY37W	Cambus	RNV485M	The Shires	SJI4424	Beestons
PWY39W	Viscount	RNY313Y	Enterprise	SJI4425	Beestons
PWY40W	Viscount	RPW189R	Eastern Counties	SJI4426	Beestons
PWY43W	Hedingham	RRB116R	Eastern Counties	SJI4427	Beestons
PWY44W	Eastern National	RRB118R	Ambassador Travel	SJI4429	Beestons
PWY45W	Viscount	RRB120R	Ambassador Travel	SJI4430	Beestons
PWY46W	Viscount	RRP812M	The Shires	SJI4431	Beestons
PWY47W	Viscount	RRP815M	The Shires	SJI4635	Osborne's
PWY48W	Viscount	RRT100W	Sanders Coaches	SJI5629	Sanders Coaches
PWY49W	Viscount	RSD978R	Morley's	SJI8100	Marshall's
PWY50W	Viscount	RSE156W	Towler	SJI8101	Marshall's
PYJ458L	Cedar Coaches	RSU231	Boon's Tours	SJI8102	Marshall's
Q394MPU	Fargo Coachlines	RTH917S	The Shires	SJI8103	Marshall's
Q475MEV	Southend	RUT684W	Beestons	SJI8104	Marshall's
Q476MEV	Southend	RVF35R	Great Yarmouth	SJI8105	Marshall's
Q552MEV	Southend	RVF36R	Great Yarmouth	SJI8106	Marshall's
Q553MEV	Southend	RVW88W	Colchester	SJI8107	Marshall's
Q554MEV	Southend	RVW89W	Colchester	SJI8286	Motts
Q684LPP	Seamarks	RVW90W	Colchester	SJI9319	Beestons
Q956UOE	Red Rose	RWC40W	Osborne's	SJI9320	Beestons
RAH129M	Eastern Counties	RWC41W	Osborne's	SJI9321	Beestons
RAH130M	Eastern Counties	RYG766R	The Shires	SLK886	Simmonds
RAH134M	Eastern Counties	RYL706R	Semmence	SM9562	Marshall's
RAH258W	Eastern Counties	RYL728R	Neaves	SMK659F	B T S
RAH259W	Eastern Counties	SBD523R	The Shires	SMK663F	B T S
RAH260W	Cambus	SBD524R	The Shires	SMK668F	B T S
RAH261W	Eastern Counties	SDA620S	Supreme	SMK674F	B T S
RAH262W	Eastern Counties	SDX21R	Ipswich	SMK686F	B T S
RAH263W	Eastern Counties	SDX22R	Ipswich	SMK694F	B T S
RAH264W	Viscount	SDX23R	Ipswich	SMK719F	B T S
RAH265W	Cambus	SDX24R	Ipswich	SMK756F	B T S
RAH266W	Eastern Counties	SDX25R	Ipswich	SMU721N	NIBS
RAH267W	Eastern Counties	SDX26R	Ipswich	SMW56Y	Stephensons
RAH268W	Cambus	SDX27R	Ipswich	SMY630X	The Shires
RAH269W	Eastern Counties	SDX29R	Ipswich	SNG436M	Eastern Counties
RAH270W	Eastern Counties	SDX30R	Ipswich	SNG438M	Eastern Counties
RBJ46R	Simmonds	SDX31R	Ipswich	SNG439M	Eastern Counties
RCH501R	Galloway	SDX32R	Ipswich	SNJ591R	Hedingham
RCS754	Spratts	SDX33R	Ipswich	SNT925H	Sander's
RDA670R	Ambassador Travel	SDX34R	Ipswich	SNV932W	The Shires
RDS82W	Whippet	SDX35R	Ipswich	SNV933W	The Shires
RDS83W	The Shires	SFC2T	Sanders Coaches	SNV934W	The Shires
RDS84W	The Shires	SFU718	Rover Bus Services	SNV938W	The Shires
RDV903	Sanders Coaches	SGF965	Sanders Coaches	SPA192R	Morley's
RDX18R	Ipswich	SGS497W	County	SPC277R	County
RDX19R	Ipswich	SHD293P	Caroline Seagull	SPU898W	Hedingham
RDX20R	Ipswich	SHL882S	Enterprise	SPW92N	Boon's Tours
REG870X	Whippet	SHR780N	Felix	SSU331	Boon's Tours
REV188R	Hedingham	SIA488	Simmonds	STK122T	Harris Bus
RFR415P	Colchester	SIB4671	Lamberts	STK123T	Harris Bus
RFR416P	Colchester	SIB4846	The Shires	STW21W	Eastern National
RFR419P	Colchester	SIB6441	Shorey	STW22W	Eastern National
RFR421P	Colchester	SIB6724	Motts	STW23W	Eastern National
RFS585V	Beestons	SIB7480	The Shires	STW24W	Cambus
RFS586V	Beestons	SIB7481	The Shires	STW27W	Eastern National
RFS588V	Beestons	SIB8529	The Shires	STW28W	Eastern National
RGS598R	Spratts	SIJ82	Simmonds	STW30W	Cambus
RGV284N	Hedingham	SJI1615	Sanders Coaches	STW36W	Eastern National
RGV684W	Emblings	SJI1616	Sanders Coaches	STW37W	Eastern National
RHD660X	Simmonds	SJI1617	Sanders Coaches	STW38W	Eastern National
RIB8815	APT	SJI1618	Sanders Coaches	SUB789W	Eastern National
RJI4668	Prestwood Travel	SJI1619	Sanders Coaches	SUB790W	Viscount
RJI4669	Prestwood Travel	SJI1620	Sanders Coaches	SUB791W	Viscount
RJI4670	Prestwood Travel	SJI1621	Sanders Coaches	SUB792W	Viscount

TET748S is a Leyland Fleetline once with South Yorkshire's Transport and now operating with Don's of Dunmow. The photograph, taken in Dunmow, displays the distinctive Roe styling applied in the late 1970s. *Geoff Mills*

SUB793W	Viscount	THX122S	Universitybus	TPC110X	County
SUB794W	Cambus	THX204S	Universitybus	TPC113X	County
SUB795W	Cambus	THX216S	Universitybus	TPD101X	County
SUP685R	Hedingham	THX225S	Enterprise	TPD102X	County
SUR283R	Motts	THX243S	Universitybus	TPD103X	County
SVA7S	Emblings	THX261S	Universitybus	TPD104X	County
SVV588W	The Shires	THX312S	The Shires	TPD105X	County
SWO70N	Amos Coaches	THX324S	Hedingham	TPD107X	County
SWW302R	Eastern National	THX332S	The Shires	TPD109X	County
SXF615	Beestons	THX345S	The Shires	TPD110X	County
TAH271W	Eastern Counties	THX480S	The Shires	TPD111X	County
TAH272W	Eastern Counties	THX481S	The Shires	TPD115X	County
TAH273W	Eastern Counties	THX493S	Buffalo	TPD117X	County
TAH274W	Eastern Counties	THX513S	Enterprise	TPD123X	County
TAH275W	Eastern Counties	THX525S	The Shires	TPE155S	Stephensons
TAH276W	Eastern Counties	THX531S	Eastern Counties	TPL292S	Southend
TAH554N	Eastern Counties	THX533S	Buffalo	TPL293S	Southend
TBB283S	Ipswich	THX560S	The Shires	TPM616X	Towler
TBU30G	Classic Coaches	THX573S	Eastern Counties	TPU67R	Colchester
TBW451P	Hedingham	THX580S	Shorey	TPU68R	Colchester
TCF496	Simmonds	THX605S	Buffalo	TPU69R	Colchester
TDL127S	Caroline Seagull	THX625S	Enterprise	TPU71R	Colchester
TDL420S	Caroline Seagull	TIB4873	The Shires	TPU73R	Colchester
TDT32S	Fords Coaches	TIB4886	The Shires	TPU74R	Colchester
TDX120W	Ipswich	TJI1670	Osborne's	TPU75R	Colchester
TDX124W	Ipswich	TJI1685	Osborne's	TPU76R	Colchester
TET748S	Don's	TJI1688	Osborne's	TPV41R	Simmonds
TEX401R	Eastern Counties	TJI3130	Osborne's	TRN470V	The Shires
TEX402R	Eastern Counties	TJI3131	Osborne's	TRN477V	The Shires
TEX403R	Eastern Counties	TJN502R	Thamesway	TSU610	Hallmark
TEX404R	Eastern Counties	TKV18W	Semmence	TSU611	Boon's Tours
TEX405R	Cambus	TND134X	Beestons	TUO255J	NIBS
TEX406R	Eastern Counties	TND439X	Buffalo	TUO260J	NIBS
TEX407R	Eastern Counties	TND440X	Buffalo	TUO261J	NIBS
TEX408R	Eastern Counties	TNH864R	The Shires	TVF620R	Eastern Counties
TGX892M	NIBS	TNH865R	The Shires	TVG397	Simmonds
THM630M	Hedingham	TNH866R	The Shires	TVN330X	Lamberts
THM705M	NIBS	TNH867R	The Shires	TWS905T	Cedric's
THM706M	Buffalo	TPA666X	Galloway	TXI2440	J B S

Registration	Operator	Registration	Operator
TXI8756	Don's	VBH605S	Neaves
TXI8762	Beestons	VEX283X	Eastern Counties
TYE708S	Spratts	VEX284X	Eastern Counties
UAR593W	Eastern National	VEX285X	Eastern Counties
UAR596W	Eastern National	VEX286X	Eastern Counties
UAR599W	Eastern National	VEX287X	Eastern Counties
UAT274R	Hedingham	VEX288X	Eastern Counties
UAV457X	Morley's	VEX289X	Cambus
UBJ847R	Hedingham	VEX290X	Eastern Counties
UCY629	Airport Coaches	VEX291X	Viscount
UEB782K	Morley's	VEX292X	Eastern Counties
UEB783K	Morley's	VEX293X	Cambus
UFX629X	Towler	VEX294X	Eastern Counties
UFX854S	Eastern Counties	VEX295X	Cambus
UHJ969Y	Neaves	VEX296X	Cambus
UJN429Y	County	VEX297X	Eastern Counties
UJN634Y	County	VEX298X	Cambus
UKE830X	Motts	VEX299X	Viscount
UKY608Y	Coach Services	VEX300X	Cambus
UNK11W	Neaves	VEX301X	Viscount
UNO100W	Hedingham	VEX302X	Eastern Counties
UPB312S	County	VEX303X	Cambus
UPB316S	The Shires	VEX304X	Cambus
UPB319S	County	VFX981S	Eastern Counties
UPB328S	The Shires	VGD779R	Supreme
UPB337S	The Shires	VHB672S	J B S
UPB341S	The Shires	VKC832V	Sanders Coaches
UPB343S	The Shires	VKC833V	Sanders Coaches
URB826S	Buckinghamshire	VKE564S	Sovereign
URF666S	J B S	VKN836X	Beestons
URF673S	Supreme	VKX539	Rover Bus Services
URL856S	Eastern Counties	VNM900S	Fords Coaches
URP942W	Buckinghamshire	VNO732S	Thamesway
URP943W	Cambus	VNO741S	Sovereign
URP946W	The Shires	VNO744S	Thamesway
URP947W	The Shires	VNO745S	Thamesway
URY598	The Shires	VNT7S	Lamberts
UUF110J	Emblings	VOD590S	Hedingham
UUF112J	Emblings	VOI5888	J B S
UUF115J	Emblings	VOI5888	J B S
UUX360S	Simmonds	VPW85S	Viscount
UVF623X	Cambus	VRP37S	Harris Bus
UVF624X	Eastern Counties	VRP39S	Harris Bus
UVF625X	Eastern Counties	VRP531S	The Shires
UVF626X	Eastern Counties	VRP532S	The Shires
UVF627X	Eastern Counties	VRP533S	The Shires
UVF628X	Eastern Counties	VRS152L	Cedar Coaches
UVG846	Angian	VRY841	Simmonds
UVO121S	Eastern Counties	VTH941T	Eastern National
UVO122S	Eastern Counties	VUR118W	Rover Bus Services
UVO123S	Ambassador Travel	VVD432S	Belle Coaches
UVO124S	Eastern Counties	VVV65S	Harris Bus
UVX4S	Hedingham	VVV951W	The Shires
UVX5S	Hedingham	VVV955W	The Shires
UVX6S	Hedingham	VVV956W	The Shires
UVX7S	Hedingham	VVV957W	The Shires
UWA93S	Beestons	VVV960W	The Shires
UWH314T	Rules	VYU753S	Semmence
UWW3X	Cambus	VYU759S	Semmence
UWW4X	Cambus	WAH586S	Eastern Counties
UWW8X	Cambus	WAH587S	Eastern Counties
UXI5357	Buffalo	WAH588S	Eastern Counties
UXI7897	Buffalo	WAH589S	Eastern Counties
VAH277X	Eastern Counties	WAH590S	Eastern Counties
VAH278X	Viscount	WAH591S	Eastern Counties
VAH279X	Viscount	WAH592S	Eastern Counties
VAH280X	Viscount	WAH593S	Eastern Counties
VAH281X	Eastern Counties	WAH594S	Eastern Counties
VAH282X	Eastern Counties	WAY456X	Semmence
VAL55S	Beestons	WBD874S	The Shires
VAR895S	Thamesway	WBD877S	The Shires
VAR897S	Thamesway	WCR819	Crusader
VAR898S	Eastern National	WDB551S	Angian
VAR899S	Eastern National	WDM345R	Eastern Counties
VAR900S	Thamesway	WDX663X	Simmonds
VAV161X	Whippet	WET880	Felix
VBH602S	Enterprise	WEX679M	Great Yarmouth
		WEX680M	Great Yarmouth
		WEX681M	Great Yarmouth
		WEX682M	Great Yarmouth
		WEX683M	Great Yarmouth
		WEX685M	Great Yarmouth
		WEX686M	Great Yarmouth
		WEX687M	Great Yarmouth
		WGE37S	Windmill Cs
		WGR66R	Fords Coaches
		WGY594S	Beestons
		WHJ869S	Waylands
		WJM810T	Golden Boy
		WJM812T	Golden Boy
		WJM814T	County
		WJM816T	County
		WJM831T	Hedingham
		WJN558S	Sovereign
		WJN559S	Thamesway
		WJN560S	Thamesway
		WJN564S	Eastern National
		WJN565S	Thamesway
		WJN566S	Thamesway
		WKH424S	Whippet
		WKH426S	Whippet
		WNH50W	Buffalo
		WNO479	Eastern National
		WNO480	Eastern National
		WNO546L	Eastern National
		WOA521P	Sanders Coaches
		WOD142X	Coach Services
		WOI607	Ipswich
		WOO903W	Hedingham
		WPH130Y	County
		WPH131Y	County
		WPH132Y	Red Rose
		WPH133Y	County
		WPH135Y	Hedingham
		WPW199S	Eastern Counties
		WPW200S	Cambus
		WPW201S	Viscount
		WPW202S	Viscount
		WRJ447X	Harris Bus
		WRJ448X	Harris Bus
		WRO438S	Prestwood Travel
		WRR396Y	Cedar Coaches
		WSF643Y	Rules
		WSU225	Boon's Tours
		WSU368	Cedar Coaches
		WSV503	Sanders Coaches
		WSV555	Beestons
		WTH949T	Eastern National
		WTH958T	Eastern National
		WTU473W	Southend
		WTU474W	Southend
		WTU484W	Cedric's
		WUL261N	Beestons
		WVF598S	Eastern Counties
		WVF599S	Eastern Counties
		WVF635S	Sanders Coaches
		WWH26L	Eastern Counties
		WWJ771M	Buffalo
		WWN191	Classic Coaches
		WWY120S	Cedric's
		WWY120S	Stephensons
		WWY126S	Beestons
		WWY130S	Cambus
		WXI4357	Buffalo
		WXI9252	Emblings
		WXI9253	Sanders Coaches
		WYV48T	Morley's
		WYV57T	B T S
		WYV820T	Felix
		XAR777S	Rules
		XBJ876	Semmence
		XCG264V	Simmonds
		XCT474T	Lamberts
		XDV607S	Cambus

XEH254M	Airport Coaches	XVG686X	Sanders Coaches	YOI7145	Golden Boy
XFE649S	Sanders Coaches	XVV537S	The Shires	YOI7353	Golden Boy
XGS763X	Simmonds	XVV538S	The Shires	YOI7373	Golden Boy
XGS767X	Osborne's	XVV539S	The Shires	YOI7374	Golden Boy
XHE754T	Neaves	XWX181S	Eastern Counties	YOI7575	Golden Boy
XHK215X	Thamesway	XYK760T	Belle Coaches	YOI7725	Golden Boy
XHK217X	Eastern National	YBF682S	Stephensons	YOI7744	Golden Boy
XHK218X	Thamesway	YBF686S	Southend	YOI7757	Golden Boy
XHK232X	Eastern National	YCD81T	Sovereign	YOI8271	Golden Boy
XHK235X	Thamesway	YDS650S	Don's	YOI949	Golden Boy
XHK236X	Thamesway	YDX100Y	Ipswich	YPF768T	The Shires
XHK237X	Thamesway	YDX101Y	Ipswich	YPF769T	The Shires
XJO46	Simmonds	YDX103Y	Ipswich	YPF770T	The Shires
XKX640X	Graham's	YDX104Y	Ipswich	YPL396T	The Shires
XNA337X	Coach Services	YDX105Y	Ipswich	YPL398T	The Shires
XNG203S	Eastern Counties	YEV305S	Thamesway	YPL404T	The Shires
XNG204S	Eastern Counties	YEV306S	Sovereign	YPL405T	The Shires
XNG205S	Eastern Counties	YEV308S	Eastern National	YPL409T	The Shires
XNG206S	Eastern Counties	YEV309S	Eastern National	YPL410T	The Shires
XNG207S	Eastern Counties	YEV311S	Thamesway	YPL415T	The Shires
XNG762S	Eastern Counties	YEV312S	Thamesway	YPL417T	The Shires
XNG763S	Eastern Counties	YEV315S	Thamesway	YPL418T	The Shires
XNG765S	Eastern Counties	YEV318S	Eastern National	YPL421T	The Shires
XNG766S	Eastern Counties	YEV319S	Eastern National	YPL424T	The Shires
XNG767S	Eastern Counties	YEV320S	Eastern National	YPL426T	The Shires
XNG768S	Eastern Counties	YEV321S	Eastern National	YPL434T	The Shires
XNG769S	Eastern Counties	YEV322S	Thamesway	YPL436T	The Shires
XNG770S	Eastern Counties	YEV323S	Eastern National	YPL438T	The Shires
XNM820S	Lodge's	YEV325S	Eastern National	YPL441T	The Shires
XNR997Y	Semmence	YEV326S	Thamesway	YPL446T	The Shires
XNV882S	Fords Coaches	YEV327S	Thamesway	YPL449T	The Shires
XPG190T	County	YEV328S	Eastern National	YPL451T	The Shires
XPG194T	County	YEV329S	Thamesway	YPL454T	The Shires
XPG195T	The Shires	YFV179R	Eastern Counties	YPL456T	The Shires
XPG199T	County	YFY5M	Eastern Counties	YPL457T	The Shires
XPP693X	Richmond's	YHA386J	Rules	YPL458T	The Shires
XPV657S	Rex Motor Services	YHN654M	Eastern Counties	YPL91T	Bordacoach
XPW877X	Hedingham	YJE3T	Kenzie's	YTU353S	Buckinghamshire
XRA397Y	Cedar Coaches	YJE9T	Sanders Coaches	YUM401S	Southend
XRF24S	Supreme	YMJ555S	Lodge's	YUM515S	Southend
XRF25S	Supreme	YNG208S	Viscount	YUM516S	Southend
XRR613M	Ambassador Travel	YNG209S	Cambus	YVF158	Simmonds
XRR622M	Ambassador Travel	YNG210S	Cambus	YVJ677	Sanders Coaches
XRR629M	Ambassador Travel	YNG211S	Eastern Counties	YVV892S	The Shires
XRT931X	Ipswich	YNG212S	Cambus	YVV893S	The Shires
XRT932X	Ipswich	YNO481L	Hedingham	YVV894S	The Shires
XRT947X	Ipswich	YNO77S	Colchester	YVV895S	The Shires
XTE221V	Southend	YNO78S	Colchester	YVV896S	Cambus
XTE222V	Southend	YNO79S	Colchester	YWF512T	Enterprise
XTE223V	Southend	YNO80S	Colchester	YWY830S	Cambus
XTE224V	Southend	YNO81S	Colchester	YXI9255	Emblings
XTE225V	Southend	YNO82S	Colchester	YYG104S	Sovereign
XTE226V	Southend	YOI1214	Golden Boy	YYL771T	Reg's
XTE227V	Southend	YOI2517	Golden Boy	YYL776T	Belle Coaches
XTE228V	Southend	YOI2642	Golden Boy	YYL778T	Belle Coaches
XTE229V	Southend	YOI2805	Golden Boy	YYL783T	Belle Coaches
XTE230V	Southend	YOI5475	Golden Boy	YYL786T	Belle Coaches
XTT5X	Cedar Coaches	YOI5997	Golden Boy	YYL791T	Semmence
XVA545T	Simmonds	YOI7079	Golden Boy	YYL795T	Belle Coaches
XVE8T	Kenzie's				

ISBN 1 897990 11 1

Published by *British Bus Publishing Ltd*, September 1995
The Vyne, 16 St Margarets Drive, Wellington,
Telford, Shropshire, TF1 3PH
Fax: 01952 255669

Printed by Graphics & Print
Unit A13, Stafford Park 15
Telford, Shropshire, TF3 3BB